Writing History

General Editors: Stefan Berger
Heiko Feldner
Kevin Passmore

Also in the *Writing History* series

Published:

Writing History: Theory and Practice
Edited by Stefan Berger, Heiko Feldner and Kevin Passmore

Writing Gender History
Laura Lee Downs

Writing Medieval History
Edited by Nancy Partner

Writing Early Modern History
Edited by Garthine Walker

Forthcoming:

The Holocaust and History
Wulf Kansteiner

Writing Early Modern History

Edited by: Garthine Walker

BLOOMSBURY
NEW DELHI • LONDON • OXFORD • NEW YORK • SYDNEY

First Published in India 2017
First published in Great Britain in 2005

Bloomsbury Academic
An imprint of Bloomsbury Publishing Plc
Bloomsbury is a registered trade mark of Bloomsbury Publishing Plc

This edition published with permission from Bloomsbury Publishing Plc
50, Bedford Square, London, WC1B3DP

British Library Cataloguing in Publication Data
A catalogue record for this book is available from the British Library

Library of Congress Cataloging-in-Publication Data
A catalog record for this book is available from the Library of Congress

ISBN: 978-93-86643-17-9
10 9 8 7 6 5 4 3 2 1
For sale in the Indian subcontinent only

Bloomsbury Publishing India Pvt. Ltd
Second Floor, Building No. 4
DDA Complex LSC, Pocket C – 6 & 7
Vasant Kunj, New Delhi 110070
www.bloomsbury.com

Exclusively Distributed in India by:
Manohar Publishers & Distributors
4753/23, Ansari Road
Darya Ganj, New Delhi 110002
Tel.: 23284848, 23289100
Email: sales@manoharbooks.com, manoharbooks@gmail.com

Typeset in II pt Adobe Garamond by Servis Filmsetting Ltd, Manchester
Printed and bound in India

Contents

Notes on contributors		vi
General editors' preface		ix
	Introduction *Garthine Walker*	xi
Part 1		
1	Marxism *David Rollison*	3
2	Modernization *Garthine Walker*	25
3	Anthropological approaches *David Gentilcore*	49
4	The linguistic turn *Susan R. Boettcher*	71
5	Gender *Merry E. Wiesner-Hanks*	
6	Psychoanalysis *Diane Purkiss*	114
Part 2		
7	Religion *Trevor Johnson*	139
8	Economy and material life *Clare Haru Crowston*	159
9	Politics *Lloyd Bowen*	183
10	The body *Kevin Stagg*	205
Index		227

Notes on contributors

Susan R. Boettcher is Assistant Professor of History at the University of Texas at Austin, where she teaches Reformation and early modern German history and researches sixteenth-century Lutheran confessional culture, especially preaching, polemic and devotional literature. Recent publications include 'Are the Cranach Altarpieces Philippist? Memory of Luther and Knowledge of the Past in the Late Reformation', in Mary Lindemann (ed.), *Ways of Knowing: Ten Interdisciplinary Essays* (Boston and Leiden, 2004) and 'Lutheran Sermons on the Turk: Jacob Andreae's Message on the Turks after Szeged (1568)', *Comparative Studies of South Asia, Africa and the Middle East* 24(2) (2004). She is currently completing a monograph on Reformation *memoria* and later sixteenth-century commemoration of Martin Luther.

Lloyd Bowen is a lecturer in History at Cardiff University. His main areas of research relate to Wales in the sixteenth and seventeenth centuries. His publications include articles on representations of the Welsh during the Civil Wars, legislation in Tudor parliaments and gentry culture in the early seventeenth century. His monograph, *The Politics of the Principality: Wales, c.1603–42*, is forthcoming from the University of Wales Press in 2005.

Clare Haru Crowston is Associate Professor of History at the University of Illinois at Urbana-Champaign. She specializes in the history of early modern France, women and gender, work, credit and material culture. Her monograph, *Fabricating Women: The Seamstresses of Old Regime France, 1675–1791* (Durham, NC, 2001), won the Hagley Prize for the Best Book in Business History and the Berkshire Conference First Book Prize. She is currently researching in two areas of French history: the intersection of credit, fashion and sex in the eighteenth century and apprenticeship from the seventeenth to the nineteenth centuries.

David Gentilcore is Reader in History at the University of Leicester and the author of *From Bishop to Witch: the System of the Sacred in Early Modern Terra d'Otranto* (Manchester, 1992) and *Healers and Healing in Early Modern Italy* (Manchester, 1998). He is currently working on a study of charlatans and charlatanism in early modern Italy.

Trevor Johnson is Senior Lecturer in History at the University of the West of England. He has research interests in two broad areas: the social, cultural and political history of seventeenth-century Germany, in particular, Bavaria and the Upper Palatinate; and the culture of the Catholic or Counter-Reformation as a pan-European phenomenon. He is currently completing a monograph, *Maximilian of Bavaria and the Thirty Years War*, for Manchester University Press, and is working on a comparative study of early modern Mariology. His publications include Bob Scribner and Trevor Johnson (eds), *Popular Religion in Germany and Central Europe, 1400–1800* (Basingstoke, 1996).

Diane Purkiss is Fellow of Keble College, Oxford. She is the author of *The Witch in History: Early Modern and Twentieth-century Representations* (London, 1996) and *Troublesome Things: A History of Fairies and Fairy Stories* (London, 2000). Her most recent works, on various aspects of the English Civil War, include *Literature, Gender and Politics in the English Civil War* (Cambridge, 2005).

David Rollison is the author of *The Local Origins of Modern Society: Gloucestershire, 1500–1800* (London and New York, 1992) and numerous articles on popular resistance and rebellion, industrial development and politics, mobility, religion and theology, language and other aspects of early modern studies, based on local ('bottom-up') microhistories. He is currently writing *The English Explosion, 1215–1649*, a study of popular influence in the evolution of the early modern English commonwealth up to the execution of Charles I. He is Senior Lecturer in History at the University of Western Sydney.

Kevin Stagg lectures in history at Cardiff Business School, Cardiff University. He is co-editor with David M. Turner of a forthcoming volume on the history of the body and disability in the Routledge Social History of Medicine series, which draws on papers delivered at the 2002 'Controlling Bodies. The Regulation of the Body 1650–2000' conference at the University of Glamorgan. His current research interests range from the body and disability in history to early modern print culture and the dynamics of early modern ports.

Garthine Walker is Senior Lecturer in History at Cardiff University. Her publications include *Crime, Gender and Social Order in Early Modern England* (Cambridge, 2003) and a number of essays on aspects of early modern gender relations, criminality and historical theory. She is co-editor of *Women, Crime and the Courts in Early Modern England* (London and North Carolina, 1994). Currently completing a book for Palgrave on crime and disorder in early modern England and Wales, her next major research project is a monograph on rape and sexual violence in early modern society.

Merry E. Wiesner-Hanks is Professor of History at the University of Wisconsin, Milwaukee. Her books include *Working Women in Renaissance Germany* (New Brunswick, 1986), *Women and Gender in Early Modern Europe* (Cambridge, 1993), *Discovering the Global Past: A Look at the Evidence* (Boston, 1997), *Gender, Church and State in Early Modern Germany* (London, 1998), *Christianity and Sexuality in the Early Modern World: Regulating Desire, Reforming Practice* (London, 2000) and *Gender and History* (Oxford, 2001). She has co-edited several volumes, including *A Companion to Gender History* (Oxford, 2004).

General editors' reface

Can historical writing tell us anything about the past given that many, poststructuralists in the lead, would deny that academic historical writing is intrinsically different from fiction? Does the study of the past serve any purpose in a society in which, according to Eric Hobsbawm, 'most young men and women . . . grow up in a sort of permanent present lacking any organic relations to the public past of the times in which they live'?

Historians have never been more inclined to reflect upon the nature of their discipline. Undergraduate and postgraduate courses increasingly include compulsory study of historiography, the philosophy of history, and history and theory. *Writing History* presents a book series that focuses on the practical application of theory in historical writing. It publishes accessibly written overviews of particular fields of history. Rather than focus upon abstract theory, the books in this series explain key concepts and demonstrate the ways in which they have informed practical work. Theoretical perspectives, acknowledged and unacknowledged, have shaped actual works of history. Each book in the series relates historical texts and their producers to the social conditions of their existence. As such, *Writing History* does go beyond a focus on historical works in themselves. In a variety of ways each volume analyses texts within their institutional arrangement and as part of a wider social discourse.

The early modern period has been one of the primary fields of historical innovation. The first professional historians saw it as a crucial period in the formation of modern states, and Geoffrey Elton took this form of writing into the late twentieth century. One also thinks of Christopher Hill's contribution to the social history of politics, Natalie Zemon Davis's introduction of anthropological methods to history through her original essays on French society and culture, and more recently the application of different forms of feminist psychoanalysis in the work of Lyndal Roper on German witchcraft.

The first part of Garthine Walker's book lucidly explains the major approaches influential in early modern history – through her concise introduction, and essays on Marxism, modernization theory, anthropology, linguistic theory, gender, and psychoanalysis – and explores the particular problems involved in the application of those theories to the early modern period. The second part of the book shifts its focus to the application of the aforementioned theories to particular subfields of early modern history: religion, economy, politics, and the body. The essays in both parts reveal that the early modern period itself is a theoretical construction, which carries the danger of serving as a substitute for analysis, but which may serve as a useful starting point.

Stefan Berger, Heiko Feldner and Kevin Passmore
Cardiff and Pontypridd, November 2004

Introduction

Garthine Walker

Discussions of history and theory rarely contain more than a few passing references to early modern (or medieval) historiography. They focus overwhelmingly on histories of the later modern period. In doing so, they sometimes perpetuate superficial generalizations about the 'pre-modern', 'pre-industrial' and 'traditional' period that supposedly preceded the modern one. These conceptual labels are not neutrally descriptive: they signify the occupation of a particular position – a theoretical perspective – on what does and what does not constitute modernity, and they assume that history has, perhaps even necessarily, passed through certain 'stages'. Even where discussions of historical theory do make reference to historical writing about the early modern period, there is little consideration of the implications of theoretical models and concepts for early modern history as a distinctive period.[1]

Early modern history's somewhat low-key status in discussions of history and theory is unsatisfactory and rather odd for two main reasons. First, there has been a tremendously rich tradition of theoretical application to the early modern period. Great nineteenth- and twentieth-century thinkers – like Jacob Burckhardt (1818–97), Karl Marx (1818–83), Friedrich Engels (1820–95), Emile Durkheim (1858–1917), Max Weber (1864–1920), Norbert Elias (1897–1990) and Michel Foucault (1926–84) – all proposed that the period between the end of the Middle Ages and the beginning of the nineteenth century witnessed crucial developments in the making of the modern world. Among such developments are the rise of capitalism, the rise of the middle class, the development of modern notions of shame, self-restraint and individualism, and the processes of secularization, rationalization, bureaucratization and industrialization. These ideas have been hugely influential not only on the work of historians but also on broader cultural understandings of what defines modern society. Indeed, some aspects of these theoretical formulations have become so widely accepted that they have entered common discourse and are assumed to be 'common sense'. This means that as well as finding their influence in the arguments of historians who engage explicitly with such theoretical formulations, it is possible, too, to identify their mark even in the writing of people who do not evoke them and who might never have read their original works. Part of the purpose of this book is to help students of history identify implicit theoretical assumptions, as well as explicit applications of theory, to writing about the early modern period. Being able to recognize the underlying assumptions of any given historian's approach is a key skill that will enrich students' critical engagements with the histories they read.

Second, early modern historians have frequently been at the forefront of innovative and interdisciplinary engagement with theoretical models and concepts. One telling indication of early modern history's vanguard position is the domination by early modernists of a book about the practice of what has been termed 'the new history' – no fewer than seven of the nine individuals interviewed are early modern historians! These are Natalie Zemon Davis (b. 1928), Keith Thomas (b. 1933), Daniel Roche (b. 1935), Peter Burke (b. 1937), Robert Darnton (b. 1939), Carlo Ginzburg (b. 1939) and Quentin Skinner (b. 1940), all of whom are mentioned (some of them several times) in the chapters that follow.[2] Nor is this list of innovative early modern historians exhaustive. From the publication in 1919 of Alice Clark's *Working Life of Women in the Seventeenth Century*, to Eric Erikson's 1958 psychobiography, *Young Man Luther*, and on to the 'new social history' of the 1970s and the 'new cultural history' of the 1980s, historians working on the centuries between 1500 and 1800 have been at the cutting edge of historical study.

As the subject of this book is the influence of theory upon historical writing about the early modern period, it is useful to establish at the outset what we mean by 'theory'. For some historians, theory provides an overarching explanatory framework for change over time and/or the nature of societies in the past. This sort of theory – Theory with a capital 'T' – is sometimes referred to as providing a historical 'metanarrative', a schematic account of historical change according to which various historical phenomena may be ordered. Opponents of theoretically informed historical writing have often singled out Marxist models as constituting this sort of theory. Marxism was apparently what both G.R. Elton (1921–94) and Gertrude Himmelfarb (b. 1922) had in mind when they warned against adopting theoretical approaches to history. Elton, when instructing historians on how to approach their primary evidence, opined that 'ideological theory' operates as a straitjacket for historians, forcing them to follow predetermined explanations and to tailor their evidence to fit the theory.[3] Himmelfarb, in her 1987 assault upon the 'new' social history that she perceived as outrageously eclipsing political history over the preceding 20 years, approvingly noted criticism of 'the prevalent ideological bias' which 'disposes the historian to identify with his subjects and endow them with his own attitude and values'.[4] Even those who are not overtly hostile to Marxism sometimes give the impression (perhaps inadvertently) that 'historical theory' is pretty much synonymous with Marxism. When delineating the contours of academic history, for instance, Ludmilla Jordanova limited her discussion under the subheading 'Theory-based history' to the waning of Marxism and the waxing of psychoanalysis. This pairing is itself significant, for psychoanalytic interpretations, like Marxist ones, have been denounced by critics as deriving 'more from a priori theories than from empirical evidence'.[5] Grand theoretical models are not, however, limited to these two. Modernization theory is one obvious addition and (although its adherents might disagree) poststructuralist histories have also accepted an overarching historical narrative in which the pre-modern, modern and postmodern periods follow each other in what looks suspiciously similar to at least one conventional periodization.[6]

In addition to discussion of influential Grand Theories, this book considers how approaches that might best be described as theoretical with a lower case 't' have informed the work of early modern historians. Important advances of this nature include the development of microhistory, for example, and the eclecticism of certain types of women's and gender history that eschew the overarching contours of, for instance, Liberal feminist and Marxist feminist accounts of historical development. In fact, even theoretical models with the potential to be adopted as a Grand Theory can operate at a more subtle and diffuse level. Thus, many historians happily accept Marxist categories and terminology such as 'class' or 'bourgeois' without necessarily agreeing with Marx about the nature and trajectory of historical change. Similarly, historians who do not subscribe to all the tenets of modernization theory might utilize unquestioningly distinctions between 'traditional' and 'modern' societies. People to whom such categories and distinctions seem like matters of 'common sense' might not regard them as 'theories' at all. As the philosopher of science, Karl Popper (1902–94), noted some half-century ago, 'Very often we are unaware of the fact that we are operating with hypotheses or theories, and we therefore mistake our theoretical models for concrete things'.[7] Whether or not practising historians are willing to acknowledge it – and not all do – all history writing 'inevitably entails taking a stand on key theoretical issues' and is 'an intrinsically theoretical as well as empirical enterprise'.[8] In fact, all our ideas, assumptions, interpretations and hypotheses about the past may reasonably be described as theoretical in the sense that they are views of history informed by our perspectives on the world.

Whatever our perspective is, it does not arise from some indisputable set of 'facts', but is coloured by perceptions that emanate from a particular mental point of view. Our attempts to understand the past 'as it was' are led by questions we ask of sources we select, and upon both of these – questions and sources – we bring to bear theoretical models and assumptions. It has long been established that historical 'facts' do not exist independently of theory; historians' selections of facts are themselves acts of interpretation.[9] Thus the 'grand narrative' tradition of historical writing in which history is presented as an unfolding story of great men and events is itself theoretically informed. It is a form of history written from a particular position and involves judgements made in the present about who and what is important in the present and the past.[10] The interpretations of self-professed anti- or non-theorists are themselves informed by theoretical models, concepts, assumptions and strategies. It is just that in such cases, historians attribute 'theoretical' perspectives to people with whom they disagree, while presenting their own views as innocently correct, and refuse to acknowledge the ways in which their own position is informed by an alternative theoretical perspective. See, for example, the discussions in chapters 2 and 9 of this volume of the ways in which theory informed the practical historical writing of that self-proclaimed anti-theorist G.R. Elton.

The essays in this volume demonstrate some important ways in which historical and social theories have informed the histories written about the early modern period. By examining the mechanics of the arguments of actual historical writing rather than focusing on abstract theory, readers will be assisted in their own attempts to recognize the theoretical assumptions that have shaped the historiographies of early modern European political, social, economic and cultural history. Part 1 of the book concerns approaches to history that we may categorize as distinct theoretical traditions – although some of these are more pluralistic than others. Each of the six chapters surveys particular theoretical models, bodies of thought or perspectives that have been used to explain the nature and course of early modern history. There are chapters on Marxism, modernization theory, anthropological models, linguistic theories, psychoanalysis and gender. In a book of this size, comprehensive coverage of *all* theoretical perspectives with which early modern historians have engaged is clearly impossible. Most notably, the French *Annales* school has not been afforded a dedicated chapter, despite its substantial contribution to early modern history. The vast array of theoretical models with which successive generations of *Annalistes* engaged was inconsonant with the present volume's format, which focuses in Part 1 on discrete bodies of theoretical thought and in Part 2 on specific subject areas. However, the influence of the *Annales* is evident throughout the volume (and is marked in the index).

In the second part of the volume, the focus moves from particular theoretical traditions to an exploration of the ways in which theoretical approaches – including but not limited to those discussed in Part 1 – have contributed to the nature and development of broad fields within early modern history. There are chapters on religion, the economy and material life, politics and the body. Readers might wonder why the chapter on gender was not placed here, and certainly it is possible to consider gender as a topic, an object of study, rather than as an approach to history that involves a particular theoretical perspective or set of assumptions. The chapter on gender has been grouped with the essays in Part 1 for a simple reason: to underline the enormous impact that the development of gender history has had upon historical writing generally. Gender, as Joan Scott argued in her 1986 theorization of the concept of gender as a category for historical analysis, is everywhere, and is interconnected with and implicit in power relationships of all kinds, not just those overtly concerned with women, the family or sexuality.[11] In organizing the volume in two parts like this, the intention is twofold: first, to provide readers with a basic understanding of theories that either have helped to define or pose challenges to the historical writing about the early modern period; second, to help readers identify the influence of theory in the history books and articles about early modern society that they will encounter in their ongoing exploration of the early modern period.

It is also worth noting that the book primarily focuses on Anglophone historiography. The decision to do so was made consciously because (sadly) the majority of history undergraduates and, increasingly, even postgraduates in the English-speaking world no longer possess the foreign-language skills necessary to read works published in languages other than English. As the authors of the chapters herein were asked to discuss works that students of early modern history in the English-speaking world were likely to come across, this meant that the emphasis is on histories written in English or available in English translation. However, it is obvious from the contributors' discussions that English-language history, whether of Britain or other European or non-European countries, has not developed in linguistic isolation. While some British and North American historians have been involved in pushing forward the boundaries of their fields of expertise, many crucial advances have been made by historians of other nationalities, especially French and German. These have had a tremendous impact on the development of Anglophone scholarship. It will also become clear that major theorists of historical change have not always been professional historians. The theorists to which historians have turned in seeking fresh perspectives and insights are frequently practitioners of other disciplines, sociology, philosophy and anthropology prominent among them. The intellectual traditions of France and Germany again stand out for their remarkable contributions to modern thought. This is worth noting because, while it is true that there has been a distinct turn to interdisciplinarity since the 1970s, when historians in the new social history school first turned to other academic disciplines for inspiration, theoretical models and concepts, historical writing has been an interdisciplinary and international endeavour ever since its inception as an academic discipline in the late nineteenth century. Indeed, one need look no further for an example of that than the indisputable impact upon professional historical writing of the German historian Leopold von Ranke (1795–1886), renowned as one of the discipline's founders, whose theory of how to 'do' history was adopted as a blueprint for historical practice throughout the later nineteenth and the twentieth centuries.

By attending to the ways in which a variety of theories have contributed to the way that historians have approached the early modern period, this volume implicitly draws attention to the constructed nature of historical periodization. We have so far taken 'early modern' as an unambiguous, self-explanatory term, a kind of shorthand for the centuries between the end of the 'medieval' period and the start of one that was fully 'modern'. When I decided upon *Writing Early Modern History* as the title for this book, and when the contributors agreed to write chapters for inclusion in it, we all took for granted that we would be examining historical writing about a period of time that extended from *c.*1500 to *c.*1800. A useful shorthand it might be, but neither the term nor the concept of an 'early modern' period is 'natural' or innocent.[12] For one thing, it has only relatively recently become a dominant designation. Before the 1970s, 'early modern' was rarely used in titles of books or articles, and was not widely adopted until the 1980s. Only since 1990 has 'early modern' outstripped all terminologies for the period other than simple centurial designations. However, the *concept* of early modernity, and with it an idea of history as progress, has a much longer pedigree. It can be traced at least as far back as the eighteenth-century philosophical thought that has informed so much of what has been taken for granted by scholars ever since, and from there to the works of the great social and historical theorists of the nineteenth and twentieth centuries – Marx, Engels, Durkheim, Weber, and Ranke prominent among them. These men's ideas about what constituted modernity and when the characteristics of modernity first developed can be seen to have played a key role in how early modern history has been written right up to the present day. Again and again, we find historians noting that what makes the early modern period distinctive is the presence of features that, with hindsight, may be seen as characteristics of the modern world. This very basic concept – the simple idea of there having been an early modern period – is itself an example of theory making a fundamental contribution to historical writing.[13]

Garthine Walker

Notes

1 See, for example, the chapter on 'Theories and Concepts' in Jeremy Black and Donald M. MacRaild, *Studying History* (Basingstoke, 2000).

2 Maria Lúcia G. Pallares-Burke, *The New History: Confessions and Conversations* (Oxford, 2002). The remaining two are the historical anthropologist Jack Goody, who has included discussion of early modern Europe in some of his works, and Asa Briggs, predominantly a

specialist on Victorian Britain. For the 'new history', see Peter Burke, 'Overture: the New History, its Past and its Future', in his (ed.), *New Perspectives on Historical Writing* (Oxford, 1991), pp. 1–23.

3 G.R. Elton, *Return to Essentials: Some Reflections on the Present State of Historical Study* (Cambridge, 1991), p. 27.

4 Gertrude Himmelfarb, *The New History and the Old* (Cambridge, MA and London, 1987), pp. 14–15.

5 Ludmilla Jordanova, *History in Practice* (London, 2000), pp. 55–7. Himmelfarb, *New History*, p. 14.

6 See, for instance, the historical narrative provided in Keith Jenkins, *Re-thinking History* (London and New York, 1991), pp. 60–3.

7 Karl Popper, *The Poverty of Historicism* (1957; London, 1989), p. 136.

8 Mary Fulbrook, *Historical Theory* (London and New York, 2002), pp. ix, 4.

9 E.H. Carr, *What is History?* (London, 1961), p. 12.

10 See, for example, Himmelfarb's assault on what she sees as the unacceptable priorities of social historians: *New History*, pp. 17–18.

11 Joan W. Scott, 'Gender: A Useful Category of Historical Analysis', *American Historical Review* 91(5) (1986), pp. 1053–75; reprinted in numerous collected works thereafter.

12 While 'early modern' in Anglophone and its equivalent (*früh Neuzeit*) in German-language scholarship have been widely adopted, the 'early' part of the term is redundant in French- and Italian-language historiographies, for the period in question is rendered respectively as *histoire moderne* and *storia moderna*, with post-1789 society being referred to as *histoire contemporaine* and *storia contemporanea* – *contemporary* history.

13 For more on the development of 'early modern' periodization, see Garthine Walker, 'What's in a Name? Early Modern Periodization', *History Compass* (forthcoming).

Part 1

1

Marxism

David Rollison

Who built Thebes of the seven gates?
In the books you'll find the names of kings.
Did the kings haul up the lumps of rock?
And Babylon, many times demolished
Who raised it up so many times? In what houses
Of gold-glittering Lima did the builders live?
Where, the evening that the Wall of China was finished
Did the masons go? Great Rome
Is full of triumphal arches. Who erected them? Over whom
Did the Caesars triumph? Had Byzantium, much praised in song
Only palaces for its inhabitants? Even in fabled Atlantis
The night the ocean engulfed it
The drowning still bawled for their slaves . . .[1]

Social revolution is the only true revolution . . .[2]

What we call the 'early modern' period has a central place in Marxism. Karl Marx (1818–83) saw early modern England as the nucleus of capitalism, the place and time of the Big Bang of modernity. In his masterpiece, *Capital Volume One* (1867), is to be found his account of the English explosion. The three volumes of *Capital* sketch the dynamics of the global processes unleashed by that explosion. They are not, let it be said, bedtime reading.[3]

Marx concentrated on the less glamorous aspects of human history that have since become the specialist fields of social, economic and demographic historians. He was interested in politics and ideas, but saw them as contingent outgrowths of the mode and social relations of production.[4] 'Mode of production' refers to society's dominant form of economic production and its technical and social organization – in other words, how a society goes about producing goods and services. Within Marxist terminology, a society with simple technology, landowning lords and bonded serfs, for example, is said to have a *feudal* mode of production, while a society with sophisticated technology, private ownership of capital (which includes raw materials, tools, and so on) and a wage system is said to have a *capitalist* mode of production. The 'social relations of production' are the class relationships that arise from that division of labour. Students who come to history for the lives of kings, queens and heroes will not find Marx congenial. The great political revolutions of 1649 in England and 1789 in France, in Marx's theory, were dramatic eruptions into the constitutional realm of a deeper and more all-pervasive 'social' revolution, a more fundamental and consequential change in the mode and social relations of production. They were 'bourgeois' revolutions, opportunities for the new capitalist class to wrench control of the state away from feudal aristocracy and monarchy.[5] Marx was well aware of the eccentricity and diversity of state-forms that arose out of these bourgeois revolutions. Constitutional forms may retain their names (as Britain has retained monarchy and aristocratic titles), but their content is transformed by *social* revolution.[6] In human history, really fundamental changes develop outside the primary contexts of states and ruling classes. One of the most fruitful approaches that follows from this has been called 'history from below'.[7] Various kinds of 'bottom-up history' have been a significant growth area in early modern studies since the early 1970s.

Marx and history

Marx's essays on the world of primitive accumulation were part of an attempt to see the whole genesis of capitalism, from its origins to his own time.[8] He was a powerful scholar. He and Friedrich Engels (1820–95) between them knew as much as anyone alive in 1870 about the economic and social history of early modern England. Keith Wrightson estimates that 'of historians writing in Britain in the mid-nineteenth century, the one most closely in touch with the older tradition of approaches to the economic and social history of the sixteenth century was . . . Karl Marx'.[9] Marx mined the British Library's collection of literature relating to English social history and political economy. He discovered, among a vast body of lesser writers, classic earlier anatomies of what Marx's contemporary, Thomas Carlyle (1795–1881), called 'the condition of England'. He discovered for himself (as we can still do) influential writers like John Fortescue (*c.*1395–1476), Thomas More (1478–1535), Thomas Smith (1513–77), William Harrison (1534–93), Francis Bacon (1561–1626), William Shakespeare (1564–1616), Thomas Hobbes (1588–1679), Edward Misselden (1608–54), William Petty (1623–87), Bernard Mandeville (1670–1733), David Hume

(1711–76), Adam Smith (1723–90), William Cobbett (1763–1835), Thomas Robert Malthus (1766–1834), David Ricardo (1772–1823), Carlyle, James Mill (1773–1836) and John Stuart Mill (1806–73).[10] Marx took his 'facts' from these commentators. As Wrightson concludes, 'the elements in Marx's history were familiar enough: its chronology and component themes were to a large extent those of his predecessors'.[11] Marx mined what we call 'secondary sources' for information about the social revolution his theory predicted.

What we find in the sources depends upon what we are looking for. Marx was interested in *what* a society produced and *how* it produced it. The 'ore' that caught his attention was information relating to the classes of people involved in production. This implied an attempt literally to construct a picture of society 'from below'. Where his sources were counsellors to kings and parliaments, who provided information that would help them govern more efficiently, Marx turned the subjects of the data (the 'commonalty' or 'common people') into a force for change in their own right.

Like the political and social commentator Tom Paine (1737–1809), Marx was a counsellor to the working classes. He taught that for all their contemporary dominance, the worlds of elite ideas and institutions, high art, religion, politics and constitutional forms were less consequential, in the long run, than the ways the work was done. If the higher thought was incompatible with the mode of production, it would become a relic. Forms of government (which Marx saw as instruments of oppression) were the last bastions of outmoded 'social relations of production', the last to give way. But give way – by gradual adaptation or violent revolution or both – they would, and to forces 'from below'. 'The rise of the industrial capitalists', he wrote, 'appears as the fruit of a victorious struggle both against feudal powers . . ., and against the guilds, and the fetters by which the latter restricted the free development of production and the free exploitation of man by man'.[12] 'Bourgeois society' was an evolutionary process, the coming into existence of a society in which wealth 'presents itself as an immense accumulation of commodities',[13] and in which there is 'a complete separation between the workers and the ownership of the conditions for the realization of their labour'.[14] The governments of the advanced capitalist societies of the nineteenth century might retain neo-feudal forms (for example, be manned by hereditary nobles), but in reality they were nothing but committees for managing the affairs of the bourgeoisie.[15]

Marx identified problems that have continued to concern us, and devised powerful explanations for them. Consider his thoughts about what we call 'the population explosion'. Mature capitalism, in his view, was a two-cornered class struggle, between Labour (or 'variable capital') and Capital.[16] One of the most fundamental driving forces in early modern England was the gradual polarization into these two classes. Power, increasingly, lay not with inherited title but with ownership of the means of production. (The French term *bourgeois* means an urban dweller and is misleading when applied to early modern England, where the masters of 'proto-industry' and capitalist farming were mainly country-dwellers.[17]) Research since has confirmed that 'industries in the countryside' led to a multiplication of units of production (households dependent on wages in various forms).[18] Marx's 'absolute general law of capitalist accumulation' stated that 'the relative mass of the reserve industrial army increases with the potential energy of wealth'. His aim was to 'consider the influence of the growth of capital on the fate of the working class'. He offers pages of argument, and references to earlier authorities on the subject, and concludes that 'accumulation of capital *is* multiplication of the proletariat'. Marx offers an explanation (not necessarily the right one) for an issue which only really came to the forefront of academic and public debate in the second half of the twentieth century. Capitalism generates population growth, is the law Marx expounded.[19]

No one today doubts that a global population explosion has taken place, and that it is possible to discern the beginnings of the process in late medieval and early modern Europe. Three hundred and fifty years ago there were maybe five hundred million individuals of the species *Homo sapiens*. Today there are six billion.[20] Marx was in no doubt that this explosion of 'the dangerous classes' was intrinsic to the capitalist world-system. This amorphous proletariat was the 'spectre' that haunted the nineteenth-century bourgeoisie.[21] Research since has confirmed Marx's assumption that in the country most affected by what he called 'primitive accumulation', England, population had been growing for three centuries before the national censuses of the nineteenth century made it an issue of public debate.[22] Marx also believed that what was happening in England was the historical nucleus of a global explosion. The practical connection between the local and the global movement was colonialism. The driving force of modern colonialism was *capital*, which, in his view, was inherently international, expansive.[23]

How did this process begin? The most influential population theorist of Marx's day, Thomas Malthus, assumed a biological regime in which the means of production remain the same. In such a system, the only way to increase production is by colonizing additional resources. Eventually population outstrips resources and the 'preventative check' (disease, famine, war and death) comes into operation. This is now generally agreed to have happened in north-western Europe in the twelfth and thirteenth centuries, when a burst of population growth was sustained by the 'internal' colonization of unused land ('waste' and forest). By the early fourteenth century this expansion reached the limits of growth, determined by the availability of wasteland and existing levels of technology. Severe famines took place throughout Europe in the first half of the fourteenth century, followed by the catastrophic Black Death, which landed in southern Europe in 1348 and reached Britain in less than a year. This combination of ecological and epidemiological 'checks' reduced Europe's population by at least a third.[24]

As a result, demand for labour increased. In his chapters on 'so-called primitive accumulation', Marx explains the 'liberation' of the proletariat from the land in terms of 'bloody expropriation of the poor'. This has been, and remains, a subject of controversy. The ruling classes of late medieval England routinely passed draconian legislation to control wages and labour mobility. But at the same time, labour was in such shortage that peasants and their children might often have left their boring manors (both Marx and Engels had a cosmopolitan, urban prejudice against 'rural idiocy'[25]) because they thought they could do better elsewhere. Whatever legislation they passed, the lords of manors and estates needed labourers. Often, given the hegemony of agrarian cycles, they needed them urgently. To attract labourers they had to pay what was being asked. They did not like the idea of a mobile, 'free' labour force, because such workers were very largely freed from the localized social disciplines which were then and were to remain for centuries the basic institutions of settled order. What we see in the statute books with regard to 'bloody legislation against the poor' was only one side of the movement, the coercive side. Many thousands of peasants were turfed off the land by enclosures, in a process that began in the late fourteenth century and continued in various forms up to the Parliamentary Enclosure Movement of the eighteenth and early nineteenth centuries. But many more were never on the land in the first place. Many left it willingly, especially in the century after the Black Death.[26] The practical effect of labour legislation from the late Middle Ages to the beginnings of the Industrial Revolution was to enable successive regimes to monitor a movement none of them proved capable of stemming: increasing proletarianization of the workforce.[27]

Marx thought that 'in England, serfdom had disappeared in practice by the last part of the fourteenth century'. As with all economic, social and demographic movements, it is dangerous to assign too definite a date, but research since tends to confirm Marx's general framework. 'The prelude to the revolution that laid the foundation of the capitalist mode of production was played out in the last third of the fifteenth century and the first few decades of the sixteenth'. The result was a massive social revolution. 'In the history of primitive accumulation', he wrote, 'all revolutions are epoch-making that act as levers for the capitalist class in the course of its formation'.

> But this is true above all for those movements when great masses of men are suddenly and forcibly torn from their means of subsistence, and hurled onto the labour market as free, unprotected and rightless proletarians. The expropriation of the agricultural producer, of the peasant, from the soil, *is the basis of the whole process.*

'The capitalist era', he concluded, 'dates from the sixteenth century'.[28] Keith Wrightson sums it up: Marx

> described the independent, self-supporting peasantry of the fifteenth century, the long history of its expropriation by ruthless landlords from the sixteenth century onwards and its replacement by a class of large-scale capitalist farmers. Then he traced the consequences. Expropriation created a landless proletariat, harassed by savage vagrancy laws, the poor laws and oppressive labour legislation into 'the discipline necessary for the wage system'.[29]

Under the noses of successive monarchical regimes, Plantagenets, Lancastrians, Yorkists, Tudors, Stuarts and Hanoverians, indifferent to constitutional, religious, political and international relations, a great collective revolution was unfolding. It was driven, not by the decisions of kings, ruling classes and states, but by changes at the grass roots, in the mode of production and then, gradually, in the whole of society. Its effects were more massive and enduring than what Marx called the 'bourgeois' revolutions in England, the American colonies and France. The political revolutions were symptoms of much more deep-seated revolution in social relations of production. A 'bigger domestic market' appeared, as 'self provisioning gave way to the need to purchase'. 'Manufacturing industries spread' and drove the movement for 'commercial supremacy in overseas markets'. A pattern emerged of 'aggressive colonialism' in foreign affairs, 'protective legislation' at home.[30] The whole movement was driven by changes in the everyday lives of ordinary people, the communities where the work went on. Marx loved to tease scholars who studied the affairs of elites and states with the suggestion that they studied symptoms, not causes.

Marx linked the 'economic' details to a dramatic big picture. The capitalist mode of production was destined to change the ways all of us live, everywhere in the world. Just as he was prescient in identifying 'the population problem', Marx took 'globalism' as his point of departure more than a century before it became a staple of academic and public discourse in the late twentieth century. Marx thought this epochal transformation took off in sixteenth-century England, was manifest in his own day as the 'first industrial revolution'[31] and would continue to spread across and occupy the entire world until there was no one and nowhere left to conquer. The agency that drove this vast social revolution was the quest for what we call 'economic growth'.

Marx was an authority on the printed sources relating to four centuries of public debate about the condition of England. For him, this debate began in the generations of 'Chancellor [Sir John] Fortescue and Thomas More', who were writing in the later fifteenth and early sixteenth centuries. What led him to conclude that 'the capitalist era dates from the sixteenth century' was that this was as far as the printed sources would take him. Much research has been done since, not least on manuscript sources, which tell of a slightly longer 'transition from feudalism to capitalism' than Marx usually conceived it, beginning perhaps in the late thirteenth and early fourteenth centuries. We would see it as a more uneven process than Marx's conception suggests. Some regions and localities were transformed earlier than others, and everywhere changes took time to sink in and take institutional forms. Early experiments in moral regulation and welfare provisions tended to take place first in the new, 'rural' manufacturing districts.[32] We may wish to adopt different terminology from his, but there can be little doubt that in the long term something very closely resembling what Marx called 'proletarianization' was taking place, more or less progressively. Social revolutions take a long time to unfold, but their effects are more sweeping than those of short-term political revolutions and *coups d'état.*

For all his eagerness to see sudden, 'revolutionary' change like 1776, 1789 and 1848 (he was, after all, a revolutionary), Marx understood the history of the capitalist mode and social relations of production as a centuries-old, *continuous* process of 'accumulation', and thus likely to be misconceived if divided up into stages like 'early modern', 'modern' and now 'postmodern'. What we call 'modern', Marx called 'bourgeois society' or 'the bourgeois mode of production'. If anything, in Marx, the stage of 'primitive accumulation', or 'age of manufactures' as he sometimes called it, gave way in the late eighteenth and early nineteenth centuries to a clearer or more 'mature' type of *industrial* capitalism.[33] It is no accident that Marx never used the term 'industrial revolution'. For him, it was an *evolution,* spanning five or six centuries up to his own time. He was mainly concerned with where this system was going in the future, but he devoted a great deal of time to the study of its origins and past development.

We know a lot more about early modern England than Marx did. In no field of historical research has the creation of new knowledge been more spectacular, especially in the last 30 years, than in the fields of demographic, economic and social history. Researchers in these fields today would regard Marx's work on the fifteenth, sixteenth and seventeenth centuries as excessively dependent upon a limited range of impressionistic, literary sources. Modern demographic, social and economic histories evaluate the old literary traditions in the light of increasingly well-organized (and voluminous) local, regional and central-state manuscript archives. Marx's account can now be measured against a much richer picture.

The British Marxist historians

Marxism was an exceptionally powerful force in early modern studies for most of the second half of the twentieth century.[34] Leaving aside historiographical breezes from abroad (which tended to be less averse to Marxian perspectives, and what the French call the *longue durée*, than Britain), no group did more than the so-called 'British Marxist historians' to provide a rich, detailed and above all exciting historical vision of what E.P. Thompson called the 'great arch' of capitalist development. All were thoroughly grounded in Marx's writing, but tended to treat it as a point of departure. It was rich in *hypotheses*, pointers to work that needed doing rather than work that had been done. As Rodney Hilton wrote:

> Any serious historian has to classify and generalise social phenomena and is not likely to get very far unless he works from a theory of social development which will provide him with hypotheses. These hypotheses have the function of acting as organising principles for the direction of his research. They will naturally have to be checked against the data and if necessary modified'.[35]

In a series of books and articles, Hilton fleshed out the view that 'conflict between landlords and peasants, however muted or however intense, over the appropriation of the surplus product of the peasant holding, was a prime mover in the evolution of medieval society'. 'The social and political crises of the late medieval feudal order cannot be understood if what Marc Bloch called "the crisis of seigneurial fortunes" is not seen as the consequence of a failure by the ruling aristocracies to keep up the level of appropriation'.[36]

It was not necessary to share Hilton's desire to confirm Marxist hypotheses to appreciate his use of manorial and taxation records in building a whole series of local and regional studies of late medieval society: history 'from below'. Hilton drew attention to the importance of the parish in the affections of late medieval peasants, artisans and townspeople. This established an important continuity with a well-known feature of sixteenth- to eighteenth-century popular culture. We need more studies that transcend the 'great divide' between the 'late medieval' and 'early modern' periods. Marxism has always been uncomfortable with the artificial divisions of 'bourgeois' historiography.

E.P. Thompson was particularly sensitive to the polemical element in Marx's work. 'Marx conceived of himself, *pugnaciously*, as a materialist', he wrote. This was partly because he was indeed a materialist by conviction, but he also set out to satirize what he saw as the naïve ('bourgeois') idealism of his contemporaries. For Thompson, *Capital* was primarily concerned to elucidate the 'logic', rather than the history of capitalism. The history, he insisted, remained to be written. 'In *Capital*', wrote Thompson, 'Marx repeatedly uses the concept of the circuit of capital to characterise the structure of the capitalist economy – and, more than that, of capitalist society more generally'. However, 'historical materialism (as assumed as hypothesis by Marx, and as subsequently developed in our practice) must be concerned with other "circuits" also: the circuits of power, of the reproduction of ideology, etc., and these belong to a different logic and to other categories'.[37] For Thompson and Christopher Hill, especially, this meant accentuating 'the enormous importance of that part of the revolutionary inheritance which may be described, in a secular sense, as the tradition of *dissent*'.[38] Both tended to place greater emphasis on what Marx had called 'superstructural' elements of social process and revolution, and were sometimes accused of being 'culturalist' or (more accurately) 'humanist' Marxists.

The 'hypothetical' approach was immensely creative. Out of various works by Maurice Dobb (1900–76), R.H. Hilton (1916–2002), Christopher Hill (1912–2003), E.J. Hobsbawm (b. 1917), E.P. Thompson (1924–93), Robert Brenner (b. 1943) and others emerged a whole series of enduring controversies: 'the crisis of feudalism', 'the transition from feudalism to capitalism',[39] 'the English bourgeois revolution',[40] 'the seventeenth-century crisis',[41] 'class-struggle without class' in eighteenth-century England,[42] criminal law and class hegemony,[43] 'moral economy' versus 'market economy'[44] and, perhaps most notoriously, the whole question of 'the making of the English working class' in the eighteenth and early nineteenth centuries. 'The storm over the gentry' was not Marxism-inspired, but historians who have read Marx will always be alert to debates about social structure and agency. Few of the social historians now working on one aspect or another of 'the middle sort' are in any sense Marxist, but their results play directly on Marx's 'hypotheses'.

Through it all, class and class struggle were the pivotal areas of controversy. Although much was made of the fact that the terminology of class only appeared in the early nineteenth century,[45] not nearly enough was made of the fact that medieval and early modern writers reflexively thought of society in class-like ways, even if the language they used ('better *sort*', 'middling *sort*', 'lower *ranks*', 'many-headed multitude', 'the multitudes around *us*', and so on) was, to put it mildly, prematurely synthetic. Hardly anyone noticed that in his explorations of the British Library sources of his day, Marx had taken no credit 'for discovering the existence of classes in modern society or the struggle between them. Long before me bourgeois historians had described the historical development of this class struggle and bourgeois economists the economic anatomy of classes. What I did that was new', he continued,

> was to prove: 1) that the *existence of classes* is only bound up with *particular historical phases in the development of production*, 2) that the class struggle necessarily leads to *the dictatorship of the proletariat*, 3) that the dictatorship itself only constitutes the transition to the *abolition of all classes* and to a *classless society*.[46]

Students of early modern society need only concern themselves with the first of these propositions. Was early modern England a class-structured society, and in what sense(s)? And if so, were these classes contingencies of any 'particular . . . phases in the development of production'? While the British Marxists certainly explored proposition (1), none of them gave anything like wholehearted assent to Marx's sense that, if it was true, propositions (2) and (3) necessarily followed.

The British Marxists, collectively, studied the 'great arch'. Individually, they specialized. It would be unfair to sum up the prolific work of Christopher Hill in a single phrase, but he tended to concentrate on the 'middling' or 'industrious sort', and for present purposes his chosen area was 'the English bourgeois revolution'. As with his Marxist colleagues, this meant a much longer period than the civil wars and commonwealth: Hill's 1967 textbook, *Reformation to Industrial Revolution*, traced the transition between 1530 and 1780

> from a society in which it was taken for granted that a fully human existence was possible only for the narrow landed ruling class to a society in which an ideology of self-help had permeated into the middle ranks. The economists were newly conscious of scarcity because of the new prospects of abundance. In these 250 years we pass from universal belief in original sin to the romanticism of Man is good. We have moved, too, from an England which had virtually no overseas possessions except Ireland to the break-up of the first British Empire and the first stirrings of Irish nationalism . . .[47]

The Marxists reminded us that some rather epochal things *had* in fact happened in early modern England. Their perspectives were always, at one and the same time, local, national and global.

After his earliest work, the Marxist framework was usually between the lines of Hill's work. In some ways everything he wrote can be seen as a critique of Marx's crude conceptions of the 'bourgeoisie'. 'The Industrious Sort of People', and in fact all the essays in his 1964 *Society and Puritanism in Pre-Revolutionary England*, are filled with insights into the worlds of what contemporaries were beginning to call 'the middling sort', still a growth area in early modern studies.[48] While it drew greatly on R.H. Tawney's (1880–1962) vision of the role of religion in sixteenth- and seventeenth-century England, many read *Society and Puritanism* as a trailblazing collection of penetrating studies of the great *social* revolution that was taking place in early modern England. Controversy focused at the time on the meaning and validity of the terms 'Puritan' and (later) 'Revolution', but this great book also pointed firmly towards the local grass roots as the places where the long, revolutionary transformation of England was taking place. Hill has seldom been given the credit he deserves for signposting this enormously important and creative area of early modern studies.

Hill's work epitomizes the refusal of the best Marxist history to conform to institutionalized periods and disciplines. His interests, developed from incomparable mastery of the printed sources, spanned 'social', 'economic', 'literary', 'intellectual' and 'political' history. Hill was a great historian of ideas; in a discipline that becomes ever more sub-specialized, this sense of the interconnectedness of every aspect of life in society remains one of the most important, if paradoxical, achievements of Marxist historiography. The book that many consider Hill's masterpiece, *The World Turned Upside Down*,[49] was criticized for reifying terms of contemporary moral panic ('Ranters', for example) into organized sects, but if read sceptically (as all history books should be) it remains the first port of call for anyone interested in the explosion of ideas that occurred in the 1640s and 1650s.[50]

Thompson and Hill are indispensable historians of 'the tradition of dissent'.[51] They grounded their work in a broadly Marxist framework, but were primarily interested, not so much in the underlying 'structures', but in what people alive at various times in their evolution *did*, what they felt and thought as a result of the circumstances they found themselves in. Both were primarily interested in ideas and ideologies in their social contexts. Thompson's *The Making of the English Working Class* (London, 1963) was very much 'bottom-up history' in its concern to 'rescue' the working people of the Industrial Revolution 'from the enormous condescension of posterity'. It was driven by a refusal of determinist conceptions of class formation, in which classes are mechanically brought into existence by forces beyond their comprehension and power to grasp. This was very much a 'New Left' reaction against Stalinist/Bolshevik 'vulgar Marxism', in which the only changes that are really consequential are economic changes. In this 'vulgar Marxist' model, 'the economy' is the 'base' and everything else (art, politics, culture, thought) is 'superstructure'. As we have seen, this was pretty much Marx's view too. The 'British Marxist historians' saw Marx's brilliant sketches as 'hypotheses' to be tested, insights to be filled out with new research. Thompson and Hill were profoundly interested in literature and culture. They were 'humanist Marxists', and for some of their critics on the Left, the humanism was stronger than the Marxism.[52]

Thompson's thesis was that the English working class made itself, in resistance grounded in custom, pre-existing senses of morality and community, intelligence and collective action. His insistence that culture and intelligence were at least as important in class formation as the mode and social relations of production was criticized by Marxists as not being Marxist enough, and by non-Marxists for being too clearly concerned with a central issue of Marxism. It is now generally agreed that Thompson's masterpiece (a best-seller that greatly influenced a generation of social historians) was as much about the development of older, artisan forms of radical and popular politics as it was about the emergence of a new 'English working class'. It included a swingeing critique of quantitative histories of the Industrial Revolution and, as we have seen, Thompson located his work in a 'bourgeois revolution' conceived as a 'great arch' of English historical development that was pretty much based on Marx's own periodization. In 1985 two Marxist sociologists filled out this idea in an inspired book entitled *The Great Arch: English State Formation as Cultural Revolution.*[53]

The classics of British Marxism are still in print. As Andy Wood commented recently, 'Marxist historical interpretation has rather more life in it than its critics have supposed'.[54] Although Thompson began his study with the 1790s, writes Wood, he 'recognized the diversity of earlier historical experiences on which the making of the English working class drew'.[55] When Thompson wrote, in the early 1960s, there were few really penetrating studies of those 'earlier historical experiences' to flesh out his intuition. Several decades later we know a great deal more about the lives of the early modern commonalty. In the light of this developing knowledge, Thompson's broad sense of the making of a national working class in the late eighteenth and early nineteenth centuries makes more sense. Wood concludes that 'we need not accept the entirety of Thompson's account to see a distinct watershed in class politics and social relations as located in the 1780–1832 period'. His crucial point is that 'the importance of this disjuncture is best discerned from a long view of class formation'.[56] A new 'long view', based in part on early modern microhistories, is starting to come into focus.

Class, politics and power

Class is the most controversial, bitterly debated and problematical facet of Marx's theory.[57] Marx and Engels were convinced that the whole history of civilization is the history of class struggle, but when Marx finally addressed the specifics of class structure in the notoriously incomplete final section of *Capital,* he faltered. The British Marxists, especially Hilton and Thompson, recognized the gap and tried to fill it with articulate dissent. The 'new' early modern social historiography distanced itself from the topic. Its exponents, dedicated to painstaking research in local, regional and national manuscript archives, saw that to engage with class would arouse violent controversy. It would cloud the vital importance of original work in fields like 'crime, kinship, social structure, urbanization, literacy, population change, household relations, sexual behaviour, riot, witchcraft and moral regulation'.[58] There were entrenched prejudices to consider. A historian of the Leveller Movement, H.N. Brailsford (1873–1958), wrote that the historical profession of the 1940s and 1950s was 'as shy in confronting the fact of class as were the novelists of the last century in facing the fact of sex'. In the 1980s, Thompson was otherwise engaged and Christopher Hill and his allies were forced to defend their conception of the 1640s as 'a revolutionary transformation which established the preconditions for the emergence of industrial capitalism in the following century' against the 'short-term causes and consequences' of triumphant revisionists. In the 1990s, historians influenced by certain aspects of postmodernism and poststructuralism confirmed the enduringly controversial nature of the topic by suggesting that 'class', 'society' and even 'history' were purely linguistic, discursive phenomena.[59]

Meanwhile, the new social historians patiently built up a more detailed picture, using archives that the British Marxists had not explored. In terms of history from below, the historiography of early modern England began again, virtually from scratch, in the 1970s. The Cambridge Group was in the vanguard; Peter Laslett's *The World We Have Lost* was the Group's manifesto, Wrigley and Schofield's *The Population History of England, 1541–1871* its most monumental product.[60] The broader implication was that we have enough knowledge about kings, counsellors and literate ruling elites. It was time to pay attention to the other millions of men, women and children alive at the time, and it seemed possible to begin that larger task, with *fresh* perspectives and *new* questions. The shoulders on which this movement stood were not the giants of British historiography, but two or three generations of archivists who had made a new kind of history ('from below') possible. These unsung heroes had identified thousands of record collections, in parish churches, manor houses, and so on, all over England, and persuaded their keepers to allow them to be located in central places (usually county archive offices), where they were categorized and classified in ways that, in spite of their volume, made them accessible and usable.

The opening up of academic history to local and regional archives was an opportunity, not to fill gaps or test hypotheses relating to existing theories and paradigms, but to effect a genuine paradigm shift.[61] The imperative to approach archives with hypotheses derived from the existing body of historiography, Marxist or otherwise, was bound to militate against such a possibility. The history of women would not have got far if it had relied on historiographical precedent. History had always been patriarchal, and it had always been written (as Marx himself wrote it) from some kind of 'centre' (men, a ruling elite, a state, a nation, the Communist Party). Local and regional archives were about the day-to-day administration of the subject population. They created a different sort of opportunity. In those early parish registers, tax lists, vestry minutes, sessions papers, settlement records and 'bawdy court' depositions are the names, addresses, actions and words of the characters in a new social history, which begins with the local and proceeds, not by means of hypotheses, but by networking trails of evidence. The spirit of the Cambridge Group was very far from that of Marx, but it was about identifying usable archives and devising methods to answer questions that were highly relevant to the 'hypotheses' of Marxism.

One of the 'unexpected revelations' that has emerged from this apparently apolitical (and extremely productive) new historiography is that 'the early modern economy and social structures *had* gone through rapid, convulsive change'. Whatever it was, early modern England was not a peaceful, harmonious commonwealth. The Peasants' Revolt (1381) and Cade's Rebellion (1450), we find, were not isolated eruptions, but peaks of endemic conflict. The English Revolution was only the greatest of a vast, enduring series of conflicts in neighbourhoods, localities, districts and provinces. The events of 1381, 1450 and 1649 stood out because only then did the rebels take London, which meant they had Westminster in their sights. While a few studies felt breezes of 'class antagonism', even 'class hatred', the dominant view that emerged was that 'the localism of [most] disturbances meant that they were pre-class, even pre-politics'.[62] The new social history of late medieval and early modern England 'reveal[ed] the effectiveness of peasant politics within the more restricted scale of [their] communities', but left completely untouched a deeper consensus that seems to have passed from generation to generation since the age it purports to describe.[63]

Shared by Marxists, non-Marxists and anti-Marxists alike, it rests on 'the conviction that peasants were incapable of political thought, unable to comprehend their political situation in terms of their own experience'.[64] To Hilton, 'the ruling ideas of medieval peasants seem to have been the ideas of the rulers of society'. Hobsbawm was slightly more hesitant:

> The great danger . . . is to equate all behaviour as equally 'rational'. Some of it is. For instance, the behaviour of the good Soldier Schweik, who had been certified as a *bona fide* half-wit by the military authorities, was anything but half-witted. It was undoubtedly the most effective form of self-defence for someone in his position. Time and again, in studying the political behaviour of peasants, we discover the practical value of stupidity. . . .[65]

He then suggests 'that many of these peasants don't just play at being dense, they really are dense'. The same, of course, can be said of any class or group. Raftis's judgement on the politics of the 1381 Peasants' Revolt has general applicability. Like Hilton, he sees 'no evidence that [English peasants] had acquired a national or political mentality . . . it was apparently non-peasants who gave the leadership, the volatile tradespeople in Kent, the disaffected clergy in Essex, the politically wise townsmen in London, burgher against abbey at St Albans and Bury St Edmunds'.[66]

Wood objects to this legend of the blinkered, parochial plebeian. 'Studies of class formation have long been hampered by modern social historians' strange obsession with the nation state', he writes.

> Ever since late nineteenth- and early twentieth-century European socialists linked their political project to the transformed national identities of that period, social historians have been mesmerized by that single definition of class-identity. The assumption that 'true' class consciousness can be manifest on the level of the nation-state has led historians to find in the closely felt local and regional plebeian identities of the early modern period one of the main barriers to the operations of class.

As he notes, 'the reductive connection between nation and class' lay behind Laslett's influential argument that class consciousness was thus necessarily limited to the only sections of English society that routinely operated on the national stage: the gentry and up.[67] More importantly,

> the history of modern European working-class political culture has often been the history of regions and localities. Whether historians are describing the insurrectionists of the Paris Commune, the mining communities of the Rhondda valley or the anarchists of Catalonia, class and local identity have in many contexts been historically inseparable.[68]

And, we may add, the English communes of 1381 and the households and countries of the commonalty from the fifteenth to the eighteenth centuries. To understand this long revolution we must begin in the communities.

The most fruitful offshoot of twentieth-century Marxism as far as these issues are concerned is the branch that runs from the Italian communist leader Antonio Gramsci (1891–1937), through E.P. Thompson and Eugene D. Genovese, historian of the North American South and slavery, to the anthropologist James C. Scott. Its prime assumption is that all human beings are necessarily sapient by virtue of being human. Gramsci contrasted this universal intellect with that of 'the intellectual', a person who is trained to think in a specific way, be it traditional, as with the clerical education of medieval times, or technical, as with modern doctors, engineers, teachers, lawyers and journalists. Gramsci called these the subalterns of the established order. Their job is to know how to do specialized and necessary jobs, like writing in Latin, using and manipulating the law, building a bridge, identifying a disease, teaching a syllabus or, as politicians, conducting affairs of state; the 'subalterns' (or 'junior officers') of the ruling class are supposed to know and work within the 'correct' or authorized intellectual contexts within which such things are, by prescribed tradition and custom, supposed to be conceived and done. These are the kind of people ruling classes and states train and employ as counsellors and administrators. To understand their politics, we must understand their perceived interests and the contexts within which they understand themselves to be operating.

If 'politics' are understood to be the study and practice of relationships of power, and power relationships are seen as intrinsic to all human contexts, it follows that 'the questions to be asked about peasants by those in pursuit of their politics are the same questions that have often been asked about non-peasants'. This kind of work rubs the magisterial tradition of constitutional history against the grain of a generation of microstudies and theoretical works like that of Scott and Wood, that 'reveal the effectiveness of peasant politics within the more restricted scale of the communities'. Given that we can now be reasonably certain that peasants routinely engaged in something closely resembling politics *within* their communities, 'there are good reasons for regarding the peasants' provincial politics as, in some respects, an extension of their family and village strategies'.[69] This still leaves us marooned in local communities, but it also alerts us to levels of dissent that are deeper and more ubiquitous than well-documented traditions of articulate dissent and collective protest.

Scott sees tactics of obfuscation and dissemblance as universal features of plebeian communities in oppressive constitutional regimes. Direct, articulate opposition results in immediate, brutal punishment. Resistance is veiled, surreptitious, subtle, restrained and resolutely patient. One of the most effective and frustrating ways in which oppressed people can resist the orders of their masters is to pretend to be too stupid to understand them.[70] Scott's theory, very influential recently among social historians of popular politics,[71] began with a study that applied Thompson's idea of 'the moral economy' to 'everyday forms of resistance' among Malaysian peasants.[72] His fieldwork led him to conclude that 'the process of domination generates a hegemonic public conduct and a backstage discourse consisting of what cannot be spoken in the face of power'.

Scott notes that 'even close readings of historical and archival evidence tend to favour a hegemonic account of power relations'. Where the British Marxists had adapted an extremely articulate tradition of dissent to the cause of class struggle, Scott identified a ubiquitous 'lower' level of dissent and resistance in the form of a 'theater of the powerless'. This theatre (a metaphor that Thompson had used to characterize eighteenth-century politics) involved 'rumours, gossip, folktales, songs, gestures, jokes . . . poaching, foot-dragging, pilfering, dissimulation [and] flight'. In this way Scott implied a *culture* of resistance in which 'peasants disguised their efforts to thwart material appropriation of their labour, their production, and their property'. Despite Scott's understandable reluctance to introduce a new jargon word into the repertoire of the human sciences, the word 'infrapolitics' and the notion of 'hidden transcripts' are useful hypotheses that remind us that absence of obvious evidence may not mean absence of the thing itself.[73]

Conclusion

Class-like features are not the only dimensions of the lives of our ancestors that the new social history has disclosed. Much of the best microhistory has been researched and written by scholars who have no Marxist leanings at all.[74] They remain relevant to Marx's hypotheses because his attempt to make holistic sense of the processes by which humanity has transformed and is transforming itself ('but never in conditions of our own making'), and his passionate belief that we can build a better future out of the accumulating mistakes of the past, still haunts us. In setting about the reconstruction of the history of what the great *Annaliste* Fernand Braudel (1902–85) called 'the civilisation of capitalism', we are already discovering a much richer, more complex and more interconnected vision than the one we inherited. It has more characters, more communities, more variants and more differences than the trail of kings and queens, parliaments, civil societies, nation states and even classes, modes and social relations of production of the old versions. Marx and Marxism are part of those old versions. What we take from them and find useful is up to us.

Guide to further reading

Philip Corrigan and Derek Sayer, *The Great Arch: English State Formation as Cultural Revolution* (Oxford, 1985).

Christopher Hill, *Society and Puritanism in Pre-Revolutionary England* (London, 1964).

Christopher Hill, *The World Turned Upside Down: Radical Ideas During the English Revolution* (London, 1972).

R.H. Hilton, *Class Conflict and the Crisis of Feudalism* (London, 1990).

David Levine, *At The Dawn of Modernity: Biology, Culture and Material Life in Europe After the Year 1000* (Berkeley, 2001).

Matt Perry, *Marxism and History* (Basingstoke, 2002).

John Seed, 'Marxist Interpretation of History', in Kelly Boyd (ed.), *Encyclopedia of Historians and Historical Writing* (London, 1999), pp. 772–8.

G.E.M. de Ste Croix, *The Class Struggle in the Ancient World from the Archaic Age to the Arab Conquests* (London, 1981).

E.P. Thompson, *Customs in Common: Studies in Traditional Popular Culture* (London, 1991).

Francis Wheen, *Karl Marx* (London, 1999).

Notes

1 Bertolt Brecht, 'Questions From A Worker Who Reads', in John Willett and Ralph Manheim (eds), *Bertolt Brecht Poems* (London, 1976), p. 252.

2 Friedrich Engels, 'The Position of England: the Eighteenth Century', *Vorwärts!* (1844), repr. in Karl Marx and Friedrich Engels, *Articles on Britain* (Moscow, 1975), p. 9: 'Social revolution is the only true revolution, to which philosophical and political revolution must lead'.

3 For a useful overview of the theoretical system that emerged after Marx's death, see 'Marxism', in Tom Bottomore (ed.), *A Dictionary of Marxist Thought* (Oxford, 1983), pp. 309–12. E.J. Hobsbawm, *Revolutionaries* (London, 1973) provides an exceptionally readable introduction to the scope and theoretical creativity of twentieth-century Marxism. Francis Wheen, *Karl Marx* (London, 1999) is a readable biography.

4 'In the social production of their existence, men inevitably enter into definite relations, which are independent of their will, namely relations of production appropriate to a given stage in the material development of their material forces of production. The totality of these relations of production constitutes the economic structure of society, the real foundation, on which arises a legal and political superstructure and to which correspond definite forms of social consciousness. The mode of production of material life conditions the general process of social, political and intellectual life. It is not the consciousness of men that determines their existence, but their social existence that determines their consciousness': Marx, *A Contribution to the Critique of Political Economy* (Moscow, 1970), pp. 20–1.

5 'The knights of industry . . . only succeeded in supplanting the knights of the sword by making use of events in which they had played no part whatsoever': *Capital*, vol. 1 (1867; Harmondsworth, 1967), p. 875. As Perry Anderson observes, 'the notion of "bourgeois revolution" that subsequent Marxists were to apply to them is scarcely to be found *as such* . . . in [Marx's] writings at all . . . the upheavals ascribed to it are seen in terms of the economic impact of large capitalist industry and the expanding world market, not in terms of a political assault by the bourgeoisie on the Ancien Régimes of the late feudal order': Perry Anderson, *English Questions* (London, 1992), p. 107.

6 For a brief sketch, see Marx, 'A Review of Guizot's Book: Why Has the English Revolution Been Successful?' (1850), in Marx and Engels, *Articles on Britain*, pp. 89–95.

7 E.J. Hobsbawm, 'On History from Below', in his *On History* (London, 1998), pp. 266–86.

8 Marx, *Capital*, vol. 1, pp. 873 ff.

9 Keith Wrightson, *Earthly Necessities: Economic Lives in Early Modern Britain* (Yale, 2000), pp. 10–13, in which a non-Marxist social historian writes a balanced epitaph of Marx on early modern England.

10 See 'Index to Authorities Quoted', Marx, *Capital*, vol. 1, pp. 1095–119.
11 Wrightson, *Earthly Necessities*, p. 11.
12 Marx, *Capital*, vol. 1, p. 875.
13 Marx, *Critique of Political Economy*, p. 27.
14 Marx, *Capital*, vol. 1, p. 874.
15 'The executive of the modern state is but a committee for managing the common affairs of the whole bourgeoisie': Karl Marx and Friedrich Engels, *Manifesto of the Communist Party*, in Marx and Engels, *Selected Works* (Moscow, 1970), p. 37.
16 'With the polarization of the commodity market into these two classes, the fundamental conditions of capitalist production are present', Marx, *Capital*, vol. 1, p. 874.
17 David Rollison, *The Local Origins of Modern Society: Gloucestershire, 1500–1800* (London, 1992), 'Introduction: Country Capitalism'.
18 David Rollison, 'Discourse and Class Struggle: the Politics of Industry in Early Modern England', *Social History* 26(2) (2001), pp.167–8, notes 9–13.
19 Marx, *Capital*, vol. 1, ch. 25 (my italic). Wally Seccombe, *A Millennium of Family Change* (London, 1992) is a broad Marxist account.
20 Andrew Goudie, *The Human Impact on the Natural Environment* (Oxford, 1990), p. 9.
21 The 'spectre' was communism; but 'the communists . . . have no interests separate and apart from the proletariat as a whole'; their theory was 'abolition of private property': Marx and Engels, *Manifesto*, pp. 35, 46–7.
22 E.A. Wrigley and R.S. Schofield, *The Population History of England, 1541–1871: A Reconstruction* (London, 1981); see also the classic line of microhistories, from Keith Wrightson and David Levine, *Poverty and Piety in an English Village: Terling, 1525–1700* (New York, 1979) to Pamela Sharpe, *Population and Society: Reproducing Colyton, 1540–1840* (Exeter, 2002).
23 Eric R. Wolf, *Europe and the People Without History* (Berkeley and Los Angeles, 1982) is an outstanding and readable Marxist account of the historical process, dynamics and global expansion of the capitalist world-system; Peter Linebaugh and Marcus Rediker, *The Many Headed Hydra: Sailors, Slaves, Commoners, and the Hidden History of the Revolutionary Atlantic* (Boston, 2000).
24 David Levine, *At the Dawn of Modernity: Biology, Culture, and Material Life in Europe After the Year 1000* (Berkeley, 2001) and David Levine, 'Industrialization and the Proletarian Family in England', *Past & Present* 107 (1985), pp. 168–203.
25 Pre-industrial peasants 'lacked any education or any mental activity; they were still at a prehistoric stage of development': Engels, 'Eighteenth Century', p. 19.
26 Levine, *Dawn of Modernity*, pp. 384–400; E.B. Fryde, *Peasants and Landlords in Later Medieval England* (Stroud, 1996); and, for example,

L.R. Poos, *A Rural Society after the Black Death: Essex, 1350–1525* (Cambridge, 1991); R.H. Britnell, *Growth and Decline in Colchester, 1300–1525* (Cambridge, 1986).

27 For quantitative estimates of this process, see David Levine, *Reproducing Families: the Political Economy of English Population History* (Cambridge, 1987), pp. 40–1.

28 Marx, *Capital*, vol. 1, pp. 877, 878, 876.

29 Wrightson, *Earthly Necessities*, p. 11.

30 Wrightson, *Earthly Necessities*, pp. 10–13.

31 For a historiographical overview, see Pat Hudson, *The Industrial Revolution* (London, 1992).

32 Marjorie K. McIntosh, *Controlling Misbehavior in England, 1370–1600* (Cambridge, 1998).

33 Wolf, *People Without History*, pp. 305–6.

34 Harvey J. Kaye, *The British Marxist Historians: An Introductory Analysis* (Cambridge, 1984); Raphael Samuel, 'British Marxist Historians, 1880–1980', *New Left Review* 120 (1980), pp. 21–96.

35 Rodney Hilton, *Class Conflict and the Crisis of Feudalism* (London, 1990), p. 41.

36 Hilton, *Class Conflict*, p. ix.

37 E.P. Thompson, *The Poverty of Theory and Other Essays* (1965; London, 1981), pp. 63, 68 (my italic).

38 Thompson, *Poverty of Theory*, p. 269 (original italic).

39 R.H. Hilton (ed.), *The Transition from Feudalism to Capitalism* (London, 1976); T.H. Aston and C.H.E. Philpin (eds), *The Brenner Debate: Agrarian Class Structure and Economic Development in Pre-industrial Europe* (Cambridge, 1985); Robert Brenner, *Merchants and Revolution: Commercial Change, Political Conflict and London's Overseas Traders, 1550–1653* (Princeton, 1993).

40 Christopher Hill, 'A Bourgeois Revolution' and Lawrence Stone, 'The Bourgeois Revolution Revisited', in J.G.A. Pocock (ed.), *Three British Revolutions: 1641, 1688, 1776* (Princeton, 1980). The best general critique of Marxist and *marxisant* approaches to 'Hill's century' is Alastair MacLachlan, *The Rise and Fall of Revolutionary England: An Essay on the Fabrication of Seventeenth-Century History* (London, 1996); MacLachlan's references (pp. 326–419) cover all angles of the controversy and testify to just how much controversy there was.

41 T.H. Aston (ed.), *Crisis in Europe, 1560–1660* (Cambridge, 1965); MacLachlan, *Rise and Fall*, pp. 160–2.

42 E.P. Thompson, 'Patrician Society: Plebeian Culture', *Journal of Social History* 7(4) (1974); 'Eighteenth-Century English Society: Class-Struggle Without Class?', *Social History* 3(2) (1978), pp. 382–405; Thompson, *Customs in Common: Studies in Traditional Popular Culture* (London, 1991), chs 1 and 2.

43 Douglas Hay et al., *Albion's Fatal Tree: Crime and Society in Eighteenth-Century England* (London, 1975); E.P. Thompson, *Whigs and Hunters: the Origin of the Black Act* (London, 1975).
44 Thompson, *Customs in Common*, chs 4 and 5.
45 Asa Briggs, 'The Language of Class in Early Nineteenth-Century England' (1967), repr. in R.S. Neale (ed.), *History and Class: Essential Readings in Theory and Interpretation* (Oxford, 1983), pp. 2–29.
46 Marx to J. Weydemeyer, 5 March 1852, in Marx and Engels, *Selected Works*, p. 669; original italic.
47 Christopher Hill, *Reformation to Industrial Revolution: A Social and Economic History of Britain, 1530–1780* (London, 1967), p. 239.
48 Steve Hindle, *The State and Social Change in Early Modern England* (Basingstoke, 2000), pp. ix–x, stresses 'the role played by relatively humble people in governing late sixteenth- and early seventeenth-century England', and 'emphasizes the extent to which state authority required co-operation at the local level'. Existing orthodoxies of political and constitutional history, he writes, 'grossly underestimated the breadth and depth of the political nation'.
49 Christopher Hill, *The World Turned Upside Down: Radical Ideas During the English Revolution* (London, 1972).
50 J.C. Davis, *Fear, Myth and History: The Ranters and their Historians* (Cambridge, 1986); MacLachlan, *Rise and Fall*, pp. 183–93.
51 Christopher Hampton (ed.), *The Radical Tradition: The Struggle for Change in England, 1381–1914* (Harmondsworth, 1984) is a broad-minded selection.
52 Perry Anderson, *Arguments within English Marxism* (London, 1980).
53 Philip Corrigan and Derek Sayer, *The Great Arch: English State Formation as Cultural Revolution* (Oxford, 1985).
54 Andy Wood, *Riot, Rebellion and Popular Politics in Early Modern England* (Basingstoke, 2002), p. 134.
55 Thompson further described some of these 'alternative intellectual traditions', contrasted them with 'the formal, classical intellectual culture', and again stressed the importance in these traditions of 'experience', in *Witness Against the Beast: William Blake and the Moral Law* (Cambridge, 1993), pp. xiv–xv and *passim*.
56 Andy Wood, *The Politics of Social Conflict: The Peak Country, 1520–1770* (Cambridge, 1999), pp. 322–4; 'Early modern plebs had been quite capable of conceiving of society in terms of stark class polarities. Class was not made in the Industrial Revolution: but it was given a different expression', p. 318.
57 G.E.M. de Ste Croix, *The Class Struggle in the Ancient World from the Archaic Age to the Arab Conquests* (London 1981), ch. 2.
58 Wood, *Riot*, pp. ix–x.

59 Gareth Stedman Jones, *Languages of Class: Studies in Working Class History* (Cambridge, 1983) started the ball rolling; Patrick Joyce (ed.), *Class* (Oxford, 1995) includes many readings; the centre of the storm in the 1990s was the journal *Social History*; see also Jacques Derrida, *Specters of Marx*, trans. Peggy Kamuf (London, 1994).
60 Peter Laslett, *The World We Have Lost* (1965) was revised as *The World We Have Lost – Further Explored* (London, 1983); Wrigley and Schofield, *Population History*.
61 Thomas Samuel Kuhn, *The Structure of Scientific Revolutions* (1962; 2nd enlarged edn, London, 1970).
62 Wood, *Politics of Social Conflict*, pp. 13–15; my italic.
63 R.B. Goheen, 'Peasant Politics? Village Community and the Crown in Fifteenth-Century England', *American History Review* 96(1) (1991), p. 43.
64 Goheen, 'Peasant Politics', p. 61; R.H. Hilton, *The English Peasantry in the Later Middle Ages* (Oxford, 1975), p. 16.
65 Hobsbawm, 'History from Below', p. 283.
66 J.A. Raftis 'Social Change *versus* Revolution: New Interpretations of the Peasants Revolt of 1381', in Francis X. Newman (ed.), *Social Unrest in the Late Middle Ages* (Binghampton, 1986), p. 18.
67 Wood, *Politics of Social Conflict*, pp. 25–6; Laslett, *World We Have Lost*, ch. 2.
68 Wood, *Politics of Social Conflict*, p. 26.
69 R.B. Goheen, 'Peasant Politics?' pp. 42–62.
70 David Rollison, 'Property, Ideology and Popular Culture in a Gloucestershire Village, 1660–1740', *Past & Present* 93 (1981), pp. 70–97.
71 For example, Michael J. Braddick and John Walter's introduction to their (eds), *Negotiating Power in Early Modern Society: Order, Hierarchy and Subordination in Britain and Ireland* (Cambridge, 2001), p. 6.
72 Thompson, 'The Moral Economy of the English Crowd in the Eighteenth Century', *Past & Present* 50 (1971), pp. 76–136, repr. in his *Customs in Common*.
73 James C. Scott, *Domination and the Arts of Resistance: Hidden Transcripts* (Yale, 1990), pp. ix–xii.
74 Eamon Duffy, *The Stripping of the Altars: Traditional Religion in England, c.1400–c.1580* (New Haven, 1992); Eamon Duffy, *The Voices of Morebath: Reformation and Rebellion in an English Village* (London, 2001) are outstanding examples.

2

Modernization

Garthine Walker

Probably few historians nowadays would list modernization theory among those that significantly inform the writing of early modern history.[1] In his entry on modernization in the *Encyclopedia of European Social History* (1993), Peter Stearns, once a leading advocate of modernization theory, accepts that it has been subject to some devastating criticisms. In the third edition of his own *European Society in Upheaval*, Stearns dropped the modernization approach. Stearns nevertheless suggests that modernization theory deserves attention as an attempt to link various processes of change in history, and that it continues to inform historical writing in a semi-casual way.[2] There is much truth in this assessment. Ideas about modernization are so deeply rooted in western culture that they appear to be common sense: 'obviously' the world has modernized; 'obviously' some societies are more modern than others. Not surprisingly, many historians have assumed that the process began in the *early modern* period and that that period is defined by a conflict between traditional and modern.

Simply put, modernization theory involves a number of assumptions about the transformation from 'traditional' to 'modern' society. Within the modernization paradigm, the nineteenth and twentieth centuries of Western Europe and North America are deemed 'modern' (capitalist, industrial, urban, individualist, bureaucratized, secular and scientifically organized) and western medieval society is 'traditional' (feudal, pre-industrial, agrarian, rural, lineage-based, religiously or magically organized). In between the medieval and modern worlds lies a period of transition from one to the other. Historians have identified in the centuries between 1500 and 1800 some nascent characteristics of modernity – such as state formation, bureaucracy, capitalism, the rise of the gentry or middle class or middling sort, modern science, secularization, rationalization and affective individualism. Modernization theory thus offers an often unacknowledged way of defining the 'early modern' period as a field of study.

Modernization theory: origins

The origins of modernization theory lie in nineteenth-century liberal ideas of progress. The tendency to cast progress as a shift from barbarism to civilization had an obvious role in legitimating imperial conquest, but it was also part of a whole set of ideas about race, class and gender. Just as elite nineteenth-century Europeans considered colonized peoples to be childlike, feminine and passive, so women and workers were frequently compared to primitive races. Such inferior groups were deemed to be unable to take responsibility for themselves or to use reason to understand and transform the world – unlike the educated, bourgeois male. 'Primitive races', women and the masses appropriated knowledge through symbols and display, rather than rationally; hence their vulnerability to sudden passions and to manipulation by the unscrupulous.

This context is important because it informed the emergence of university disciplines as we know them. Particularly important is that of sociology, under the influence of Emile Durkheim (1858–1917) and Max Weber (1864–1920). The founders of sociology are often seen as having invented a new social science, free from the prejudices of the age. Actually both Durkeim and Weber were especially concerned with the problem of integrating the working class into a liberal and democratic society. Both retained a fundamental distinction between barbarous and civilized. Durkheim described the shift from one to the other in terms of increasing specialization of function, while Weber spoke of desacralization and rationalization. Weber focused in particular on the origins of capitalism and individualism in the Protestant Reformation. Durkheim, meanwhile, emphasized the non-rational ways in which traditional societies obtained knowledge, especially through the myths and rituals of religion. Durkheim's ideas on this greatly influenced anthropology, which was concerned with the study of *primitive* races, and which developed special techniques to interpret primitive peoples' symbolic and non-rational modes of expression. Before Claude Lévi-Strauss (b. 1908) developed structural anthropology (which assumes that cultural forms are based on universal underlying properties of the human mind), the barbarous/civilized, traditional/modern distinction was an article of faith among anthropologists.

The modernization paradigm arrived in historical writing by two routes. First, the French historical school, the *Annales*, was heavily influenced by Durkheim. Mark Bloch (1886–1944), for example, used anthropological techniques to understand the rituals of kingship and healing. *Annales* historians, like protagonists of modernization, tended to view history as a process of slow, evolutionary change, affecting all areas of life. Second, and more explicitly, modernization theory entered historiography through the influence of American sociologist Talcott Parsons (1902–79). Parsons systematized the scattered ideas of Weber and Durkheim as 'modernization theory'. His ideas were particularly influential in social scientific and historical writing during the 1950s and 1960s. Modernization theory was applied particularly to so-called 'Third World' societies entering the global political stage and, increasingly, to history.

Modernization theory: some characteristics

Classic modernization theory has six key characteristics that pertain to early modern historiography. First, is the dichotomous periodization of 'traditional' and 'modern'. Modernization theory defines 'traditional' society in terms of what is not modern. Thus, in traditional society, the masses do not participate in the conduct of public affairs, unlike in modern democracy. In traditional society, individuals carry out a range of tasks without differentiation of employment, with a self-sufficient peasantry growing their own food and making their own clothes, whereas in modern society a range of different specialized occupations are involved in the various stages of food and clothing production. Traditional society is organized on lines of kinship and small communities rather than on the individual and the nation state. The culture of traditional society is imbued with religion in contrast to the secularity of modern society. Moreover, traditional societies possess only a limited capacity for dealing with change – people with a traditional mindset do not believe in the possibility and desirability of change – whereas modern people embrace change and can adapt to it easily. Inhabitants of traditional societies passively accept conventional social hierarchies, expecting continuity in nature and society. At the same time, not having learned 'modern' self-restraint, they are more spontaneous, less concerned about their bodily functions and more likely to lash out violently than modern people. Indeed, people in traditional societies are sometimes described as childlike, not having mastered themselves like modern adults.

Second, modernization theory assumes that history necessarily moves from tradition to modernity, even though the precise paths might differ from country to country. All societies are deemed to be 'traditional' or 'modern', or in a transitional state. Modernization theory is teleological and particular periods are judged not in their own terms, but according to whether they contribute to or hinder the process of modernization.

Third, modernization theory is *functionalist*. It analyses societies as systems (organic or machine-like) that have an innate tendency towards stability and to reproduce themselves. Therefore the motor of change is found in the system itself, not in people's intentional or inadvertent actions. The bureaucratic state, for instance, developed because it enabled the system to operate more efficiently. This systemic view of society emphasizes the interconnectedness of all areas of human thought and activity: economy, politics, religion, family life, sexual interaction, and so forth. These various spheres of society are all connected. Changes in one sphere produce complementary changes elsewhere. Despite the importance of industrialization to modernity, modernization theory does not posit that change emanates from the economic foundations of society as Marxism does. Ideas (including religion, rationality and the cult of the individual) are frequently presented as leading the process of change.

Fourth, again unlike Marxism, which emphasizes the role of conflict in history, modernization theory stresses that the normal state of society is one of consensus and social harmony. Ideas are seen as a social cement that produces social cohesion. In traditional society, for example, religion binds everyone together within a world-view in which the prevailing social hierarchy is natural. Conflict is exceptional and tends to be associated with periods of transition as a result of *resistance* to change. (For Marxists, by comparison, conflict creates change.) In times of rapid change, old ideas are destroyed before new ones are sufficiently established. Therefore, people become disoriented and search for new ideas with conflict as the result. Note the contradiction here: the emphasis on consensus fits uneasily alongside the common characterization of traditional people as lacking in self-restraint and prone to spontaneous acts of violence.

Fifth, modernization histories assign a prominent role to elites. This does not mean that they are concerned only with the upper classes. Rather the middling and upper classes are said to modernize first, in the process leaving behind the peasants, who continue to behave with traditional irrational violence, but usually modernize 'in the end'.

Finally, modernization theory tends to be associated with moral judgement. However, it is important to remember that moral judgement is not *intrinsic* to the theory, for the same set of changes have been variously assigned a positive and negative value. The Parsonian version of modernization theory was seen, rightly, as anti-Marxist. It arose during the cold war as a non-Marxist blueprint for developing societies and contained a value judgement about the superiority of the western model of society. This kind of modernization theory was not, though, a purely conservative ideology. It was espoused by liberals of right and left – and even socialists – who placed their faith in progress and reason and opposed the dogmas of religion as much as inflexible Marxism. Both Durkheim and Weber were associated with liberal democracy and anti-conservatism, and their work influenced many twentieth-century historians who were sympathetic to a non-dogmatic Marxism. Historians like R.H. Tawney (1880–1962) and Christopher Hill (1912– 2003) applied and developed variants of modernization theory. Norbert Elias's (1897–1990) *Civilizing Process* drew on the works of Weber as well as Karl Marx (1818–83) and Sigmund Freud (1856–1939). Nevertheless, not all those who identify a process of modernization in history view it positively. Many conservatives see it as destructive of religion, family and community, while some socialists, notably the Frankfurt school, saw it as reducing people to mere commodities. Weber himself, although critical of conservatives, feared that rationalization would imprison the individual in a gilded cage of routine. This critical stance is echoed, as we shall see, in the work of post-structuralist philosopher and historian Michel Foucault.

Ironically, given that Foucault is usually associated with undermining narratives of progress, poststructuralists have ensured that the categories of tradition and modernity remain central to historical writing and have reinforced the notion of the early modern period as a transitional period. In spite of some devastating critiques of modernization theory,[3] its categories remain deeply rooted in western cultures, of both left and right, and influential in early modern historiography at the level of 'common sense'. This means that historians sometimes articulate theoretical positions – in this case, that of modernization theory – without knowing that they are doing so. The extent to which it has pervaded intellectual thought is evident in the paradox that many critiques of modernization theory themselves use the language of modernization.

A 'modernization' overview of early modern Europe

General accounts of what constituted early modern society often owe much to modernization theory, probably in part because textbooks tend to paint pictures of the past with broad brushstrokes. Take, for instance, the 1989 edition of H.G. Koenigsberger, George L. Mosse and G.Q. Bowker's, *Europe in the Sixteenth Century.* First published in 1968, this work exemplifies the modernization tenor of historical writing in the late 1960s and early 1970s, while also indicating how the same assumptions are perpetuated in works published more recently.

The authors situate a conventional narrative of sixteenth-century events within a modernization framework. The sixteenth century is presented as a time when many 'traditional' characteristics prevailed, despite the emergence of some modern trends. 'Traditional attitudes and modes of thought only slowly gave way; there was no abrupt break with the past . . . The violent tenor of life and its cruel publicity, which J. Huizinga has described so well for the fifteenth century, continued through to the sixteenth', they write.[4] Sixteenth-century society's traditionalism is associated with violence, religious attitudes, lack of privacy and lack of self-restraint. Both non-official and official attitudes bordered on the barbaric:

> . . . violence was close to the surface of daily life, whether in public executions or popular festivals, or through the cruel treatment given to public

> and private enemies. Thus the dead bodies of criminals were dragged through the streets, dismembered and displayed, and corpses of those killed for religious or political reasons were given the same treatment. Riots might break out wherever a crowd assembled . . . Religious issues which dominated the age inspired most, if not all of the riots: even those whose cause was economic, like bread riots in times of famine appealed to some religious sanction . . . [V]iolence was taken for granted, and human life, constantly at risk to disease and natural catastrophes, was held cheap . . . The violent tenor of life [was] uninhibited by modern restraints on feelings and gestures . . .[5]

This was a world in which all the classes 'shared an attitude towards life, not just Christian, but linked also by irrationalism and fear'.[6]

Yet the features of modernity were inexorably beginning to take hold: the 'impetus towards change could not be arrested'. Despite witnessing 'heightened religious sensibilities', the sixteenth century saw a 'shift towards secularization'. There was a 'slow growth of constitutional government' and a 'profound malaise infected the class which included the vast majority of men in sixteenth-century Europe [who were] excluded . . . from political and economic power'. As with many accounts of modernization, it is the middling and upper classes who modernize first. The peasant class was 'far removed from the other classes which were rapidly becoming more sophisticated in their attitudes towards life'. The court elite, for example, devised tournaments and festivals in order 'to tame and civilize this society and its propensity towards violence', albeit without surrendering 'traditional' masculine ideals.[7] In these ways, the sixteenth century is portrayed as a period of transition from traditional to modern society, exhibiting some characteristics of both.

Indeed, the sixteenth century, the authors assert, 'is a crucial age in the development of European supremacy . . . because it laid the foundations for an attitude towards life which, in the end, proved favourable to those political, economic and social changes essential to the evolution of Europe into the modern age'. In keeping with the modernization view that transitional periods are marked by conflict as some sections of society resist change, Koenigsberger, Mosse and Bowler tell us that the 'traditional peasant rebellions of the Middle Ages now became both more frequent as well as more violent, and no decade remained free from such disturbances'.[8] Yet consensus and harmony nonetheless remain the 'normal' state of affairs. We learn that 'the dramatic qualities of change and upheaval . . . can mislead the historian' not only because of continuities from the medieval period but also because of society's prevailing 'impulse towards social, political, and intellectual harmony'.[9] They present a functionalist explanation of change. The Roman Catholic Church structures had fulfilled the needs of a 'backward' Europe, but now, in the sixteenth century, 'the need for this sort of an international organization had diminished'; it had 'outlived the functions that had made it uniquely valuable in earlier centuries'. Moreover, its traditional nature meant that it was 'unable to adapt to new and difficult circumstances' heralded by modern challenges from the printing press and state formation.[10] In numerous ways, some central assumptions of modernization theory provide the conceptual framework for Koenigsberger, Mosse and Bowler's representation of sixteenth-century Europe.

Histories of the family

The heyday of modernization theory's influence on early modern history was the 1970s, when many historians were interested in charting large-scale changes over time. Both Edward Shorter's (b. 1941) *Making of the Modern Family* in Western Europe and Lawrence Stone's similar project on the family in England, published respectively in 1976 and 1977, are cases in point. Modernization is crucial to Shorter's story of how the early modern period witnessed changes in the family life of ordinary people, not just the elite, in Western Europe. Industrialization – a central feature of modernization – is said to depend on the increasing separation of the economic sphere from the religious sphere that dominated in traditional society. In addition, as industrialization created a need for labour outside the household, the family had to adapt to a new separation of work and home. As the household ceased to be a productive unit, there arose affective (loving and empathic) relations within the family. In Shorter's words, 'modernization was the tugboat of domesticity'.[11]

Shorter characterized early modern society as 'traditional'. The superiority of modern western society is explicit in his description of the sixteenth, seventeenth and much of the eighteenth centuries as 'the Bad Old Days'.[12] The argument is teleological in that periods are judged in the light of the necessary movement from tradition to modernity: 'Every village in every province in every land has sooner or later undertaken the long trek toward the sentimental family, for the changes in intimate life that modernization fosters are essentially the same everywhere'. Shorter also judged his evidence against the idea of the 'spirit of the age', for '"Traditional" denotes a *kind* of attitude that coincides closely with a certain *period* of time'. Although certain individuals might be placed anywhere on a traditional-modern spectrum, 'the central tendency – the typical behaviour of the average person – was toward one end in traditional society and toward the other in modern society'. Part of the 'spirit' of traditional society was mothers' lack of attachment and indifference to their babies. Shorter sees this as 'impossible' within the 'twentieth-century spirit'.[13]

Shorter is uncertain of the reasons *why* traditional society is replaced by modern. Because the modernization process is accepted as 'common sense', it remains unanalysed. For example, when stating that increased geographical mobility is a feature of modernization, Shorter does not consider whether an increase in migration broke down the social stability of village life, or whether migration began as a result of that breakdown. The nearest he comes to offering an explanation for the shift from traditional to modern family life remains vague: 'market capitalism', he says, 'was probably at the root of the revolution in sentiment'.[14] But the problem of causation remains: was the development of market capitalism cause or consequence of modernization? Shorter fails to engage with such questions. Instead of analysing change, Shorter merely describes 'traditional' and 'modern' dichotomies. Whatever is identified as a 'modern' feature is either absent from or present in the form of its opposite in 'traditional' society. So if the modern family is nuclear, private and regulated by affection and intimacy, the traditional family is extended, public, regulated by ties to wider kin and community, and lacking affection and emotional expression. In modern society, courtship is an individual concern; in traditional society, courtship was monitored by the community. In modern society, individual self-realization allegedly takes precedence over community stability; therefore, in traditional society, people put the demands of the community above their personal ambitions and desires. If 'good mothering' – a term which carries a value judgement – 'is an invention of modernization', then in traditional society, 'mothers viewed the development and happiness of infants younger than two with indifference'.[15] And so on.

Shorter dismisses any supposedly modern characteristics present in traditional society by ascribing a more modern outlook to the social groups to which they pertain. Hence, eighteenth-century peasants had no sense of spousal intimacy, which was 'already present among middle-class urban couples'; the 'grief of upper-class men at the loss of their wives' is compared to the 'indifference' of the lower orders. Similarly, as the libido of adolescents and young adults, which had previously been successfully sublimated by traditional society, was aroused by modernization, middle-class youths masturbated 'earlier and more frequently than did lower-class ones'. Among the upper bourgeois and noble groups, maternal indifference began to give way in the sixteenth and seventeenth centuries, but this 'had not yet filtered down' to ordinary people, among whom 'this traditional insouciance persisted until at least the last quarter of the eighteenth century'.[16] '"Traditional" behaviour undoubtedly prevailed . . . for virtually everyone other than the middle classes and intellectuals'; the 'great surge of sentiment' that comes with modernity 'begins earlier in the cities than in the countryside, and sooner among the middle classes than the lower'. Eighteenth-century North American Puritans are also described as having more 'modern' relationships; the United States of America was apparently 'born modern'. If the European cities were the nurseries of modernization, which Shorter suggests elsewhere in the book, it is not clear how the isolated, non-nucleated communities of the American frontier spawned inhabitants with modern personality traits.[17] The ascription of 'modern' characteristics to variously the urban middle class, the upper class, middle-class youth, the upper bourgeoisie and nobility, the middle class and intellectuals, city dwellers and Puritan Americans makes for a somewhat muddy argument about precisely who was 'modernizing', in what way and why.

Unacknowledged or modified modernization theory

It is easy to identify the influence of modernization theory in the works of some historians, Koenigsburger et al. and Shorter among them. Multiple problems with modernization theory quickly became apparent. However, the influence of modernization theory often crops up elsewhere. It is possible to find problematic modernization assumptions present not only in the work of historians who have attempted to rescue and modify modernization theory by accepting certain criticisms but also even in that of some historians who claim to have rejected modernization theory altogether.

The Tudor revolution in government

Geoffrey Elton (1931–94) is known to generations of history students for his controversies with E.H. Carr (1892–1982), author of *What is History?* (1961). Among Carr's crimes, in Elton's view, was the importation into history of a priori theories of social science. Elton did not target modernization theory in particular, but he advanced criticisms of social science which apply well to it. Social scientists, Elton argued, mistakenly believed that history was subject to general laws and that it was the task of historical investigation to produce such laws. Historical facts were forced into this procrustean bed. In addition, social scientists were concerned with structures at the expense of human agency.[18] These criticisms are pertinent. Yet Elton's own practice of history owed more to the assumptions of a certain social science than he conceded.

Elton attacked social science in the name of Rankean professional history. Following Leopold von Ranke's (1795–1886) dictum that the task of the historian is 'simply to show how it really was', and that 'the strict presentation of the facts . . . is undoubtedly the supreme law',[19] Elton argued that interpretations should arise from careful source criticism after the historian had freed his or her mind from a priori assumptions. Yet professional history issued from the same intellectual climate as the social sciences and was not wholly separate from them. Most early professional historians wrote narratives of national development in the fashion of German philosopher G.W.F. Hegel (1770–1831), in which nations gradually became aware of themselves and constituted themselves politically as nation states. Nations overcame incoherence and barbarism, and became rationally organized political entities.

Elton's idea of the 'Tudor revolution in government', presented in the 1950s, first in a highly technical eponymous monograph and then in a textbook, illustrates perfectly the influence of unacknowledged modernization assumptions in national histories.[20] Elton argues that the origins of the modern English state were to be found not, as some had claimed, in the first Tudor king Henry VII's 'new monarchy', but in the administrative and ecclesiastical reforms in the 1530s of Henry VIII's minister, Thomas Cromwell (1485–1540). The fact that the nub of the debate concerns the dating of the origins of modernization, and that modernization originates at the top of society, alerts us immediately to the influence of modernization theory. Our suspicions are confirmed by Elton's characterization of Henry VII's mode of government as essentially that of the traditional Christian commonwealth. In contrast, Cromwell's reforms built a national, rational state. Feudal privileges were rooted out and the influence of the Catholic Church removed. Cromwell began to create a modern nation state in which all were subject to statute law. The sixteenth century remained transitional, however. In the 1536 Pilgrimage of Grace – when some 30,000 people in the north of England protested against Henry VIII's dissolution of the monasteries – 'conservative and feudal' northern forces defended ancient 'liberties'. Cromwell was obliged to use the 'traditional' method of patronage to buy off opposition and bind allies to his progressive cause.[21]

Elton's interpretation, like modernization theory, is structured as a linear narrative. Only occasionally does he stop to explain a particular structure. Moreover, his narrative is teleological and value-loaded. In his view, the English people possessed an innate tendency towards moderation and measure. They had discovered the correct balance of liberty and authority; Thomas Cromwell's revolution in government worked because he never broke the lifeline with the past. In other words, as a liberal conservative, Elton preached the reconciliation of tradition and modern. National history consists in the gradual realization of this innate character in practical institutional form (Hegel is influential here). Elton's interpretations were not entirely new. Before him, historians James Anthony Froude (1818–94) and A.F. Pollard (1869–1948) had located the origins of modern liberty in the Henrician Reformation.[22] But whereas Froude and Pollard had seen parliament as the carrier of liberty, Elton gave a greater role to the principle of the king in parliament. The king himself, however, was less important than Thomas Cromwell. The decisive role attributed to Cromwell might appear to introduce an element of human agency into a teleological narrative. In fact, Cromwell was a 'great man' precisely because he worked with the grain of history – he was in tune with the English national destiny towards modernity. Of course, some parts of the realm modernized before others. Elton sees the establishment of the Council of the North in 1537 as a means 'to bring the north [of England] into line with the more advanced south'. This advanced condition is explicitly associated with modernity: 'it may be said that the medieval history of the north came to an end in 1537 when its separatism fell before the centralization of the modern state imposed by Henry VIII and Cromwell'. The advanced orderliness of the modern south of England is extended to more traditional, disorderly parts of the realm: Wales and, especially, Ireland. The latter two peoples required the more 'modern' English government to drag them out of the abyss of tradition. Indeed, Elton follows some English contemporaries in wondering whether English policy in Wales was 'premature'. The Welsh, Elton suggests, were perhaps still too traditional; even the elite Welsh gentry were incapable of the self-government needed to govern impartially. Their country had not reached the appropriate stage of historical development. Happily, however, in this instance tradition worked positively for the English Crown: the Welsh ancestry of the Tudors provided just 'enough loyalty to make the policy workable'. The 1536 Act of Union between England and Wales 'was of utmost service to the tranquillity of the country [England] and did much more good than harm also for Wales'.[23] Cromwell's greatness, again, lies in his ability to harmonize his policy with the movement of history: the process of modernization.

Elton rejected social science methods entirely and yet modernization assumptions structure his work profoundly. Ironically, his belief that the origins of the modern state lay in Henrician England gave new life to the idea, evident as much in the sociologist Weber as in the historian Froude and, later, the social historian Keith Thomas (b. 1933), that the Reformation represented the beginnings of modernity. This idea has been hard to shake off. Thus Euan Cameron's *The European Reformation* (1991) concludes with the assertion that the mass politics, political commitment and universal ideology of the Reformation makes it the first *modern* ideology.[24]

The civilizing process

Other historians, more favourable to social science methods, turned to Norbert Elias's classic *The Civilizing Process* (first published in 1939, but particularly influential since the 1970s), in the belief that it represents a more usable formulation of the concept of modernization. Elias's supporters maintain that he does not insist that 'our civilized mode of behaviour is the most advanced of all humanly possible modes of behaviour'.[25] Nor was the transformation he identified predetermined or caused by the 'needs' of social structures to reproduce themselves or to become ever more efficient. Rather than seeing barbarous and civilized societies as static antithetical conditions, Elias envisioned long-term processes as continuous and ongoing, with no fixed beginning and no end point. In these ways, Elias's modernization narrative departs from classic modernization theory. Yet I remain unconvinced that Elias breaks fundamentally with the modernization programme. The fact that he puts a different moral gloss on the civilizing process is merely a further example of the ambivalence of sociologists and historians towards modernization. Elias was especially concerned with *habitus* – a Weberian term (later elaborated upon by sociologist Pierre Bourdieu) meaning social habits that are so ingrained in people that they are second nature – and he believed that a certain kind of society produces a certain kind of personality. Like Weber, Elias identified the early modern 'capitalist spirit' as 'the development of a particular *habitus*', behaviours that arose from the psychological impact of ascetic Protestantism.[26] More important from a historiographical perspective is Elias's method, which remains deductive and teleological. However incomplete and uneven, the civilizing process is a means of uncovering the meaning of history.

This is clear in Pieter Spierenburg's *The Broken Spell: A Cultural and Anthropological History of Pre-industrial Europe* (1991), which is essentially a history of mentalities. Spierenburg dedicates the book to the memory of Elias, his 'greatest teacher', and expresses an intellectual debt to both Elias and Weber. Spierenburg draws on the modernization aspects of Elias's argument, especially that in which mental changes, as part of long-term developments, are mutually related to other developments in society, particularly to processes of state formation. Spierenburg also adopts Weber's stance that the world-view of various groups became less saturated with magic a few centuries before the Industrial Revolution – a process of secularization that Weber referred to as 'the disenchantment of the world'. Spierenburg uses Elias's and Weber's theoretical frameworks in order to throw light upon three fundamental large-scale changes in the early modern *mentalité*. First, emotional life became less attuned to rank and hierarchy. Second, there was a gradual shift from a public to a private sphere. Third, perceptions of the cosmos and society became increasingly impersonal and secular; magical beliefs survive into the twentieth century only in 'remote regions'.[27]

Following Elias, Spierenburg posits no starting and end points to these changes. The development of self-control, first among elites and then among broader sections of the populace, had 'no beginning': 'There is never an absolute starting point to any development; it is always a matter of degree'. Nor does he argue for a unified, linear, progressive process of change. He points out, for example, that the geographical pattern of witch trials reveals no pattern of urban–rural, Protestant–Catholic, or any other distinction that might be associated with modernity versus tradition. How far this breaks with conventional modernization theory is arguable, however. In the latter, transitional periods frequently exhibit features of both tradition and modernity. Thus, Spierenburg identifies as a precondition of witch persecution not only the 'traditional' conflicts endemic in village social life and the emergence of a Weberian 'ideal type', or stereotype, of the witch, but also a modernizing impulse in the form of the juridical change that was 'a function of processes of state formation and urbanization'.[28]

Moreover, Spierenburg accepts modernization theory's categories. What constitutes 'traditional' or 'pre-industrial' society is everything that is not 'modern' or 'industrial'. So when discussing the experience of death in 'traditional' or 'pre-industrial' societies, Spierenburg includes examples drawn from classical Greece and Rome, the twelfth and thirteenth centuries, the fourteenth century and periods of time ranging from the sixth to the fourteenth, and the sixteenth to the eighteenth centuries. In the chapter on family relations, we shift between the unmodernized societies of ancient Roman Europe, eighteenth-century Poland, nineteenth-century Russia and thirteenth-century France. Connections between the carnivalesque 'world turned upside down' and revolutionary traditions are made for the fourth century, ancient Roman civilization and mid-seventeenth-century England. Although Spierenburg's examples suggest the existence of temporal and regional variations, the category of 'pre-industrial society' here is clumsy and amorphous, and lacks precision and coherence. Describing all sorts of non-modern societies (that might differ in as many ways as they resemble each other) as 'pre-industrial' societies explains little about what is distinctive about them. As many types of pre-modern societies exist, the heterogeneity of the term 'pre-industrial', like that of 'traditional', prevents it from being analytically useful.[29]

In other ways, too, Spierenburg's work contains conventional modernization assumptions. The very idea that there was a distinctive pre-industrial world-view, even one subject to gradual and uneven changes, suggests modernization theory's emphasis upon consensual attitudes and reinforces the idea that each age may be defined by its 'spirit'. This assumption is found also in the functionalist anthropology that has greatly informed the development of the history of mentalities. A 'basic tenet' of this approach, Spierenburg tells us, is that 'the entire personality structure of people in the past was different from what it is today'. For instance, Spierenburg argues that in medieval times up to the early sixteenth century, people of all social classes acted violently upon 'suddenly infuriated passions', but that the rise of stable and pacified nation states curbed this reaction among the upper classes over the course of the early modern period. Furthermore, the superiority of the modern West is assumed in Spierenburg's depiction of pre-industrial people's emotional immaturity. He evokes as a 'keen insight' Johan Huizinga's (1872–1945) view of pre-modern mentalities: 'Joy and sorrow, happiness and disaster were experienced directly and passionately, as only small children do today'.[30] Modernization theory is recalled also in Spierenburg's account of the weakening of patriarchy by the end of the Middle Ages. Changes in one sphere are a consequence of evolution towards modernity in other spheres: 'processes of state formation had set all this in motion', while 'urbanization and geographic mobility weakened the rule of fathers as well'. A further modernization assumption is found in Spierenburg's account of conflict arising as a consequence of change. From the sixteenth century onwards, traditional popular culture clashed with the new 'civilized' culture of the court and cities after the aristocracy and bourgeoisie adopted new models of behaviour. Otherwise, conflict is seen in terms of the non-rational and non-political – quintessentially non-*modern* – forms of protest within popular culture.[31]

Like modernization theorists, Spierenburg observes changes first among elite groups, either in court circles or among wealthy urban dwellers, while parallel changes occur among the masses 'at a later time, usually in the industrial period'. He argues that

> The social circumstances during the closing centuries of the preindustrial period merely facilitated the acquisition of a novel personality structure by European elites. In principle, every human being is capable of this development. Indeed, this personality structure became characteristic of broader groups, made possible by the changing circumstances in an industrial society.

What he appears to mean by this is that as 'social inequalities decreased' and 'power differences grew smaller' in the modern period, emotional life was 'democratized' and the masses developed the same sensibilities as the elites. The explanatory power of Spierenburg's theoretical framework is strained. He asserts that pre-industrial social change enabled elite personality change while industrial social change facilitated non-elite personality change. But the grounds upon which elite personalities developed towards the end of the pre-industrial period are not elaborated upon. Despite Spierenburg's claim that the modernization theories of Elias and Weber allow him 'to describe and explain . . . systematically' change over time, vague and amorphous concepts of modernization inform his *description* of such change but do little to explain it.[32]

Religion and the decline of magic

Whereas Elton rejected all forms of social science history and Spierenburg sought to use a particular and modified version of it, some historians, such as Keith Thomas and Lawrence Stone (1919–99), argued against modernization theory in the name of an alternative conception of the social sciences. Yet they too found it difficult to eliminate the concept of modernization from their work.

In the final chapter of *Religion and the Decline of Magic* (1971), Thomas engages with and refutes the anthropologist Bronislaw Malinowski's (1884–1942) position on the decline of magical beliefs. Like many anthropologists of his time, Malinowski accepted the traditional/modern dichotomy. He offered a functionalist explanation for the existence of magical beliefs, arguing that, although inefficacious in themselves, beliefs in magic served the positive functions of lessening anxiety, relieving frustrations and providing people with a sense of agency in an environment over which they had little real control. Once 'modern' scientific and technological techniques gave people more control in the sixteenth and seventeenth centuries, magical beliefs became redundant and so declined. The aspects of modernization associated with these new technologies included agricultural improvement, economic diversification, industrialization, development of communications, the growth of insurance and increased literacy. At first glance, Malinowski's narrative of modernization does seem to correspond with the decline of magical beliefs. However, Thomas argues that on closer inspection the idea that magic gave way to technology is flawed. Magic, he maintains, lost its appeal *before* new kinds of knowledge superseded beliefs in supernatural causes. It was the abandonment of magic that made possible the upsurge of technology, not vice versa.

Despite refuting the conventional modernization narrative, Thomas retains certain of its characteristics in his own account. This is hardly surprising given his widely acknowledged debt to functionalist anthropology. Thus Thomas talks of the 'conservative' nature of 'traditional' magical beliefs: early modern magic was rooted in the medieval and classical past and was slow to adapt to new situations. Drawing on Weber, he argues both that magic was potentially a serious obstruction to the rationalization of economic life and that changes in belief preceded changes in social and economic structure – change in the seventeenth century was more mental than technological. Hence, a new 'spirit' was born: the difference between the eighteenth and sixteenth centuries lies not in achievement but in aspiration, a new practical, optimistic, *modern* attitude, 'a spirit of self-help'. Faith in self-help replaced the traditional faith in providence. With an implicit value judgement, Thomas sees early modern people having 'emancipated' themselves from magical beliefs before effective technologies had been devised to replace them. Most fundamentally of all, Thomas retains an underlying belief in the appropriateness of the categories of 'traditional' and 'modern' and applies them to the early modern attitudes that he explores.[33] Despite Thomas's rejection of Malinowski's modernization narrative, his readers have nonetheless recognized modernization assumptions in Thomas's alternative. The changes he himself charts are seen to be socio-economic, bound up with 'the breakdown of traditional life in favour of new, impersonal, perhaps urban forms of living, which changed the psychological and intellectual needs of society and individuals'.[34] These are conventional changes associated with the transition from traditional to modern society.

The family revisited

Even more energetically, Lawrence Stone denies the validity of modernization theory *per se*. The idea of modernization 'marching relentlessly through the centuries appears less than convincing'. The unilinear nature of the theory ignores

modernization theorists, Foucault focuses on the practices and ideas of the elites, and argues that their ideologies are internalized by the masses through a process of repetition and ritual. Where Foucault differs from many modernization theorists is in viewing this process *negatively*. Like Weber himself, Foucault saw the freedom of modern society as an illusion. Even when individuals think they are free they are actually in the grip of insidious power, and Foucault celebrates the spontaneous agency of the medieval crowd. Ironically, both the barbarity of tradition and the unfreedom of modernity are implicitly judged against 'modern' enlightenment ideals like restraint and liberty.[39]

Implicit modernization is especially evident in an early application of Foucauldian ideas to the history of punishment in seventeenth-century England. J.A. Sharpe applies the insights of chapter 2 of *Discipline and Punish* to the reported confessions on the gallows of condemned criminals. Sharpe argues that such speeches were carefully stage-managed endorsements of royal justice at a time when the social order was under threat following the Reformation. They demonstrated also that propaganda through stereotype and ritual was 'internalized' by ordinary people. Thus, nineteenth-century prejudices adopted by modernization theorists about the masses' non-rational appropriation of knowledge remain intact in late-twentieth-century historiography. Sharpe argues, as does Foucault – and modernization theorists – that this system of law enforcement eventually declined because it was 'inefficient'. Here there is an obvious contradiction. If the inhabitants of traditional society had internalized the dominant ideology, where did change come from? Aware that other historians have demonstrated, precisely, the refusal of the masses to internalize ruling ideas, Sharpe admits perplexity on this point and fails to come up with a solution.[40]

Modernization assumptions in the twenty-first century

The strength of enduring unacknowledged assumptions about progress and societal differences, together with the implicit endorsement of modernization metanarratives in some forms of poststructuralist history, have ensured the survival of modernization theory's influence in much contemporary historical writing. Modernization provides the interpretative framework, for example, for the essays in *Early Modern Europe: An Oxford History* (1999). Indeed, Euan Cameron's introduction explicitly draws attention to it. 'Early modern', he correctly notes, 'is a description born of hindsight. It assumes that European culture was travelling towards something called "modernity", but had not yet reached its goal'.[41] Robin Briggs's contribution on religion and natural philosophy in the seventeenth century serves as a case in point. Briggs acknowledges that the old distinctions between the (traditional) supernatural and (modern) science are untenable. The great mathematician-astronomer Johannes Kepler (1571–1630) was not only a practising astrologer, but was 'driven by an almost mystical fascination with celestial harmonies'. Similarly, Francis Bacon (1561–1626), 'who has often been claimed as the standard-bearer of a new rationalist mode of scientific proof, also turns out on closer inspection to have been much influenced by the magical tradition'. Yet despite this, Briggs falls back upon a conventional modernizing narrative. For 'In the end modern distinctions between hard science and occultist nonsense are almost impossible to make *until late in the seventeenth century*'. Thus the familiar distinction between superior, modern, scientific 'fact' and inferior, traditional, supernatural 'nonsense' is reiterated, with the transition between the two as dominant forms of intellectual expression falling in the late seventeenth century.[42] Moreover, while beliefs in malevolent witchcraft – 'traditional notions' – are ascribed to 'peasants and artisans', only weak, non-centralized states witnessed endemic witch-hunts, and the decline in prosecutions of witches reflects the development of the modern nation state. Again, the modernization metanarrative is clearly present.[43]

As befits a transitional period, religious (traditional) and secular (modern) motives in politics and war mingled profoundly in early modern Europe. Self-interest had not yet overtaken religious belief as 'the real driving force' in history as it was to do, Briggs implies, in the modern period.[44] Briggs's discussion of religion also reinforces a modernizing schema in which the Protestant Reformation is seen to lay the foundations for the development of modern attitudes. By the seventeenth century, religious conflicts mobilized clerics and laity of the major religious denominations in ways that challenged the elites' traditional ideas of authority and hierarchy, and reformers criticized (Briggs notes approvingly that this was 'to their credit') elites' greed, ostentation and worldliness. Moreover, popular ignorance and superstition (both marks of traditional masses) as well as sinfulness were identified as problems to be overcome.[45] By the late seventeenth century, religion began to lose its hold over society. Briggs presents secularization as the paradoxical and inadvertent consequence of the churches' attempts to assert their doctrines rationally and in relation to all spheres of life; the 'endless compromises and difficulties' they were forced to confront ultimately ensured that secular values came to prevail over sacred ones.[46] A modern rationality is here the motor of change.

It is worth highlighting these aspects of modernization theory in Briggs's essay, not because the evidence he presents is 'wrong' or his argument unconvincing, but, on the contrary, because he presents a nuanced overview of his subject with which most scholars of the seventeenth century would concur. Briggs gainsays the binary opposition between magic and science which ascribes magical beliefs to the masses and rational scientific beliefs to the elite. He emphasizes the durability of conventional religious beliefs and the multiple limitations of early modern natural philosophy. He presses home the point that

> We must always remember the crucial distinction between what contemporaries perceived and the historian's retrospective view. This is particularly important here, because what is at stake is the massive and complex set of shifts which can be seen as the birth of modernity, to which we must ascribe such huge significance.

In Briggs's vision of emerging modernity, as in conventional modernization theory, a traditional agrarian *ancien régime* of kings, nobles and priests was replaced by modern industrial society, but the driving force for this long-term process was in the realm of ideas. It was made possible 'only . . . through a vast intellectual revolution'. From the late seventeenth century, 'this evolution was inevitable; Pandora's box had been opened, and the ideas which had been released were simply unstoppable'.[47] The fact that such changes are shown to be 'neither uniform nor one-sided, or that older assumptions persisted long and changed only gradually and imperfectly' merely assimilates new research into the conventional framework. Allowing for lags, hesitations and even temporary reversals, as we saw with Stone, ultimately does little to challenge a theory of modernization that has become so diffused within our contemporary western intellectual landscape that it is rarely acknowledged as a theoretical position.

Conclusion

This chapter's primary aim has been to examine how modernization assumptions, acknowledged and unacknowledged, have shaped historical writing. In my view, modernization theory's worth to the historian is dubious. This is not the place to engage in a detailed critique, for that would involve the elaboration of complex alternative methods.[48] Nevertheless, I wish to conclude with the following points.

First, modernization theory's explanation of change is inadequate. It posits either inexorable forces outside history or vague ideas about mutually reinforcing changes. Historical change is more usefully seen as the product of conscious and unconscious actions of human beings within the constraints of cultural and social structures.

Second, modernization theory is teleological. Even versions of the theory that do not claim that modernization is inevitable tend, in practice, to derive the meaning of particular periods from the process of modernization, civilization or progress. A more historical method examines meaning within the very specific context of a given period. Meaning arises not from the movement of history, but from the social and cultural beliefs and actions of human beings in a given context.

Third, the traditional/modern dichotomy is fruitless. We need a variety of concepts to understand a given period and, using them, we find that societies are far too variable to be captured in a simple dichotomy. Neither is it possible to characterize any period in terms of a single idea, for all periods exhibit a great variety of often conflicting and contradictory ideas, including both rational and irrational elements. For instance, medievalists can find the 'origins' of the self and of rationality in the twelfth century, while modernists show that rationalist philosophies depend on unacknowledged, irrational prejudices. Likewise, seemingly irrational religious beliefs appear to hold great sway in the contemporary USA, conventionally considered by modernization theorists to provide the benchmark of modern society.

Fourth, conceptualizing modernity as the opposite of tradition, with modernity being the standard, leads to erroneous assumptions about earlier societies. Because modern society is associated with change, for example, traditional society is presented as static and characterized by stability. This in turn leads to suppositions such as that early modern people are resistant to change. Meaning is thus ascribed by theory, not by people through ideas and practice.

Finally, the idea that elites are (increasingly) able to appropriate ideas rationally, while the masses are still motivated by myth and shapable ritual, needs to be heavily qualified. Elites are far from free from prejudice, while the masses are often highly sceptical of the so-called dominant ideology.

Guide to further reading

Euan Cameron (ed.), *Early Modern Europe: An Oxford History* (Oxford, 1999).

Pieter Spierenburg, 'Punishment, Power, and History: Foucault and Elias', *Social Science History* 28(4) (2004), pp. 607–36.

Peter N. Stearns, 'Modernization', in *Encyclopedia of European Social History: From 1350 to 2000. Vol. 2* (1993; London, 2001), pp. 3–11.

Dean C. Tipps, 'Modernization Theory and the Comparative Study of Societies: A Critical Perspective', *Comparative Studies in Society and History* 15(3) (1973), pp. 199–226.

Garthine Walker, 'What's in a Name? Early Modern Periodization', *History Compass* (forthcoming).

Notes

1 This chapter benefited enormously from the input of Kevin Passmore. Thanks are also due to Andy Wood for his helpful comments.
2 Peter N. Stearns, 'Modernization', in *Encyclopedia of European Social History: From 1350 to 2000. Vol. 2* (1993; London, 2001), pp. 3–11. Peter N. Stearns and Herrick Chapman, *European Society in Upheaval: Social History Since 1750* (New York, 1992).
3 For example, Samual P. Huntington, *Political Order in Changing Societies* (New Haven, 1968); Dean C. Tipps, 'Modernization Theory and the Comparative Study of Societies: A Critical Perspective', *Comparative Studies in Society and History* 15(3) (1973), pp. 199–226.
4 H.G. Koenigsberger, George L. Mosse and G.Q. Bowker, *Europe in the Sixteenth Century* (1968; London, 1989), p. 7.
5 Koenigsberger et al., *Europe*, pp. 4–6.
6 Koenigsberger et al., *Europe*, p. 128.
7 Koenigsberger et al., *Europe*, pp. 155, 9, 6, 128, 83.
8 Koenigsberger et al., *Europe*, p. 10.
9 Koenigsberger et al., *Europe*, p. 6.
10 Koenigsberger et al., *Europe*, p. 160.
11 Edward Shorter, *The Making of the Modern Family* (London, 1976), p. 273.
12 Shorter, *Modern Family*, pp. 3–4, 5, 8, 20, 75, 206, 245.
13 Shorter, *Modern Family*, pp. 14, 18–19 (original italic), 169.
14 Shorter, *Modern Family*, pp. 49, 255.
15 Shorter, *Modern Family*, p. 168.
16 Shorter, *Modern Family*, pp. 55–6, 58, 65, 250, 99, 101, 170.
17 Shorter, *Modern Family*, pp. 60, 61, 137.
18 G.R. Elton, *Political History: Principles and Practice* (London and New York, 1970), pp. 125–6; see also his *Practice of History* (Oxford, 1967). E.H. Carr, *What is History?* (London, 1961).
19 Ranke, quoted in Beverley Southgate, *History: What and Why? Ancient, Modern, and Postmodern Perspectives* (London and New York, 1996), p. 22.
20 G.R. Elton, *The Tudor Revolution in Government: Administrative Changes in the Reign of Henry VIII* (Cambridge, 1953); G.R. Elton, *England Under the Tudors* (London, 1955). For an excellent account of the assumptions present in political histories of the nation state, see Kevin Passmore, 'Historians and the Nation State: Some Conclusions', in Stefan Berger, Mark Donovan and Kevin Passmore (eds), *Writing National Histories: Western Europe Since 1800* (London and New York, 1999), pp. 281–304.
21 Arthur J. Slavin, 'G.R. Elton: On Reformation and Revolution', *History Teacher* 23(4) (1990), pp. 405–31; Arthur J. Slavin, 'Telling the Story

Straight: G.R. Elton and the Tudor Age', *Sixteenth Century Journal* 21(2) (1990), pp. 151–69.

22 James Anthony Froude, *History of England from the Fall of Wolsey to the Defeat of the Spanish Armada* (London, 1856–70). A.F. Pollard, *Political History of England, 1547–1603* (London, 1910); A.F. Pollard, *Thomas Cranmer and the English Reformation* (London, 1927); A.F. Pollard, *Wolsey* (London and New York, 1929).

23 G.R. Elton, *England Under the Tudors* (1955; London, 1974), pp. 178, 176.

24 Euan Cameron, *The European Reformation* (Oxford, 1991), p. 422.

25 Norbert Elias, cited in Johan Goudsblom and Stephen Mennell (eds), *The Norbert Elias Reader: A Biographical Selection* (Oxford, 1998), p. 44.

26 Robert van Krieken, *Norbert Elias* (London and New York, 1998), p. 47.

27 Pieter Spierenburg, *The Broken Spell: A Cultural and Anthropological History of Pre-industrial Europe* (New Brunswick, 1991), pp. 2, 3–13, 56.

28 Spierenburg, *Broken Spell*, pp. 3, 100–2, 90.

29 The 'pre-modern' period is similarly applied to cultures ranging from classical Rome to various parts of early modern Europe in Anne L. McClanan and Karen Rosoff Encarnación (eds), *Material Culture of Sex, Procreation, and Marriage in Premodern Europe* (Basingstoke, 2002).

30 Spierenburg, *Broken Spell*, pp. 1, ix, 195–7, 200.

31 Spierenburg, *Broken Spell*, pp. 26, 29, 13, 78–80.

32 Spierenburg, *Broken Spell*, pp. 4–5, 2. Other of Spierenburg's works in which Elias's vision of modernization figures include 'Violence and the Civilizing Process: Does it Work?', *Crime, Histoire & Sociétés/Crime, History & Societies* 5(2) (2001), pp. 87–105 and 'Punishment, Power, and History: Foucault and Elias', *Social Science History* 28(4) (2004), pp. 607–36.

33 Keith Thomas, *Religion and the Decline of Magic: Studies in Popular Beliefs in Sixteenth- and Seventeenth-Century England* (London, 1971), ch. 22.

34 Jonathan Barry, 'Introduction: Keith Thomas and the Problem of Witchcraft', in Jonathan Barry, Marianne Hester and Gareth Roberts (eds), *Witchcraft in Early Modern Europe: Studies in Culture and Belief* (Cambridge, 1996), p. 29.

35 Lawrence Stone, *The Family, Sex and Marriage in England, 1500–1800* (London, 1977), p. 658.

36 Robert A. Nisbet, *The Sociological Tradition* (New Brunswick and London, 1966).

37 Stone, *Family, Sex and Marriage*, p. 659.

38 H. Aram Veseer (ed.), *The New Historicism Reader* (London, 1994), p. 14.

39 Michel Foucault, *Discipline and Punish: The Birth of the Prison*, trans. Alan Sheridan (1975; London, 1977). Lois McNay, *Foucault: A Critical Introduction* (London, 1994), pp. 91–5.

40 J.A. Sharpe, ' "Last Dying Speeches": Religion, Ideology and Public Execution in Seventeenth-Century England', *Past & Present* 107 (1985), pp. 144–67.

41 Euan Cameron, 'Editor's Introduction' to his (ed.) *Early Modern Europe: An Oxford History* (Oxford, 1999), p. xvii. (The volume was first published in paperback in 2001.)

42 Robin Briggs, 'Embattled Faiths: Religion and Natural Philosophy in the Seventeenth Century', in Cameron (ed.), *Early Modern Europe*, p. 173; my italic.

43 Briggs, 'Embattled Faiths', p. 188.

44 Briggs, 'Embattled Faiths', pp. 176–7.

45 Briggs, 'Embattled Faiths', pp. 174–5.

46 Briggs, 'Embattled Faiths', pp. 184–5.

47 Briggs, 'Embattled Faiths', pp. 204–5.

48 For critiques, see note 2, above. For a claim for modernization theory's fruitfulness in early modern European history, see Heinz Schilling, *Religion, Political Culture and the Emergence of Early Modern Society: Essays in German and Dutch History* (New York, 1992), esp. ch. 7, 'The History of the Northern Netherlands and Modernization Theory', pp. 305–52.

3

Anthropological approaches

David Gentilcore

The appeal of anthropology to early modern historians is varied: its concern with the everyday, the small-scale, with alien mentalities, with a concept of culture that includes attitudes and values (and is not simply concerned with 'high' culture), the construction of reality.[1] The early modern period is different enough from the present day to make the approach insightful, while the records are rich enough to make it viable. Why historians turned to anthropology at a specific point in time has much to do with the trends then being followed within both disciplines and with the kinds of history historians were trying to write. And while many historians have called their work 'historical anthropology', on closer inspection their approach is generally more modest: not really trying to 'do' anthropology, but borrowing according to perceived usefulness and applicability.[2] My aims here are similarly modest. This is not a survey of the entire range of anthropological approaches, touching on all the subjects which have benefited from anthropology – from kinship to ritual, from gender relations to gift exchange. This would require a volume of its own. Rather, I offer a critical discussion of a few 'classic' studies in which historians of early modern Europe have made use of anthropology. Most of these concern the problem of culture. Indeed, there are many kinds of anthropology, but the socio-cultural is the approach that has most influenced historians. Where possible, I have paired the studies with the reactions of anthropologists, as well as other historians. The exchanges serve to highlight the strengths – and some of the limitations – of an anthropological approach. It also suggests some of the evolving concerns of both disciplines over the last four decades, and, I hope, why the approach continues to be of value to historians. Some of the issues raised concern the intelligibility of past beliefs, expressions and usages; the apparent otherness or alienness of the past and the people (at least some of them) who inhabited it; the homogeneity or diversity within cultures; and cultural change and how it happens.

In 1961 one of Britain's best-known anthropologists, E.E. Evans-Pritchard (1902–73), published a lecture in which he advocated a rapprochement between the by-then very separate disciplines of anthropology and history.[3] The response of one anthropologist was less than enthusiastic. Isaac Schapera's (1905–2003) answer to his own highly charged question of whether anthropologists should be historians was a firm 'no'. At most, the past might be an aid to understanding the social systems of the present, Schapera argued.[4] But at least one historian was quite keen to take the dialogue forward. Keith Thomas (b. 1933) argued in 1963 that historians could learn much from anthropologists: their 'discipline and precision of thought', their skill at relating 'their findings to their understanding of the wider social system', their 'experience of matters about which historians have only read in books' (like witchcraft and blood-feud) and their knowledge of 'primitive mentality'. Thomas's 'case for anthropology' rested on two broader points. First, he suggested that it could widen the subject matter of academic history, to include subjects that historians now take for granted but were then little studied: the family, children's education, attitudes to birth, adolescence and death, to name but a few. Second, it could enhance historians' methods of historical explanation, providing them with new techniques. The historian familiar with 'the findings of the anthropologist', Thomas modestly (if somewhat vaguely) proposed, would be better able 'to ask intelligent questions of his material and more likely to come up with intelligent answers'.[5]

'Functional' or 'structural'? Keith Thomas and Hildred Geertz

In the book that followed a few years later, Thomas practised what he preached. His 1971 *Religion and the Decline of Magic* has justly become a classic, never out of print and the subject of a retrospective study 25 years after its initial publication.[6] It is a seminal work for the study of early modern witchcraft in particular, for it gave an importance to what had previously been dismissed by early modern historians as a marginal phenomenon. The study employed a wide range of sources to explain witchcraft and magic on a variety of levels – intellectual, sociological and psychological – and account for their subsequent decline. The work is generally associated with *functionalist* anthropology, a school that explains phenomena in terms of the function (or purpose, utility) they purportedly serve. Thomas explored witchcraft in terms of social tensions by means of village-level analysis.[7] For Thomas, 'function' meant the way magical beliefs in general, and witchcraft beliefs in particular, provided a meaningful explanation for the apparently inexplicable in individual life. Magic, interconnected with religion, provided a coherent 'system of belief'. To understand this, Thomas urged historians to take early modern magic beliefs as seriously as they had taken religious beliefs of the time. Thomas succeeded in rendering the apparently irrational rational, an aim which owes a great debt to anthropology (and to Evans-Pritchard's study of Azande witchcraft in particular).[8]

For all his advocacy of anthropology, Thomas was actually quite cautious in his own use of it. He cited anthropologists to suggest hypotheses and provide analogies, but never to prove a point or sustain an argument – he preferred to quote contemporary Tudor and Stuart writers for that. His use of anthropology is most evident in his focus on the accused–accuser relation in witchcraft accusations. Thomas suggested that most accusations of witchcraft developed out of social situations where the accused was refused charity by the accuser. The latter would then feel guilt and attribute subsequent malady and misfortune to the ill will of the person refused. Witchcraft was thus a gauge of social tension. Known as the charity-refusal model, this has become common currency among historians of early modern witchcraft. While it is true that discussion of this model occupies only one chapter in his witchcraft section, Thomas can be accused of placing more weight on the model than it could bear. More recent historians have been careful to reconstruct the precise nature of the social relationships of those involved in specific accusations, and to study how the cases themselves were affected by the wider judicial context.[9]

Inevitably, Thomas's use of anthropology now appears dated. Indeed his preference for the language of primitivism and his concentration on African anthropology were outmoded in anthropological circles when the book was published. 'Primitive', as the anthropologist Hildred Geertz pointed out in her critique, was used by Thomas as a synonym for 'magical' (beliefs and practices that were goal-orientated, though ineffective, and incoherent), both of which were quite distinct from 'religious' (seen as less goal-centred, but comprehensive and organized).[10] Besides the obvious artificiality of the magic–religion distinction, Geertz argues, Thomas employs the terms in such a variety of ways that we are not always sure whether we are dealing with contemporary (that is, pre-modern) cultural ideas or the historian's. Thomas stands accused of taking 'part in the very cultural process that he is studying' (anachronism, in other words).[11] In hindsight, this is doubly ironic: first, in view of the fact that Thomas had praised the distancing from one's subject matter as one of the skills that anthropology could offer the historian; and, second, since the imposition of the anthropologist's own (western, white, frequently male) world-view on the society under study was one of the main criticisms which would be levelled at anthropology itself from the mid-1980s onwards (on which, more below), though of course Geertz could not have known that. In his reply, Thomas stressed that he had written English history and not cross cultural analysis. 'Magic' was therefore used as a convenient label, one that was derived from various contemporary usages, rather than as a category awaiting application to 'some more exotic context'. The question of effectiveness did not come into it, he explained. If there was a distinction between magic and religion, it was the one originally formulated by sixteenth-century Protestant reformers, later exported to other societies by early anthropologists like E.B. Tylor (1832–1917) and James Frazer (1854–1941). Thomas did concede, however, that his study would have benefited from greater attention to vocabulary and classification, in particular a discussion of the shifting boundaries between 'religion', 'magic' and 'science', in terms of the varying outlooks of the different social and religious groups. Thomas put his finger on one of the key issues in the ongoing history–anthropology debate when he wrote that 'from the anthropologist's point of view, much of what historians call social change can be regarded as a process of mental reclassification, of re-drawing conceptual lines and boundaries'.[12]

Thomas was also criticized by Geertz for rejecting *structuralism*, a then dominant theoretical approach most associated with the French anthropologist Claude Lévi-Strauss (b. 1908). This would have meant studying witchcraft as part of a broader system or language of cultural classification. As a theory of anthropology, structuralism seeks to identify cultural codes as a means of exploring important themes in human thought and action. In his book Thomas dismissed structuralism's applicability to complex societies like that of early modern England (relegating it to the analysis of culturally homogeneous societies). His response to Geertz a few years later is more helpful. Here he questioned the model of unitary cultural systems, favouring instead something more pragmatic and practical, and firmly rooted in its social and technological context. Changes in the context helped account for changes in beliefs and practices. If this meant empirical observation and a historical approach to the problem, instead of Lévi-Strauss's advice to examine the 'unconscious foundations' of social life, then so be it.[13]

Thomas viewed culture as a resource, a concept that has stood the test of time, outliving structuralism among cultural anthropologists. It is therefore somewhat surprising that Thomas did not pay more attention to the processes of cultural transmission. We need to know more about social differentiation: how ideas circulated among different levels of society throughout the period. Compare this to the approach taken by French historian Robert Muchembled a few years later. Here witchcraft beliefs are seen as an example of acculturation: how popular culture was reformed by the elites though the imposition of learned notions of magic and associated legal mechanisms, as part of a broader programme of social and ideological control.[14] It is worth noting that if the 'decline of magic' referred to in Thomas's title occurred when it ceased to occupy a central position in educated thought, during the eighteenth century, then a depiction of popular beliefs during that period in survivalist terms is inadequate. Why, for instance, did educated beliefs change, while village ones did not, despite the modernization that apparently affected both levels? In describing the former, Thomas refers to the role of faith and science and to a new commitment to self-help in marginalizing magic. Geertz found this explanation problematic, since there was no reason to consider recourse to magic any less self-reliant than other responses.[15]

An authoritative ethnographic document? Emmanuel Le Roy Ladurie and Renato Rosaldo

Thomas regarded his own work as a contribution to what anthropologists refer to as ethnography: the product and process of fieldwork which is one of the building blocks of anthropology but which generally eschews contributions to the theory of anthropology. In this sense, 'ethnographic history' is a much more accurate label of what historians have tried to do. This is how we might categorize another significant contribution to the approach: Emmanuel Le Roy Ladurie's (b. 1929) study of the southern French medieval village of Montaillou.[16] His introduction to the original French edition of 1975 is entitled 'De l'Inquisition à l'ethnographie' (From Inquisition to Ethnography) and the bishop-inquisitor behind the trial which forms the basis of the book is styled an 'ethnographe et policier' (ethnographer and detective).[17] The implication is that interpreting a historical document could resemble undertaking anthropological fieldwork. Though the chronology was medieval, the book's impact upon early modernists was great. This was due as much to its use of an inquisitorial trial as an ethnographic source for the study of peasant life, as its focus on a single community. The influence of the American anthropologist Robert Redfield (1897–1958), pioneer of village ethnography, on both aspects was clear.[18] As the last village that actively supported the Cathar heresy, or Albigensianism, Montaillou was the subject of an inquisitorial investigation lasting some seven years and carried out by the tireless bishop Jacques Fournier (b. *c.*1280). While Fournier diligently recorded evidence of heresy in this mixed Catholic-Cathar village of some 200 souls, he also inadvertently provided posterity (in the form of Le Roy Ladurie) with an extraordinarily detailed and vivid picture of the villagers' everyday lives.

Historians had hitherto used Inquisition records either to study the institution itself or to explore the nature of heresy. Instead, Le Roy Ladurie used what he referred to as 'the direct testimony of the peasants themselves' to explore the villagers and their society. This represented a shift away from historians siding with the producers of documents, towards those whose lives might be tangentially reflected in them. The book's layout reflects the author's place in the French *Annales* school, in its preoccupation with historical geography and the setting of economy, society and culture. It is divided into two sections. The first, 'ecology', deals with structures that remained unchanged over a long time-span (physical environment, household, transhumant pastoralism); the second, 'archaeology', delineates apparently equally long-lived cultural forms (body language, life cycle, social relationships, religion and magic). The descriptions are lively and detailed, interspersed with direct quotations from the depositions. The effect is to give to the reader the impression of overhearing the peasants' own speech from centuries ago. The peasants themselves seem to come across as reliable informants, articulate and aware, their evidence assembled and collated by the capable (and invisible) hands of the expert and meticulous inquisitor.

What was the role of the book's author in all this? Le Roy Ladurie was aware that the evidence he was using was not an objective ethnographic document. The depositions – peasants under suspicion of heresy interrogated by an inquisitor – were the fruit of what he called, in his introduction, an 'unequal dialogue'. And yet, as the anthropologist Renato Rosaldo (b. 1941) pointed out some years later, despite this caveat, it is as if the rest of the book takes the evidence at face value, presenting it as authoritative.[19] Rosaldo used his critique to make wider points about the distorting effects of authority in ethnography, pairing *Montaillou*'s inquisitor with the once influential voice of Evans-Pritchard, whose *The Nuer* was long regarded as an exemplary ethnographic study.[20] Yet Rosaldo's discussion of *Montaillou* is just as thought-provoking for the historian. Le Roy Ladurie confines his (brief) methodological discussion to the introduction; even the figure of Fournier, the inquisitor-cum-ethnographer, makes no significant appearance in the rest of the book. This gives the false impression that what follows is objective, disinterested and unproblematic. This is much too reminiscent of traditional ethnography for Rosaldo, where the ethnographer appears briefly in the preface only to disappear from the main text. The ethnographer's role in fashioning the text is thus not reflected upon. With regard to *Montaillou*, Rosaldo argues that the reader needs to understand more fully the implications of power relations and cultural differences between judge and accused. Rosaldo's criticism boils down to Le Roy Ladurie's failure to take Fournier's role as mediator into account and to consider the implications this mediation had on the testimony and its use as evidence by the historian. Gaps in the record – as when female witnesses do not go into detail about courtship practices – are more than 'cultural silence'. They stem from the very structure of what were after all inquisitorial proceedings: of women testifying before male judges, unwilling to talk about possibly heretical love magic. In Le Roy Ladurie's defence, however, he was reading the depositions 'against the grain'. That is, to learn, not about the inquisitor's chief concern, heresy, but about everyday life from the peasants' point of view. Le Roy Ladurie's target is thus distinct from the inquisitor's and should be less affected by his perceptions. However, Le Roy Ladurie fails to go into any detail about another potential problem: the implications of the language of testimony, which would have been the vernacular Occitan, then translated into Latin by scribes (in turn read back to the witnesses in Occitan for corroboration), transcribed into a fair copy and finally translated into modern French by Le Roy Ladurie. The different usages of terms such as 'family' and 'household', for instance, tend to get blurred as a result. The rather ecclesiastical Latin of the document and

Le Roy Ladurie's not always careful use of it have been pointed out by another critic, the medievalist Leonard Boyle.[21] Finally, for a purported ethnographic account, Le Roy Ladurie makes too many undocumented assumptions regarding the nature and behaviour of the villagers, emphasizing their sameness or difference from the modern (French) reader, as he sees fit. At the same time, he follows the practices of much traditional ethnography in ascribing a timelessness to pastoral life, as evinced in the figure of 'the happy shepherd', Pierre Maury.

Clues, signs and new standards of proof: Carlo Ginzburg and Paola Zambelli

If Le Roy Ladurie can be identified with a particularly French historiographical tradition, Carlo Ginzburg (b. 1939) can be identified with intellectual traditions that are particularly Italian. Ginzburg can also be said to have identified somewhat with the subject of his study, the sixteenth-century Friulan miller Domenico Scandella (1532–99), whom he calls by his familiar name of Menocchio. Moreover, he too is able to tell this story thanks to an inquisitorial trial for heresy. Menocchio is much more contextualized in time, place and circumstance than the shepherd Maury. But like Le Roy Ladurie, Ginzburg aims to present the reader with 'a story as well as a piece of historical writing'.[22] And like him, he tells a good one. Ginzburg still dazzles with the virtuosity of his methods and the boldness of his conclusions. From a village focus in *Montaillou*, we move to a single individual, the miller Menocchio. This may not seem particularly 'anthropological': the exploration of the life and thoughts of a single individual certainly was not then an approach favoured by anthropology.[23] But Ginzburg saw Menocchio as a privileged informant, who might serve as a gateway to the wider world of traditional oral culture. The use of the single informant, identified as expert in some aspect of their own culture by the ethnographer conducting fieldwork, is one of the key techniques employed to access another society. That said, it is not without its risks. This is especially so for the historian, for whom the problem of ascertaining typicality is ever present. Menocchio, a literate and widely read miller, freethinking, eccentric and outspoken, was hardly representative of peasant culture. At the same time, by closely analysing the trials of 1582–86 and 1599 to reconstruct what Menocchio read and how he read it, Ginzburg sought to explore the filter of peasant culture that Menocchio interposed unconsciously between himself and the books he read. This filter was the patrimony of a vast segment of sixteenth-century society, peasant culture. On the one hand there is Menocchio's philosophical system: pantheist, egalitarian and materialist. On the other hand there is the filter: a matrix of primordial oral culture, partly Asian in origin (we are told), partly independent of (while contributing to) contemporary learned culture. This is where the cheese and worms of the title come in: for Menocchio, life emerged from the sea like worms from cheese. This notion of spontaneous generation out of chaos, Ginzburg explains, was the echo of an ancient myth, which had survived by 'oral transmission from generation to generation'.

Ginzburg once described himself as 'halfway between history and anthropology'.[24] In his case it is a very particular anthropology, part cross-cultural, part European (that is, Europeans studying Europeans). In Ginzburg's case there are close links with the Italian anthropological tradition, with its distinct disciplines of ethnology, the history of popular traditions and cultural anthropology, and its concentration on religion, subaltern groups and cultural complexity, emphasis on historical approaches and tendency to study Italian society.[25] All these are summed up in the work of Italian anthropologist Ernesto de Martino (1908–65).[26] Consistent with this tradition is Ginzburg's notion of circularity between the culture of the dominant classes and the subordinate classes in pre-industrial Europe. What he hoped Menocchio's case demonstrated was a cultural relationship composed of 'reciprocal influences', where ideas travelled 'from low to high as well as from high to low'.

Ginzburg went to great pains to stress the nature of this relationship in the preface to the English translation of his work. This was in response to a lengthy criticism from Paola Zambelli, a historian of philosophy with a specialization in natural magic.[27] Zambelli brings to the fore some of the difficulties inherent in Ginzburg's approach, the first regarding origins, the second touching the nature of peasant culture. Zambelli pointed out that at the university of Padua, not far from Menocchio's village, there were scholars putting forward ideas on spontaneous generation. Menocchio may simply have had contact with someone who was a student there, rather than come up with such a notion himself based on an ancient myth. Using the well-travelled, office-holding Menocchio as a spokesman for popular culture thus has serious risks. At times the ideas are said to be his own; at other times they are a refraction of peasant culture. This may show the circularity of culture in the period, but it also points out a circularity in Ginzburg's own argument. The only testimony for this peasant culture is Menocchio himself.

For all his stress on cultural transmission – and this remains the most fascinating and ambitious aspect of the book – Ginzburg still has a gut sympathy for the immemorial and collective nature of popular tradition. Zambelli questioned Ginzburg's notion of the 'autonomy and continuity' of peasant culture. Both aspects pose difficulties for historians. How can we believe that such long-term and autonomous, but almost hidden, structures exist, if their existence is not amply and independently ascertained and documented? What is most interesting about Ginzburg's response to Zambelli is his suggestion that what was needed for any investigation of popular culture was a new standard or criterion of proof.[28] In the unequal struggle between dominant and subordinate cultures, the latter – largely oral – was obviously going to be the loser, leaving fewer traces in the records for historians to pick up. In Ginzburg's view, when it comes to determining the origin of ideas, our conventional standard of proof exaggerates the importance of the dominant culture, as against what can only remain the hypothesis of an origin in remote oral tradition. This justification of his approach is somewhat lame, confined as it is to a footnote, but he did expand on it elsewhere.[29] Historians, he suggested, must be like detectives or medical doctors in looking for clues and signs. He called it the 'evidential paradigm': identifying unknown objects through single, seemingly insignificant signs, rather than through the application of laws derived from repeatable and quantifiable observations. The historian should carefully select exceptional documents and read them to neutralize distortions. Using the atypical to get at the normal meant ascertaining and exploring what another Italian historian, Edoardo Grendi, termed the 'normal exception'.[30] In this way the apparently exceptional or unusual could be turned on its head to shed light on the experience of the everyday world in the past.

The issue of evidence is crucial: historians of past societies cannot interact with their sources as anthropologists do. This is one of the main sources of difficulty in the dialogue between historians and anthropologists. In another article in his collection, Ginzburg explored the use of inquisitorial records by historians as sources of ethnographic data.[31] To what extent could the inquisitor stand in for the anthropologist, and the defendants for the 'natives'? The records were far from neutral. Nonetheless Ginzburg believed it was possible to get beyond the judges' own convictions, and the psychological and physical pressures they exerted, in order to mine the rich evidence available. He argued that the inquisitorial trial resembles the anthropological approach in the sense of being a permanent confrontation between different cultures. Borrowing from the literary critic Mikhail Bakhtin, he called this a 'dialogic disposition'. Most defendants simply echoed the interrogator's questions, which was easier and safer. This was 'monologic', in that what was expressed seemed to come from a single, unified source, the perspective of the inquisitor. Occasionally, however, we can detect a clash between different, even conflicting voices. (Bakhtin argued that all discourses are multivocal.) This clashing cultural reality could be turned to the historian's advantage, allowing us 'to disentangle the different threads which form the textual fabric of these dialogues'. Ginzburg concluded that a close reading of a relatively small number of texts, related to a possibly circumscribed belief, could be more rewarding than the massive accumulation of repetitive evidence.

You say 'historical anthropology', I say 'anthropological history'

It is ironic that just when some historians were turning to anthropology for evidence of what was timeless and unchanging – *l'histoire immobile* in the French phrase – some anthropologists were turning to history as a means of escaping the assumptions of a timeless and unchanging native culture. As a sort of intermezzo it might be useful to examine the state of the relationship at this midway point in our survey. A 1981 collection of articles in the *Journal of Interdisciplinary History*, a journal that prided itself on being cutting edge, took stock of 'anthropology and history'.[32] By then it was quite common to refer to a dialogue between history and anthropology. But what sort of dialogue was it? It was also quite common to use 'historical anthropology' as a label. How accurate or useful was it?

It is possible to have a foot in both camps, as in the case of Alan Macfarlane,[33] William Christian[34] and Richard Trexler,[35] to name but three. This is not the same as saying that historical anthropology is itself a specialized discipline, however. It was, and continues to be, more of an approach. Here history and anthropology overlap and collaborate with one another. However, what we are dealing with is not so much 'historical anthropology' as 'anthropological history'. The latter suggests the pragmatic use of certain of anthropology's themes and methods by historians, who nevertheless never cease to see themselves first and foremost as practising historians. E.P. Thompson (1924–93), commenting on the Thomas–Geertz exchange, suggested it was all well and good to be stimulated by anthropologists, but historians should avoid becoming ensnared in their debates and ulterior assumptions.[36] Natalie Zemon Davis (b. 1928), herself one of the pioneers of an anthropologically informed history, affirmed that historians needed to know about the different schools of anthropological interpretation in order to be able to integrate it into their own vision. Yet she asked whether it was necessary 'to import all the special reservations that anthropologists have about each other's work or all their in-fighting'. After all, historians turn to anthropology for suggestions rather than prescriptions, comparisons rather than universal rules. There was 'no substitute for extensive work in the historical sources'.[37] This remains salutary advice. But if historians were to contribute to anthropological theory, rather than simply borrow from it, as Davis hoped, would it not be necessary to pay more attention to what she belittled as 'in-fighting'? To give this disputatious habit a more positive connotation, it is potentially the kind of reflexive exercise that benefits any discipline. Failure to give internal debates a more important place may be one of the reasons why historians have tended to borrow from a few key, established anthropological names – Clifford Geertz (b. 1926) and Victor Turner (1920–83) are the obvious ones – giving the impression that these were the winners and that the debates were settled.[38] By and large, historians have eschewed a deeper engagement with anthropology as a whole. They have 'dabbled', according to the anthropologist John Adams. They have borrowed concepts from anthropology without attempting to make a contribution to anthropology in return.[39]

Historians have made off with the expression 'historical anthropology', Adams might have added. In Germany, for instance, it was used from the 1960s onwards by historians as a (partly critical) parallel to the then dominant 'historical social science'.[40] It was linked to *Alltagsgeschichte* (the study of everyday life), as well as the study of *mentalités* and popular culture, and eventually spawned its own journal.[41] As this suggests, history as a discipline has a seemingly unique capacity for adding on bits and pieces from other disciplines without ceasing to be 'history'. Debates range round the edges without affecting the core. 'Historical anthropology', though it occupies history's boundary zones, comes closer to the status of a sub-discipline within anthropology.[42] Most of those calling themselves historical anthropologists are to be found in departments of anthropology. In this context it is viewed as one way of doing anthropology. Other historical anthropologists, who have written and taught as anthropologists, include Marshall Sahlins, who writes about Hawaii and Fiji, Bernard Cohn on India and Eric Wolf. The latter's most famous work, Braudelian in sweep, typifies the aims, dealing as it does with the troubled interactions between Europe and 'the people without a history', an ironic reference to traditional western notions about 'the natives'.[43] Most work in the field is colonial and postcolonial, studying native North America, Africa, Asia, Australia and Oceania. One of the key areas of interest is how local people coped with change.

The historical anthropologists proper raised a range of issues regarding the overlapping efforts of historians. Bernard Cohn praised some historians for being aware that anthropology suggested a certain reading of documents, providing hypotheses rather than clear-cut answers. They sought to build this ambiguity into their narratives. But he took to task historians in general for concentrating on the version of anthropology 'concerned with stability, structure, regularity, the local, the common, the small scale, and the expressive symbolic, and magical'. Even when studying fast-changing, complex societies, historians focused on 'immobile' groups within them – the peasantry, working class, women – and the relevant anthropology, Cohn argued. It is worth noting, however, that this was due not only to a (perhaps misplaced) perception of what anthropologists were good at. These were just the kinds of issues that historians were then keen on exploring in a serious and purposeful way, after being preoccupied with 'mobility' for so long. It turns out that what was once perceived as unchanging and ahistorical, and as such incidental to the historical process, can both be historically significant and possess a complex history during the early modern period. In historiographical terms this importance and complexity is exemplified by the shift from women's history to gender history,[44] and by the lively debate on conceptions of popular culture.[45] Sociocultural anthropological ways of seeing can shake us from our unilinear historical complacency. Apparently marginal phenomena, like begging, can suggest important new ways of understanding broader developments, like economic changes or attitudes towards the poor.[46] It can bring to the fore new meanings for long-studied subjects, as well as suggest possible contours for new areas, as Davis argued.

A question of scale: Peter Burke and Rosario Villari

This is just what Peter Burke (b. 1937), one of the historians to use the label 'historical anthropology' with most confidence and flair, attempted in a 1987 collection of essays.[47] The collection was praised for its narrative style: a series of detailed cases or vignettes where the theory and analysis is embedded into the story.[48] In one of the essays, a study of an urban revolt which took place in Naples in 1647, Burke illustrates how the smallness of scale can suggest new interpretations of a much-studied event, permitting an alternative reading of the 20 or so contemporary narratives that have survived.[49] In particular, Burke reinterprets the revolt through the lens of ritual. The study of ritual has been one of the most exciting contributions of anthropologically minded historians to the study of early modern Europe.[50] In this case, ritual is seen as a means of communication, providing collective actions with a meaning for those involved. This is particularly applicable to the first phase of the revolt, the second week of July 1647, led by the fisherman Masaniello against the introduction of a tax by the Spanish. Burke uses the notion of 'social drama', developed by the Scottish anthropologist Victor Turner.[51] In a symbolic way, the various events of the riot had three functions: expressive (sending a message to the authorities), legitimating (as popular justice, lynchings became executions) and organizing (exemplified in the coherence of crowd actions). As Burke puts it, 'the rituals both expressed community cohesion and created it', the community in question being located near the city's Piazza del Mercato and the church of the Virgin of the Carmine.

Burke's radical new approach to the insurrection goes beyond earlier interpretations based on social and economic grievances. It is an attempt to add a dimension based on the culture of the crowd to a behavioural approach based on economic determinism. In this respect it is a model of the microhistorical style, which looks at the small-scale to ask new questions and suggest hypotheses, with the aim of relating these back to larger questions and trends. However, the article has been criticized for sacrificing historical detail to anthropological structure and hypothesizing. Rosario Villari, an authority on the riot and among the scholars cited by Burke, commented on the 'value and deceptiveness of symbols' for the historian in his critique.[52] Villari is less than clear in identifying what he thought the 'value' of Burke's approach to be, or even the 'symbols'; but he made the 'deceptions' clear enough: singling out the first ten days of a 'revolution' which lasted nine months and went through several phases (and whose demands were at least partially met); underplaying the revolt's political content and its appeal to the masses (in the process exaggerating the function of the Carmine as a focus, as well as the centrality and personality of Masaniello); all but ignoring the particular social, political and economic context of the city itself (then Europe's largest); and, finally, following the well-worn stereotype of the city as one lacking in urban structure and organization (a distortion which began with literary accounts of the event immediately afterwards).

The anthropological approach, as exemplified by Burke, risks satisfying neither the historian nor the anthropologist. For the anthropologist, it papers over the theoretical cracks between different anthropological theories and interpretations, reducing everything to a kind of diluted functionalism, of the kind generally favoured by early modern historians. For the historian, it downplays the bread and butter of historical research: context and detail. In addition to these cross-disciplinary perils, there are the pitfalls inherent in the narrative style historians have often adopted in the presentation of their 'anthropological' material: the in-depth microhistory, as developed in the form of an essay. These can fall short of the mark, however, with densely presented detail masquerading as the 'thick description' advocated by Clifford Geertz, storytelling at the expense of analysis, the problematic relationship between the 'exceptional' and the 'normal' in legal records, the failure to relate the microhistorical to the macrohistorical.[53] There is the risk of 'atomizing' the past, as John Elliott has put it.[54] At the same time, the best microhistory excels in turning the small-scale into an opportunity to shed light on the previously unnoticed or marginalized, delving into unexplored social attitudes, behaviours and structures, by means of a narrative strategy rich in explanatory value.[55] The best microhistorians are actually trying to discover very big things with their microscopes and magnifying glasses.[56] However small the scale, the same criteria of relevance and applicability apply. The 'archives are full of stories of unknown people', Ginzburg has said apropos of *The Cheese and the Worms*; 'the problem is why one has to choose that story instead of another story, why that document instead of another'.[57]

Related to this is what is the 'small' in small-scale, the 'micro' in microhistory? And how can we relate the macro (the major processes of the past) to the micro level? Relating local-level responses to the Protestant and Catholic Reformations – in terms of continuities and changes in beliefs, attitudes and practices – would certainly qualify as an exploration of the complex relationship, with each level shedding light on the other. I sought to do this for the Terra d'Otranto in southern Italy and, more recently, Margo Todd has done this for Scotland.[58] Both works are influenced by anthropology, in particular the notion of religion as a cultural system. Neither are examples of microhistory as such, although each is profoundly rooted in their different locales and in individual experiences. In this regard, however, at least two anthropologists have referred to historians' 'analytical sleight of hand' in stressing the 'local' while at the same time picking useful examples from a range of different localities.[59] Historians, especially early modernists, do not have the anthropologist's luxury of laying down roots in a single community; our data are far too scarce and we are forced to roam. Then again, scale reduction should be as much about widening horizons beyond the village, the small group or the individual as a self-contained unit of activity, and therefore of study. The point is that small-scale data must be made to speak to large-scale or abstract and conceptual issues. They will not do so by themselves.[60] Historians often have difficulty accepting a description of past phenomena that does not treat these phenomena as homogeneous. Microhistory, by contrast, takes advantage of the exceptional normal, relating in concrete detail how actual entities, personal experiences or events can relate the micro with the macro. It represents a new way of describing and analysing the micro–macro link.

Texts and meanings: Robert Darnton and Roger Chartier

If the influence of Clifford Geertz looms large in much microhistory, if only as an obligatory point of reference, in the final exchange his contribution is more significant. It concerns Robert Darnton's 'great cat massacre'.[61] In the study, Darnton (b. 1939) uses a 1762 account of a gruesome prank to explore the lore of a group of Parisian artisans. It and the book of which it is part are significant in another way: as an attempt to abandon the distinction between elite and popular culture and look at how both coped with the same sort of problems. Darnton is an expert guide to what he calls the 'anthropological mode of history', not least because he has taught a course on history and anthropology together with the anthropologist Clifford Geertz. Indeed, Geertz's influence as ethnographer-essayist is evident throughout the chapter. From Geertz, historians learn to see culture as consisting in systems of often ritualized meaning. Actions are systems of meaning; they are symbolic. They can be read as 'texts', and texts have meaning without reference to anything other than themselves. Geertz was able to 'read' a foreign culture as a 'text' – both metaphors drawn from the post-structuralist work of anthropologist Paul Ricoeur, because he was there. It is to Darnton's credit that he gives the reader of his essay the illusion of his (Darnton's) having been there, too.

When a group of apprentice printers stage a trial and execution of the neighbourhood cats, including their mistress's favourite, and retell the event to much hilarity on later occasions, we are confronted with an alien culture. Where a culture is at its most opaque the anthropologist seizes the opportunity to unravel a different system of meaning. This is what Geertz did with his analysis of the Balinese cockfight;[62] this is what Darnton attempts to do here. The meaning of the cat massacre revolves around identifying and understanding different parts of the cultural repertory of the time which the workers drew upon: fears of witchcraft and sorcery, the carnival mock trial, the charivari, their code of sexual relations, and so on. To do so means reconstructing the social and cultural world of the apprentice printers, which Darnton does in an effective and lively way.

Underlying this is Darnton's working conviction that this meaning, however multivalent, is fully recoverable through a close reading of the text.

Both meaning and text were called into question by poststructuralist-influenced historian Roger Chartier (b. 1945). He worried that certain borrowings from anthropology would create problems 'by destroying the "textuality" of the texts that relate the symbolic practices being analyzed'.[63] On the one hand, there is the text itself, the 1762 account of the event, taken from Nicolas Contat's *Anecdotes typographiques.* Contat was a participant in the event. However, Chartier argues that his *Anecdotes* belong to a literary genre, and yet Darnton treats it as a transparent vehicle for the full recovery of meaning. Then there is the meaning itself. Surely, Chartier suggests, we would be better off seeking out contemporary commentaries on symbols, rather than trying to come up with our own interpretations. For example, we have 'the native's point of view', in the form of Antoine Furetière's dictionary of 1727.

Darnton took the opportunity of a reply to Chartier to elaborate on his own symbolic approach, rather than comment point-for-point on Chartier's remarks.[64] This has been called a non-exchange, a dispute not over facts but over preferred narratives of the past.[65] The dispute highlighted the differences between the two scholars, downplaying the more significant aspects of the history of reading and cultural practices on which they agree.[66] Doubtless, Darnton asks a lot of his text. Indeed his belief in the authority of the text recalls Le Roy Ladurie. Basic questions remain: was this a typical form of popular ritual? Did it actually happen? Darnton has also been called to task for reducing clashing anthropological definitions of culture to a shared 'general orientation', one that was based on seeing things from the native's point of view and exploring the social dimensions of meaning. He was criticized for using anthropology as a 'quick fix' for certain historiographical difficulties. We have certainly heard this before. Finally, Darnton was criticized for the overall argument in the book: that there was both a significant shift in 'mental worlds' between the *ancien régime* and the present and a persistence in 'Frenchness' throughout. Seeing culture in terms of shared symbols risks missing the variety of contemporary voices, sometimes in conflict or negotiation. It risks painting a picture of uniformity.

A 'pidgin paradigm'?

The late 1980s was just about the time when interest in sociocultural anthropology among early modernists showed signs of declining. This was due in part to anthropology's crisis of postmodernism. An increasingly reflexive anthropology began pondering its own claims to authority in a fragmented world. We saw an element of this in Rosaldo's critique of *Montaillou.* Some fields of early modern history actively engaged with anthropology's encounters with postmodernism. Ideas concerning cultural relativism and social construction have been particularly useful in the history of medicine and science. Here, we also see a complementary tendency among anthropologists: the return to detailed, empirical, comparative ethnography in an expanding range of sub-fields, such as medical anthropology.[67] Meanwhile, other areas of history have transposed their version of sociocultural anthropology into a paradigm with an almost canonical range of authors, methodologies, interpretations and topics. It has become a 'pidgin paradigm', with its implications of simplification and debasement, on the one hand, and fluidity across boundaries and flexibility, on the other.[68] If anthropology does not provide early modern historians with the 'buzz' it once did, that is because some of its basic premises and approaches have entered the historical mainstream (actor's categories, native's point of view, symbolic interpretations). Some of its themes – ritual being the most obvious – are now widespread among historians and have been applied to more traditional historical genres, now revitalized, like the study of elite groups and politics. But there is still much anthropology can teach us. For instance, historical anthropology reminds us not to take our archival sources for granted: that the archive itself (to say nothing of the individual holdings) is the result of a historical process. Rather than worrying solely whether a historical source can stand in for fieldwork, we should also be conducting 'extensive fieldwork on the archive itself'.[69] How did it come into being and with what purpose? How is it structured, used and read today?

Just how much anthropology is good for early modern historians? When does the law of diminishing returns set in? Lawrence Stone (1919–99) argued that anthropology is useful at shedding light on, but not explaining, phenomena in the past.[70] This is certainly true; but it seems more than enough to ask of a related discipline. At least one of anthropology's fervent advocates, Bob Scribner, was actually lukewarm when it came to applying it to his own work. This was partly because he was aware of its limitations and pitfalls, partly because he wanted to be free to choose from other interpretations and methodologies as he saw fit. The use of 'theory' for the historian lay in its applications, Scribner believed.[71] Historians are probably wise to stress the practical applications of 'theory', of whatever sort. At the same time, it would do us no harm to be more reflexive about our choice and use of theories from other disciplines. We should aim to reduce the theory–practice dualism that mars much historical research and writing (as if theory did not lie at the root of all practice). Whatever role it assumes in historical theory and practice, sociocultural anthropology has much to offer. We are still a long way from understanding the belief systems, range of social relationships, change and persistence underpinning early modern cultures. As historians continue to explore how things fit together in the past, we are conscious of acting as mediators, in this case between the past and the present. Whenever we want to investigate people's thoughts and actions we shall benefit from the translation and interpretation skills and experience provided by anthropologists.

Guide to further reading

Brian Axel, 'Introduction: Historical Anthropology and its Vicissitudes', in B. Axel (ed.), *From the Margins: Historical Anthropology and its Futures* (Durham, NC, 2002), pp. 1–44.

Peter Burke, *The Historical Anthropology of Early Modern Italy: Essays on Perception and Communication* (Cambridge, 1987).

Elizabeth Cohen and Thomas Cohen, 'Anthropology and History', in D.R. Woolf (ed.), *A Global Encyclopedia of Historical Writing* (New York and London, 1998), vol. 1, pp. 33–6.

David Gentilcore, 'The Ethnography of Everyday Life', in John Marino (ed.), *Early Modern Italy, 1550–1796* (Oxford, 2002), pp. 188–205.

Don Kalb, Hans Marks and Herman Tak (eds), *Focaal: European Journal of Anthropology* 26/27 (1996): monograph issue entitled *Historical Anthropology: the Unwaged Debate*.

Matti Peltonen, 'Clues, Margins and Monads: the Micro-Macro Link in Historical Research', *History and Theory* 40 (2001), pp. 347–57.

Renato Rosaldo, 'From the Door of his Tent: the Fieldworker and the Inquisitor', in J. Clifford and G. Marcus (eds), *Writing Culture: the Poetics and Politics of Ethnography* (Berkeley, 1986), pp. 77–97.

Robert Scribner, 'Historical Anthropology of Early Modern Europe', in R. Po-Chia Hsia and R.W. Scribner (eds), *Problems in the Historical Anthropology of Early Modern Europe* (Wolfenbüttel, 1997), pp. 11–34.

Notes

1 I am indebted to Elizabeth Cohen and Thomas Cohen, who commented on an earlier draft of this chapter. Their entry on 'Anthropology and History', in D.R. Woolf, *A Global Encyclopedia of Historical Writing* (New York and London, 1998), vol. 1, pp. 33–6, provides a useful starting point.

2 On history and theory, see Ludmilla Jordanova, *History in Practice* (London, 2000), pp. 59–90.

3 E.E. Evans Pritchard, *Anthropology and History* (Manchester, 1961).

4 Isaac Schapera, 'Should Anthropologists be Historians?', *Journal of the Royal Anthropological Institute of Great Britain and Ireland* 92 (1962), pp. 143–56.

5 Keith Thomas, 'History and Anthropology', *Past & Present* 24 (1963), pp. 3–24.

Sixteenth-Century France (Oxford and New York, 2000), Davis has been one of anthropological history's most eloquent exponents.

38 Jordan Goodman, 'History and Anthropology', in Michael Bentley (ed.), *Companion to Historiography* (London and New York, 1977), pp. 787–8.

39 Adams, 'Consensus, Community, and Exoticism', p. 265.

40 Hans Medick, ' "Missionaries in the Row Boat"? Ethnological Ways of Knowing as a Challenge to Social History', *Comparative Studies of Society and History* 29 (1987), pp. 76–98.

41 *Historische Anthropologie* has been published since 1993. Michael Mitterauer, 'From Historical Social Science to Historical Anthropology?', in M. Jovanović, K. Kaser and S. Naumović (eds), *Between the Archives and the Field: a Dialogue on Historical Anthropology of the Balkans* (Belgrade, 1999), http://www.udi.org.yu/article/archives/MM.html (accessed February 2005).

42 Brian Keith Axel, 'Introduction: Historical Anthropology and its Vicissitudes', in his (ed.), *From the Margins: Historical Anthropology and its Futures* (Durham, NC, 2002), pp. 1–44.

43 Eric Wolf, *Europe and the People without History* (Berkeley, 1982).

44 Olwen Hufton, 'Women, Gender and the *fin de siècle*', in Bentley (ed.), *Companion to Historiography*, pp. 929–40.

45 Compare Peter Burke, *Popular Culture in Early Modern Europe* (London, 1978) and the collection of essays in Tim Harris (ed.), *Popular Culture in England, c.1500–1800* (Basingstoke, 1995), particularly the editor's contribution, 'Problematising Popular Culture', pp. 1–27.

46 For instance, Norbert Schindler, 'The Origins of Heartlessness: the Culture and Way of Life of Beggars in late Seventeenth-Century Salzburg', in his *Rebellion, Community and Custom in Early Modern Germany*, trans. Pamela E. Selwyn (1992; Cambridge, 2002), pp. 236–92.

47 Peter Burke, *The Historical Anthropology of Early Modern Italy: Essays on Perception and Communication* (Cambridge, 1987).

48 Review by Randolph Starn, *Journal of Modern History* 62 (1990), pp. 628–30.

49 Peter Burke, 'The Virgin of the Carmine and Revolt of Masaniello', *Past & Present* 99 (1983), pp. 3–21, reprinted in his *Historical Anthropology*, pp. 191–206.

50 Edward Muir, *Ritual in Early Modern Europe* (Cambridge, 1997).

51 Victor Turner, *Schism and Continuity in African Society* (Manchester, 1957) was the first of several books exploring ritual and symbols.

52 Rosario Villari, 'Masaniello: Contemporary and Recent Interpretations', *Past & Present* 103 (1985), pp. 117–32, reprinted in his *The Revolt of Naples*, trans. J. Newell (Cambridge, 1993), pp. 153–70.

53 'Thick description' refers to how even the smallest detail of human life is embedded in layers of contextual significance. On 'microhistory', see Edward Muir's entry in Woolf's *Global Encyclopedia*, vol. 2, pp. 615–17.

For an exploration of the link between anthropology and microhistory, see David Gentilcore, 'The Ethnography of Everyday Life', in John Marino (ed.), *Early Modern Italy, 1550–1796* (Oxford, 2002), pp. 188–205.

54 John Elliott, *National and Comparative History: An Inaugural Lecture Delivered before the University of Oxford* (Oxford, 1991).

55 In support: Edward Muir, 'Introduction: Observing Trifles', in Edward Muir and Guido Ruggiero (eds), *Microhistory and the Lost Peoples of Europe* (Baltimore and London, 1991), pp. vii–xxviii and Giovanni Levi, 'On Microhistory', in Peter Burke (ed.), *New Perspectives on Historical Writing* (Cambridge, 1991), pp. 93–113. Against: Thomas Kuehn, 'Reading Microhistory: the Example of *Giovanni and Lusanna*', *Journal of Modern History* 61 (1989), pp. 512–34 and Samuel Cohn, *Women in the Streets: Essays on Sex and Power in Renaissance Italy* (Baltimore and London, 1996), esp. pp. 98–136.

56 Matti Peltonen, 'Clues, Margins and Monads: the Micro-Macro Link in Historical Research', *History and Theory* 40 (2001), p. 350.

57 Maria Lúcia Pallares-Burke, *The New History: Confessions and Conversations* (Cambridge, 2002), p. 197.

58 David Gentilcore, *From Bishop to Witch: the System of the Sacred in Early Modern Terra d'Otranto* (Manchester, 1992); Margo Todd, *The Culture of Protestantism in Early Modern Scotland* (New Haven and London, 2002).

59 Marilyn Silverman and P.H. Gulliver, 'Inside Historical Anthropology: Scale-reduction and Context', *Focaal: European Journal of Anthropology* 26/27 (1996), pp. 149–58.

60 Don Kalb, Hans Marks and Herman Tak, 'Historical Anthropology and Anthropological History: Two Distinct Programs', *Focaal: European Journal of Anthropology* 26/27 (1996), pp. 5–13.

61 Robert Darnton, *The Great Cat Massacre and Other Episodes in French Cultural History* (New York, 1984), pp. 79–104.

62 Clifford Geertz, 'Deep Play: Notes on the Balinese Cockfight', in *The Interpretation of Cultures: Selected Essays* (New York, 1973), pp. 412–53. But see William Roseberry, 'Balinese Cockfights and the Seduction of Anthropology', *Social Research* 49 (1982), pp. 1013–28.

63 Roger Chartier, 'Texts, Symbols, and Frenchness', *Journal of Modern History* 57 (1985), p. 690.

64 Robert Darnton, 'The Symbolic Element in History', *Journal of Modern History* 58 (1986), pp. 218–34.

65 Dominick LaCapra, 'Chartier, Darnton, and the Great Symbol Massacre', and James Fernandez, 'Historians Tell Tales: of Cartesian Cats and Gallic Cockfights', both in *Journal of Modern History* 60 (1988), pp. 92–112 and 113–27.

66 For Darnton's take on it, see Pallares-Burke, *New History*, pp. 169–70.

67 Michael MacDonald, 'Anthropological Perspectives on the History of Science and Medicine', in Pietro Corsi and Paul Weindling (eds), *Information Sources in the History of Science and Medicine* (London, 1983), pp. 61–80; Jordan Goodman, 'History and Anthropology', in Bentley (ed.), *Companion to Historiography*, pp. 796–8.

68 Mary Fulbrook, *Historical Theory* (London, 2002), esp. pp. 47–8, 86.

69 Nicholas Dirks, 'Annals of the Archive: Ethnographic Notes on the Sources of History', in Axel, *From the Margins*, p. 51. See also Stephen Milner, 'Partial Readings: Addressing a Renaissance Archive', *History of the Human Sciences* 12 (1999), pp. 89–105.

70 Lawrence Stone, 'History and the Social Sciences in the Twentieth Century', in his *The Past and Present Revisited* (London, 1987), p. 30. The article was first published in 1977.

71 Robert Scribner, 'Historical Anthropology of Early Modern Europe', in R. Po-Chia Hsia and R.W. Scribner (eds), *Problems in the Historical Anthropology of Early Modern Europe* (Wolfenbüttel, 1997), pp. 11–34; Thomas Brady, 'Robert W. Scribner, a Historian of the German Reformation', introduction to R.W. Scribner, *Religion and Culture in Germany (1400–1800)*, ed. Lyndal Roper (Leiden, 2001), pp. 9–26.

4

The linguistic turn

Susan R. Boettcher

A growing body of scholarship challenges the use of the terminology 'early modern',[1] a label for the fifteenth to eighteenth centuries that appears to have been adopted (with the exception of the German-speaking world) practically without discussion.[2] This material charges that the term does not describe most of the world effectively, is entwined in questionable Marxist categories for describing economic development and, most crushingly of all, is unacceptably teleological.[3] Still, the label 'early modern' has indeed served as an attractive refuge from vitriolic debates about the meaning of terms like 'Renaissance', 'Reformation' and 'scientific revolution', with the result that its definition has remained, perhaps intentionally, hazy.[4] A number of factors influence the wide and apparently growing alliance between early modern historiography and the broader 'linguistic turn' in the humanities. Linguistic theories have provided alternative paths for circumnavigating some of the interpretive dilemmas (to be discussed below) inherent in the subject of 'early modernity'.

The attraction of linguistic theory to early modern historians in part stems from a more general 'linguistic turn'. Linguistic theories have penetrated the humanities and social sciences in recent decades, becoming popular in philosophy, literature, anthropology, law, psychology, sociology and political science before historians addressed them.[5] The increasingly interdisciplinary nature of historical inquiry amplifies their attractiveness. For example, the vision of the historian as an ethnographer of past societies – researching topics like kinship networks and inheritance systems – has fostered a growing conversation with the theoretical framework used by anthropologists, which is heavily influenced by structuralism and poststructuralism.[6] Literature scholars have examined Geertzian 'thick description' as a rhetorical activity akin to their own traditional strategies.[7] Recognition of the textual quality of sources has intensified discussions about the critical tool kit for textual analysis in philosophy.[8] General interest and broader acceptance of interdisciplinarity, however, only partially explain early modernists' attraction to linguistic theories.

Both detractors and practitioners might claim that in association with 'new cultural history',[9] the use of linguistic theories has achieved the status of a new orthodoxy. However, it is hard to think of a practising early modern historian whose work fully exemplifies this trend, because the precarious definitions of the 'linguistic turn' make it harder to categorize its frequently haphazard applications. At its most general, 'the linguistic turn' conflates a number of theories, including both the structuralist linguistics of Ferdinand de Saussure (1857–1913) and Jacques Derrida's (1930–2004) reformulations, which emphasize the relationship of knowledge to language. These theories are often referred to as 'postmodern' or 'poststructural', but the 'linguistic turn' also includes theories more properly considered 'modernist' and 'structuralist' (like Saussure's, in fact), and some theories that are simply 'literary' (Russian formalism, reader-response theory). Literary scholars employ a kindred method called 'new historicism'.[10] Terminological slippage is an unavoidable effect of the lengthy discussions of these matters.[11] While many historians have read the works of the most influential theorists, in practice few have employed them with strict intellectual stringency. For the purposes of explaining the early modernist affinity to such theories, we can usefully characterize these concepts by generalizing: first, about their views on language and, second, about their views on the nature of human existence. Rather than attempt to cover the full range of linguistic theories available, this essay provides a general introduction which focuses in particular on the approach of the French post-structuralist philosopher, Michel Foucault, whose theories have been the most broadly influential in the field of early modern history.

Linguistic theory for historians: some key features

To understand the role that language plays in our understanding of human experience, according to followers of the linguistic turn, it may be useful to consider a banal example. Imagine that you are sitting under an apple tree and an apple hits you on the head. In general, proponents of the linguistic turn would suggest that in essence this experience is a linguistic one. You cannot report this experience or even think about it without language. (It is crucial to note that the sceptical presuppositions of this axiom apply neither to your actual existence nor to that of the tree or apple. We may confidently assume that you, the tree and the apple all exist and that the apple indeed fell on your head independently of your own will, without trespassing upon the fundamental assumptions of poststructuralism.)

This unavoidable linguistic intrusion in all human experience involves certain culturally constituted, powerful patterns of language that we will call 'discourses'.

No matter what you say to tell us about your experience or how we respond to your report, our statements are inextricably bound up in discourses. Even if you say something apparently neutral, like 'the apple fell on my head', your statement reflects a number of assumptions about your location and role in the universe, most notably that the apple fell on your head (hence your head did not fall on the apple), and that this event was empty of larger meaning (presumably, an accident). After all, you did not say, 'I hit the apple with my head' or, alternatively, 'God caused the apple to fall on my head in order to turn me from sin', or even 'The spirit of the tree has blessed me with its food'. In our culture, the explanation of random events is controlled by a quasi-scientific discourse about the mechanisms of events (people who sit under trees with ripe fruit are likely to be hit by it when, as it must, it falls). But as little as four hundred years ago, when the religious discourse of providentialism affected people's perceptions of random events in the West, the response elucidating divine action might have been more typical in this situation.

Thus, what exactly you say after the apple has fallen on your head bears on your relationship to the relevant 'metanarratives', or narrative discourses, that control everyone's abilities to speak about events. (The extent of the control exercised by the discourse is a matter of dispute among theorists and historians; some scholars would prefer to say that discourses 'affect' the possibility of speech.) Even if you say nothing in response to the fall of the apple, you can be assumed to participate in a discourse (such as one in which you are unsurprised due to mystic foreknowledge of the falling apple or of toughness in response to physical challenge). Moreover, you are certainly not the first person upon whose head an apple has fallen and who has lived to tell the tale. 'Intertextuality', another component of linguistic theories, suggests that narrative accounts of events are unavoidably influenced by other accounts of similar events, known in whole or in part to the speaker. Sometimes intertextuality is reliable (if this incident influenced you to describe your experiences in terms of those of the mathematician and scientist Isaac Newton (1642–1727), who first theorized about gravity, for example), but at other times it can be blurry (for example, if you made a stretched association in your narrative with William Tell or Adam and Eve, in both of whose stories apples play a prominent role). Either way, it unavoidably shapes your spoken perception of your experiences.

Furthermore, a conventional response on our part, perhaps to say, 'I'm sorry', is similarly bound up in cultural and linguistic assumptions determined by the discourse of politeness or appropriate response to random events in a mechanistic universe. The power of these discourses makes it inappropriate for us to bow our heads in prayer or exclaim 'Congratulations!' in response to your misfortune. That we are aware that we have other options for response than the one dictated as most appropriate in this example does not lessen the power of the discourse in constituting this experience for you and us. The power of the discourse can be seen precisely in the instance of intentional transgressions against it, as, for example, if we were to laugh uproariously at your misfortune – a response that might be permitted if we were either more powerful than you, or outside of the hierarchy entirely (as in the case of a mentally ill individual). An 'inappropriate' response not only outlines the limits of the discourse, but also has the effect of delineating the relative social power of the powerful speaker or marginalizing the less powerful one wherever the discourse is in force. Thus the employment of discourses can also be seen to reveal the structure of power relationships in a society, which poststructuralists in particular have often formulated in terms of binary oppositions (such as good/bad, active/passive, powerful/weak). Moreover, the fact that some people (the child or the fool) can transgress against powerful discourses points out their fundamental instability and the gaps in their control over accounts of experience (a point to which we will return).

In practice, historians are usually one additional step removed from this situation, since we often do not observe the events we analyse. We are dependent on sources that reconstitute an event, again ostensibly by means of language and discourse. We might examine your doctor's record of your medical treatment, for example, in which case we would encounter discourses of health and science – did you receive a concussion? We might interview a witness to the incident, such as the owner of the tree sued for property liability, in which case legal and insurance discourses would enter the picture. We might watch a videotape of the incident, which raises other discursive questions with regard to technology and visual aesthetics. These source examinations would open us up to the further experience of discourses to be critiqued before we could understand what the source tells us.

Analysing the operating discourse(s) in such situations means taking a further step than simply identifying the interests of the different observers who contribute to the creation of historical sources and attempting to neutralize them in one's own account. It means more than the idea that language is conditioned by social context. Historians writing before the linguistic turn carried out critical activity in response to social aspects of language as well, by trying to construct a full picture of an event in evaluating the reliability of their primary sources. Historians following the linguistic turn add an additional element to this activity by analysing the ways in which language as discourse constitutes events and circumstances.

The conclusion that discourses control the constitution of sources implies a radical challenge to the activities of historians who believe that sources merely reflect the intent of a speaker. Indeed, linguistic theorists may speak of the 'decentred' self, which is not capable of expressing an individual intent but is itself created by discourses. Thus, for the linguistically influenced historian, sources are evidence of the discourses and power relationships of their context(s) rather than reflecting the intentions of their authors. And this relationship is not limited to texts but extends in the view of some to the whole of the perceived world. As Gerhild Scholz Williams writes, 'discourse does more than identify the spoken or the written word: it also stands for the whole spectrum of cultural signs'.[12] The most important methodological outcome of this way of thinking is a focus on the decisive role of language. Language systems, which condition historical, material and political circumstances, are seen to fix and limit the range of possible meanings in any particular situation. Discourses determine human experience by creating centres of power. Here the study of linguistics converges with that of sociology, or what might be called 'social constructivism'.[13] Given these occasionally tyrannical assumptions about the importance of language in controlling reality, the fundamental unit of analysis for historians writing in a linguistic key must be that of discourse.[14] Typically, discourse analysis focuses on interaction and dialogue, and is thus heavily concerned with the sociological aspects of language. Discourse is to be understood in such theories not as a product of language, however, but as the determining agent or process in the constitution of the object that language describes.[15] We might think of discourse as language, working in its capacity as actor – it is itself the agent and hence is the constructing force in the power relations that influence the preconditions for any knowledge.[16] Texts do not respond to or reflect situations or events (a fundamental recognition about the texts of political theory found in the work of scholars like John Pocock and Quentin Skinner) – instead, texts construct events and circumstances.[17]

The focus on language alone is not sufficient to characterize the 'linguistic turn', however; philosophical views that influence this attitude towards language must also be included in its description. The particular world-view customarily associated with the linguistic turn appears to dictate a general mood of interpretation as well. Many linguistic theories are sceptical about the possibility of unified, universally applicable knowledge about the universe, as it has been constructed or theorized since the later seventeenth century – because this knowledge is itself the product of a discourse. The task of assembling such knowledge, sometimes termed 'the Enlightenment project', is also frequently referred to as 'logocentrism', a term that describes the dominant narrative centre in the West since the Enlightenment. Postmodernists argue that logocentrism has tended to emphasize the primacy of the *logos* (Greek for 'word') or rationality. French philosopher Jean-François Lyotard (1924–98) defined the interpretive mood resulting from postmodern criticism as one of 'incredulity toward metanarratives'.[18] This incapacity (critics would say refusal) to believe stems from an ontological uncertainty or confusion about the nature of human existence in response to the decentring of traditional assumptions about life, human experience and knowledge.

This erosion of confidence has its roots in the Renaissance, but has accelerated in the chaos of the post-World War II world. Such philosophical views either reluctantly admit or joyfully proclaim a fundamental incoherence of world, self and meaning that questions inherited ideas about the absolute quality of truth. Whether they are completely successful in achieving this rejection is a matter of some contention.[19] Such views are often associated with an espoused 'hermeneutic of suspicion' that questions the face value and the governing context of statements, even when emphatically affirmed or empirically supported. The act of interpretation on this view, which is called 'deconstruction' by postmodernists, challenges interpretively the metanarrative of a text, an age or an interpretation by noting the indeterminacy of texts in the tension between the binary dichotomies ('rational/irrational', 'fact/fiction', 'observer/subject') assumed to govern intellectual discourse in the modern West.[20] A ubiquitous metanarrative found in the sources of modern western history that has been crucial to constituting the field of early modern history, for example, is that of 'progress', the idea that 'things are always getting better and better'. The interpretive act necessary in response to this metanarrative is assumed to be a rigorous examination of the ways in which the discourse influences the content of the sources it creates – and the conclusions we come to from reading them.

Most 'linguistic' scholars agree that discursive systems are unstable in that they fail to be internally consistent and completely effective – hence their openness to critique and transgression by contemporaries as well as historians. They argue further that the self, an object that cannot be understood except in its relationship to dominant discourses, nonetheless shapes itself or undergoes shaping in response to the discourse – the self is thus flexible within its 'prison' of language.[21] As Stephen Greenblatt argued, the self has no essential characteristics but responds to the structures of power glimpsed in the discourses peculiar to any particular cultural or historical sphere.[22] While not everyone would agree to such a radically deracinated conception of the human self and its possibilities for agency, at its most simple, the linguistic turn in historical writing amounts to the admission both that historians cannot penetrate 'the veil of language' and that the results of thinking through the consequences of this idea are valid in its ramifications for understanding one's sources and conclusions.[23]

Textual readings that follow linguistic theories tend to prioritize reading 'against the grain', which means that the historian looks not at the stated or implicit intention of the author (since most poststructural theories deny the possibility of understanding authorial intention), but rather at the way that metaphors and other elements of the text work. The hermeneutic of suspicion leads historians working in this vein to pinpoint apparent holes, contradictions or gaps in texts, thus showing the way that arguments undermine themselves as a way of looking at culture in tension with itself. They conclude that despite the 'death of the author'[24] as a consequence of the decentring of the self, texts betray cultural information both in the sense that they allow us to glimpse such cultural presuppositions, and in the sense that texts are not always faithful to them. When we read an individual text in this mode, we should ask ourselves what cultural and generic constraints were operating upon the text, and pinpoint locations where the text fulfils these constraints and where it does not. Such analysis reveals the places in which particular discourses are more or less powerful, and at points of discursive transformation, the matter of what is said or not said in a text can be symptomatic of the successful and less successful points of cultural change. Such a textual approach can admittedly sometimes lead the historian to heavily speculative conclusions. The discussion of 'what is missing' may also provoke counterfactual approaches, both of which play a role that is at best controversial.[25]

While the names mentioned so far are widely familiar to historians, and their works deserve more consideration, the most influential intellectual in this tradition for early modern historians has clearly been Michel Foucault (1926–84). For Foucault, discourses in their relationship to power and knowledge were a key analytical unit. Although not every historian who makes reference to his ideas can fairly be called Foucauldian, Foucault's thinking has been central to the intellectual development of many historians, even those who ultimately reject it.[26] Historians have mostly left the painstaking examination of Foucault's thinking to philosophers, and his most important conclusions about history, especially about the concrete progression, timing and qualities of disciplining processes, have never been completely embraced, even by sympathetic historians, and are largely rejected by others.[27]

Still, a number of Foucault's insights stand out. Probably the most persisting image from Foucault's oeuvre is his exposition of British philosopher and jurist Jeremy Bentham's (1748–1832) design for the panopticon, which became a metaphor for the development of modernity in the West. The panopticon was a prison in which a single observer could monitor all the inmates without them ever being certain whether they were being observed at any particular moment. The design thus fostered a constant discipline for fear of discovery. Foucault expanded upon this metaphor in *Discipline and Punish* (1977), in which he described the growth of systems of discipline in the West. He had more generally explored this theme in its relationship to deviance and health in the more narrowly historical *Madness and Civilization* and *Birth of the Clinic*.[28] The matter of discipline and punishment of deviance in the West was one aspect of what Paul Rabinow, Foucault's most influential popularizer, characterized as a project to examine the different processes by which human beings are constructed as subjects, processes such as science, discipline, religion and sex.[29] A central object of this process of uncovering has been the elucidation of the location of power in any particular historical situation and its relationship to knowledge. The panopticon embodies such power – the most powerful is the person with the knowledge of what the observed is doing – and he, in turn, is connected to a network of people who observe him. That the possibility and development of such a network of 'power/knowledge' is a desirable aspect of modernity is a central insight of Foucault's thought. Studying the discourses of discipline, madness, medicine and other aspects of civilization allowed Foucault to examine how human subjectivity was constructed by the human sciences in relationship to these developments. The structure of this discursive development was the central focus of *The Order of Things* (1966).[30]

Foucault's thinking was taken up so readily partly because his work was accepted by early modern historians working in the influential *Annales* school. One outcome of the *Annales* approach in its attempt to write a 'history from below', as exemplified in the works of its most eminent practitioner Fernand Braudel (1902–85), was to reduce relationships of power to the ephemera of history. *Annales* historians eventually turned to the history of *mentalité* as a means to redress this gap.[31] The results often led to overgeneralization, as in Jean Delumeau's *Sin and Fear* (1983),[32] or to intriguing but anecdotal microhistories such as Emmanuel Le Roy Ladurie's *Montaillou* (1975) and *Carnival in Romans* (1979).[33] Historians of *mentalité* had always been short-changed by the Braudel model, and linguistic theories offered new vistas on this matter.[34] Foucault's discussion of the human subject and the process of its creation, despite his early emphasis on ruptures, bears strong resemblance to this historiographical strain.[35] Moreover, a decisive factor in the linguistic turn's appeal was wider dissatisfaction with the quantitative social history of the 1960s, particularly *Annales* and Marxist methods.[36] Discourse analysis offered an additional, complementary way to study the effects of historical change and hierarchical structures of early modern society on the individual, which had been a traditional concern of 'history from below'; at the same time, the linguistic turn seemed to lessen the importance of looking for the essential self of historical actors, which could be studied primarily via the activities of discourses in creating reactions to social change.

Case study: the French Revolution

The fortunes of these different approaches are clearly apparent in ongoing attempts to explain the causes of the French Revolution. In this field (shared by early modern and modern historians), the early triumph of economic and social history was manifested in Marxist explanations of class struggle as propounded by Albert Mathiez (1874–1932) and followed by Georges Lefebvre (1874–1959), Albert Soboul (1914–82) and, more recently, Michel Vovelle, successive holders of the Sorbonne Chair in the History of the French Revolution. These scholars elucidated the victory of the bourgeoisie over first the aristocracy and then the working classes, arguing that the Revolution represented the transition from a feudal to a capitalist economic order. The Marxist paradigm began to disintegrate in the mid-1950s in response to Alfred Cobban (1901–68), who argued that although the French Revolution was a social event, it was not due to the triumph of the bourgeoisie. For Cobban, feudalism had long been dead by 1789, and the Revolution was conducted by a group of notables who were neither bourgeois nor interested in reform; instead, these lawyers and landowners allied with the nobility in order to stop monarchical reform. The culmination of this 'revisionist' point of view, supported by George Taylor and Colin Lucas, was a rejection of economic and social causes of the Revolution. This stage was reached with the work of François Furet, *Interpreting the French Revolution* (1981).[37] In rehabilitating the early explanations for the Revolution offered by Alexis de Tocqueville (1805–59), Furet moved to an explanation that stressed the Revolution as a response to tensions between the political culture of eighteenth-century France and the increasing demands of the centralizing state. Furet thus moved explanations of the French Revolution back to politics and intellectual history, even if he felt that politics were ultimately related to their social origins.

This move left explanations of the Revolution ripe for a crop of historians with linguistic sympathies. While Lynn Hunt's first book had, like Furet, postulated the importance of the political qualities of the revolution based on a thorough archival examination of social conditions in the cities of Troyes and Reims, her second book turned to a focus on language, symbol, rhetoric and imagery as motivators in revolutionary activity, even arguing that language had a special quality during the French Revolution.[38] She challenged Furet by arguing that the causes of politics were cultural and hence linguistic, rather than social. Following Foucault, Roger Chartier (b. 1945) forced into question the received understanding that events have origins and causes, then argued that the French Revolution occurred not because of specific causes, but because it became conceivable in the public sphere.[39] Perhaps paradoxically, Carol Blum formulated the consideration of all the writing and speech of Rousseau and his followers as discourse as a means of rehabilitating the individual writer, whom she felt had been unfairly pushed out of history by (Marxist) social historians.[40]

But the linguistic turn in the Anglophone study of the French Revolution was most fully exemplified in the work of Keith Michael Baker. In his treatment of the intellectual origins of the Revolution, Baker stated firmly that 'to the extent that social and political arrangements are linguistically constituted in any society, efforts to change them (or to preserve them) can never occur outside of language. Language is constantly deployed as an instrument of social and political change, or, to be precise, social and political changes are themselves linguistic'. When discussing Louis XVI's (1754–93) fall from the French throne as a consequence of a loss of charisma, he continued,

> charisma itself must be understood as a linguistic effect: The sense of the monarch as the sacred center of the corporate social order, expressing its very ground of being as the public person in whom a multiplicity of parts became one, sprang from traditional symbolic representations constituting the nature of human existence and social identity in essentially religious terms. To say that the charisma of the monarch eroded (as it did . . .) is to say that the symbolic representations upon which it depended had been rendered increasingly discursive practices

which were then up for analysis.[41] With this argument, discussions of the French Revolution had not only moved miles away from the bourgeois revolution or any other social explanation of the problems of French absolutism, they were opened up to questions that uncovered acres of terrain under commonplaces of the field. Chartier, for instance, did not ask *why* Louis lost legitimacy; he asked *how*. In doing so, Chartier diffused the cause and responsibility throughout the Revolution to the public sphere rather than locating them either in the irresponsible cavorting of the court at Versailles or the virtuous politics of the revolutionary sans-culottes.

The example of the French Revolution in its position on the brink of modernity illuminates one of the peskiest problems of early modern history: that is, the very conception of the term 'early modern' requires us to think of the period as a sort of anteroom for modernity. This is the period in which the sweeping changes thought to have given birth to the modern world took place: the information revolution caused by the printing press, the scientific revolution, the Reformation, the birth of democracy, the beginnings of capitalism and industrialization, the triumph of the bourgeoisie, and so on. The broadest, simplest and most pressing question for this period has been how such monumental transformations affected people. Social history as 'history from below' was supposed to illuminate this question, but while historians learned a great deal more about what happened to a larger mass of people, we learned relatively little about how people experienced these changes. The linguistic turn, despite its professed inability to say anything about the 'real' self, allowed a return to the sort of sources that appear to say more about such issues, and which early modernists will always have in abundance: the written text.

Early modern historians and textual analysis

Textual sources were not new sources for historians. Critics, however, had always insisted on questions about the reception of the text among wider social groups.[42] Uncertain knowledge about early modern literacy rates complicates any conclusions drawn from the amazing number of texts available to early modernists. In medieval studies, when literacy rates are assumed to have been low, reception is a technical problem, involving identifying who read whose work by tracing textual traditions through a series of manuscripts. In modern history, when literacy rates are relatively high and the public sphere more fully developed, multiple sources for the question of reception are usually available. Early modern history, however, is characterized by rising literacy rates, but an often inchoate public sphere and a paucity of sources that allow us to examine how average people received ideas.

Discourse analysis is attractive because it provides new ways of evaluating old sources and new arguments about the reception of ideas. If authors are embedded in a discourse peculiar to a society, then the discourse can be traced through other parts of a society, in actions, architecture, politics and religion – even if the discourse is itself unstable and inconsistent, it is nonetheless legible. Arguments about the reception of ideas or discursive responses to social transformations can be made without resort to ego-documents, which are relatively rare before the eighteenth century. Also, following Chartier, the idea of a discourse in which all are embedded has proved useful in ending the traditionally understood elite/popular cultural split, since discourses are assumed to connect all people in society, not just those who are literate.[43] Discourse analysis has revalorized the text as such, along with its close reading, by skirting traditional problems of reception. At the same time, however, by tying discourses to the social construction of reality, these theories neatly invalidate the charge that texts are insignificant or 'elitist'.

Moreover, because of their assumptions, linguistic theories have been helpful even in interpreting one of the most interesting, and simultaneously compromised, sources for social history – the legal transcript. Early modern historians are plagued by the problem that ordinary people often show up exclusively in records adversarial to them, especially criminal court, inquisitorial/consistorial and welfare records. Statements under interrogation or torture were long seen as a source of lesser value because they were assumed not to reflect the authentic self.[44] In so far as individual statements appeared in the records of poor relief it was assumed that individuals were 'saying what they needed to say' in order to achieve the desired effect. If we abandon the search for the coherent self and instead focus on the discourse of social disciplining, we can more easily use sources that did not meet historicist standards for objectivity. Moreover, we begin to see the people upon whom the institutions worked not merely as victims of totalizing processes, but rather as creative actors who learned to function within the discourse and shaped their responses to it.

This has been the general approach of Natalie Zemon Davis (b. 1928) in one of her most frequently cited books, *Fiction in the Archives* (1987).[45] Davis employs literary techniques that analyse the form, genre and elements of narrative to discuss the ways that those found guilty of crimes sought to avoid punishment. She found a number of particular narrative conventions operating in the statements of individuals who were successful in obtaining pardons from punishment for their crimes. Tellers of pardon tales thus responded to cultural discourses about punishment and pardon in attempting to persuade authorities to be lenient with them. This interpretive style leaves obscure the matter of what happened in early modern crime in favour of discussing how people understood what they had to do to be perceived in a certain way – a matter that also provides a great deal of information about the role of crime in early modern society. Although it has never been Davis's authorial practice to overwhelm the reader with methodological propositions, her approach to the language of her sources carries both structuralist aspects (in that she looks for constitutive narrative elements) and poststructuralist moments (in that she only tangentially considers evidence from social history on the 'real' referentiality of the texts, considering them primarily as political constructions). Her work postulates a relation of narrative elements in judicial texts and popular and literary narratives as the standard for believability. It has become one of the most frequently cited sources for a method of cultural history in the linguistic turn.[46]

Navigating the shoals of modernity: rationality and progress(?)

If the textual methods of the linguistic turn inaugurated new perspectives on the sources, still we cannot ignore the fundamental assumptions of the postmodern world-view that accompany it as a creator of sympathy for such approaches – for we also need to explain why the historiography of the linguistic turn tends to abandon the traditional themes of historical writing, frequently focusing on culture rather than diplomacy, war or economics. In order to do so, we must consider how the narrative of modernity in the West partitioned European history. This narrative constructed modern history as a period differentiated by the triumph of progress and rationality (and the spread of these to all peoples on earth) via the birth of empirical science, the discovery of the New World, the emergence of religious tolerance, the victory of democratic politics, the sighting of the invisible hand of market economies, and the like. These transformations were located in the fifteenth through to the eighteenth centuries. Constituting and central to this narrative were the very assertions about the possibility of objectivity and the prioritization of forms of intellectual inquiry that the narrative claimed were pursued and achieved on the path to modernity. Baldly stated: objectivity and rationality as intellectual tools constructed a historical narrative dedicated to tracing the development of objectivity and rationality. The origins of our scholarship as a profession are deeply rooted in just such ideas about the possibility of historical pursuits, even if descriptions of the degree to which its seminal figures espoused objectivity as a goal are overstated.[47]

Historicists and postmodernists may debate whether rationality as the discourse of modernity referred to some actual or real activity. However, it is unquestionable that its schedule of priorities marginalized phenomena like piety and religious experience that appeared non-rational from the modernist perspective. The lens of modernity thus made activities that were fully self-explanatory in their own contexts appear primitive and irrational. Phenomena like religious wars, the burning of heretics, witch-hunts, the blood libel, Eucharistic miracles, healing the 'king's evil' and veneration of saints were relegated to the pre-modern past. Their disappearance proved the gradual triumph of modernity. Only in the move towards secularism, textbooks suggested, did Europe succeed in consummating the tasks that concerned it in modernity: central and important activities like the extinction of religious privilege, the constitution of a public sphere, the building of a nation state and the development of a rational orientation on the part of factory labourers. In German Reformation history, dominant modes of history writing marginalized religious concerns as a subject belonging to the theological sub-field of 'church history', abandoning piety as a motivating aspect in favour of political and social explanations. In its interrogation of rationality, the linguistic turn responded effectively to such claims because its world-view offered the opportunity to reintegrate central early modern activities and sentiments into the historical narrative.

Brad Gregory has charged that the use of poststructural and other cultural theory to discuss religion delegitimates the lived experience of religious people.[48] It is equally possible, however, that the linguistic turn and its associated world-view offer scholars a hermeneutical path towards a more sympathetic explanation of the sort of activities and sentiments that occupied early modern Europeans, but which the modernist narrative designated as irrational or irrelevant. In *The Myth of Ritual Murder*, R. Po-Chia Hsia analysed violence against Jews in German towns of the late fifteenth and early sixteenth centuries in terms of a discourse of ritual murder with recognizable elements associated with the exercise of power in local communities. His work explained how the same people who prayed to a loving God and venerated the sorrowful Virgin could espouse bizarre superstition and participate in cruel persecution.[49] Sigrid Brauner related the increasing focus of early modern persecution of witchcraft on women to a religious discourse that emerged during the Reformation about the complementarity of partners, so that the witch was constructed by Protestant authors as a transgressor of roles.[50] Phil Soergel's study of Counter-Reformation propaganda analysed narratives in pilgrimage literature. He suggested that this literature codified explanations for holy events and re-enacted didactically the holiness ascribed to particular shrines and locations.[51] These works not only provided descriptions of the content and relationship of ideas, which had always been in the purview of traditional intellectual history. They also made statements about why particular ideas were diffused, based on the continuing persistence of certain discourses. In no way did these studies attempt to undermine the seriousness of the religious piety or emotional conviction of early modern people, in so far as these were discernible in the sources; on the contrary, they sought to show how this piety worked and the effects that it could have been expected to have on its listeners through the agent of discourse.

Dealing with the idealized picture of modernity has been an issue of particular interest for early modernists. Admittedly, even as an element of the modernist assertion of objectivity, historicism had self-critical features.[52] But by the mid-twentieth century, many questioned the narrative of progress, rationality and objectivity. It turned out that the monsters of progress depicted in Francisco de Goya's (1746–1828) engravings were more than wraiths lurking in the imagination of the artist. If the world-view behind the linguistic turn questions the modernist consensus about rationality, unity and progress as well as objectivity as the measure of knowledge, then the process whereby these elements came to dominate the modernist narrative might reasonably be assumed to be located in the fifteenth to eighteenth centuries. If the linguistic turn is a manifestation of postmodernism, then, it is only natural that it should seek to debunk the myths of modernism, casting its sceptical hermeneutical gaze on the moments in which the modernist narrative claims that these elements were conceived and engendered.

This tendency is most visible in the application of the linguistic turn to the history of science, not least because the triumph of science is one of the cornerstones of the modernist narrative.[53] Peter Dear, a historian of science who turned to studying the rhetorical and literary aspects of science as a discourse, comments, 'if the knowledge-making practices of the early modern period were not admitted as a part of the history of science, then historical understanding of the creation and character of modern science would become impossible'.[54] In this body of literature, the linguistic turn relies on discussions about the sociology of knowledge in scientific communities conducted by David Bloor, Barry Barnes and Harry Collins (among others) during the 1970s. In this sub-field, interest in language serves as a means of interrogating questions about the production of knowledge.[55]

An examination of the development of studies of the Copernican Revolution shows how the linguistic turn has affected histories of science. In 1543, Nicolas Copernicus (1473–1543) discovered that, rather than being the centre of the universe, the earth was simply one of several planets that rotated upon their own axes around the sun. This argument was condemned by many, including the Roman Catholic Church, but over time it convinced certain thinkers, notably the Italian mathematician Galileo Galilei (1564–1642). In the early seventeenth century, Galileo argued for a non-literal interpretation of the Bible on matters where a literal interpretation was contradicted by scientific facts. Such Copernican views were outlawed by the pope and Galileo was eventually found guilty of heresy and sentenced to life imprisonment. The modernist narrative on this topic blamed the Catholic Church and the Inquisition for condemning Galileo's obviously rational position,[56] or at least for disobeying its own legal and intellectual rules and allowing politics to contaminate the legal and scientific process.[57] Galileo emerges from such descriptions as the heroic champion of scientific truth or the tragic defender of principle. Following Foucault, however, in his *Galileo, Courtier* (1993), Mario Biagioli outlined the relationship between Galileo's intellectual commitment to Copernicanism and his decision to become a client in the Tuscan and Roman courts. This narrative presents Galileo not as an investigator or defender of truth, but as a navigator of the channels and shoals of power, an insufficiently deft client who failed to adapt his self-construction to the discourses of power at court. Biagioli considers science not as the uncovering of objective content, but as the result of a series of political practices mediated through the particular circumstances of power and language in the scientist's context.[58]

Another path-breaking study was Steven Shapin and Steven Shaffer's *Leviathan and the Air Pump* (1985), which conceives of scientific fact as a shared truth testified to by witnesses and hence controlled by social relations and their applicable rules of discourse. Hence, Robert Boyle (1627–91) came to be considered the archetype and progenitor of successful experimental science, while Thomas Hobbes's (1588–1679) science was discredited – not because Boyle was right and Hobbes was wrong about the natural world, but because Boyle more successfully employed conscious rhetorical techniques to make his ideas *appear* more reliable.[59] Shapin pursued this idea further in another central text for early modern historians, *The Social History of Truth* (1994), in which he argued that early experimental and natural science proceeded not by means of scepticism, but by emphasizing the trustworthy quality of information that could not be reproduced, and then exploring the discursive criteria for that consensus of truth.[60]

Because of the explicit relationship between language and power that the linguistic turn postulates, its method has emerged most convincingly in fields of study where literary texts were considered to be particularly important and indicative of such relationships. In the study of the English Renaissance and Tudor-Stuart histories, theatre, court politics and propaganda have long played a central role in political narratives. Similarly, the linguistic turn takes on an important role in the study of court societies and intellectual movements or professions where representation or artifice is central to the historical record.[61]

As even its opponents concede, the linguistic turn has provided an intriguing addition to the repertoire of historical methods. I have argued that it may succeed in circumventing some problems set up by modern social history. Some would argue, however, that writing history according to these assumptions runs the historian into problems, some more serious than others. Many historians have been suspicious of theories in general. The relationship outlined above between theories about language and knowledge peculiar to the post-war period is important because the interpretive methods of the linguistic turn are often criticized for applying anachronistic standards.[62] No one in early modern Europe, it is argued, even before the beginnings of the Enlightenment project, with its optimistic confidence in the unity of knowledge, could possibly have subscribed to such notions about language and power. In this criticism we observe the tension in historical writing, since the late eighteenth century, between two versions of history. In one, history invokes verisimilitude via the *narrative interpretation* of the past (most recently deconstructed in the works of literary critic Hayden White and sociologist Pierre Bourdieu). In the other, history performs a solely accurate *reconstruction* of the past. Histories that rely on the linguistic turn negate the possibility of the latter project, abandoning it in favour of a critical, actively self-conscious version of the former – a radical abandonment of the fundamental premises of historicism, or scientific historical inquiry, which has been dominant for almost two centuries. This position has been frustrating to those historians who, for intellectually plausible reasons, guard the notion that historical writing says something 'true' about history and that historical accounts can be prioritized according to such criteria.[63] Moreover, it is clearly in the political interest of historians to defend the often shaky boundary between history and fiction. Still, despite the willingness of historians writing after the linguistic turn to admit multiple interpretations of an event, their willingness to accept an ultimate relativism is overstated – even if postmodernists cannot exclude certain readings of history completely, they still prioritize readings that emphasize the relationship of discourses to power relationships and tend to discard those that discern a fundamental rationality or coherence in the source.

Some criticisms of the linguistic turn

Many critics wonder, however, whether everything about human history is effectively described discursively, particularly if the agency of discourse cancels out the possibility of the active, human self. At the end of *Renaissance Self-Fashioning*, Greenblatt vividly underlined his argument that individuals enjoy no 'unfettered subjectivity' and thus have no freedom from the discourse of self-fashioning.[64] His argument raises questions about aspects of historical experience outside of discourse and speech; one thinks immediately of embodiment, but other factors symptomatic of nagging 'reality' also come to mind. Many of these, like demographics, childbirth, war, famine, and so on, appear to be more appropriate topics for social history. The perceived embodiment of human subjects casts doubt on the primacy of discourse as a component of historical writing. It is unlikely that the French King Louis XVI, by then referred to as 'Citizen Capet', experienced his decapitation on the guillotine before the masses in 1793 as an erosion of charisma, or that Jews tortured in early modern Germany experienced their bodily pain purely as discourse. Most scientists would deny that the primary standard for successful experimental science is its basis in discourses of civility.

Because of these tricky questions, some history in the linguistic mood has an eerie quality to it; aspects of what we perceive as reality may be too unmediated, physically painful or ethically troubling to be responsibly or finally characterized as outcomes of discursive verisimilitude. If it occasionally appears to ignore aspects of human experience that seem obvious to most observers, however, the focus on discourses and relationships of power has worked to reveal aspects of political and physical oppression and the mechanisms by which they occur, particularly in studies of conquest and the New World. Here, heirs of the linguistic turn have been the most vehement critics of the ideology, technology and practice of conquest and colonization.[65] As in the case of historians who deny the occurrence of the Holocaust, ethically questionable interpretations can also successfully hide behind a scrupulously 'objective' or 'positivistic' evidentiary method. The role of any ethics as an aspect of historical writing remains highly contested, not merely with reference to the linguistic turn.[66]

The curious detachment of some linguistic analysis from putatively real circumstance also raises questions about the most traditional of the historian's activities, that is, to explain 'change over time'. It has been objected that a great deal of the linguistically influenced literature on the French Revolution does not deal especially well with the traditional historical question of *why* things happened.[67] Of course, any method that emphasizes the practice of close reading tends to present static accounts rather than narratives of transformation. However, little has been done to interrogate the conventional grounds upon which historians decide that an explanation is convincing. Those who find linguistic analyses unconvincing may be influenced by the materialist priorities of social history or the political priorities of historicism – and may not accept language as a motive force in history. Potentially the most serious objection to linguistically minded early modern histories, however, comes on the home ground of historians, that is, their ability to read and interpret the text. Histories of postmodern sensibility have constantly been accused of tendentious misrepresentation, either of social reality, context or the source itself.[68] Such histories have tended to emphasize playful and speculative readings of texts in order to underline their creative historical potential; in fact, this quality is probably what practitioners of such theories like most about them – the way that they leave textual readings open or multivalent.

Conclusion

As indicated by the dates of the major works discussed above, the linguistic turn experienced its heyday in the 1980s and 1990s, at the height of the general furore about postmodern and linguistic theories. Although the more self-conscious employment of such theories has waned, their influence has made itself felt in every area of the profession. Early modernists in particular have been attracted to such theories because of their rehabilitation of textual sources and their proposal of a way round the problematic narrative of modernity that in part has constituted the term 'early modern'. Whether early modern historians will succeed in using the linguistic turn to reconstitute that narrative completely, however, remains to be seen. Perhaps because of the critical stance of the linguistic turn towards metanarratives, no larger reassessment, however provisory, of the significance or trajectory of early modern history has emerged. This happens not only because of the 'local knowledge' preferred by scholars in this mode, but also because the level of attention to textual detail demanded by this historical style may preclude a broader perspective. Despite the inroads of the linguistic turn, then, the modernist narrative of history still dominates both textbook presentations and public perceptions of early modern history.

Guide to further reading

Catherine Belsey, *Poststructuralism: A Very Short Introduction* (Oxford, 2002).

Dipesh Chakrabarty, *Provincializing Europe: Postcolonial Thought and Historical Difference* (Princeton, 2000).

Michel Foucault, *Discipline and Punish: the Birth of the Prison* (New York, 1977).

Stephen J. Greenblatt, *Renaissance Self-Fashioning: From More to Shakespeare* (Chicago, 1980).

Keith Jenkins (ed.), *The Postmodern History Reader* (London, 1997).

Adrian Johns, *The Nature of the Book: Print and Knowledge in the Making* (Chicago, 2000).

Kevin Passmore, 'Poststructuralism and History', in Stefan Berger, Heiko

Feldner and Kevin Passmore (eds), *Writing History: Theory and Practice* (London, 2003), pp. 118–40.

Mark Poster, *Cultural History and Postmodernity: Disciplinary Readings and Challenges* (New York, 1997).

Notes

1 Alison Frazier and the members of University of Texas at Austin History Department Brown-Bag Seminar and the Ekeby in Emden Seminar made fruitful comments on drafts of this essay.

2 Wilhelm Kamlah, 'Zeitalter überhaupt, Neuzeit und Frühneuzeit', *Saeculum* 8 (1957), pp. 313–32; Johanes Kunisch, 'Über den Epochencharakter der frühen Neuzeit', in Eberhard Jäckel and Ernst Weymar (eds), *Die Funktion der Geschichte in unserer Zeit* (Stuttgart, 1975), pp. 150–61; Hans Erich Bödecker and Ernst Hinrichs, 'Einleitung', in their (eds), *Alteuropa – Ancien Regime – Frühe Neuzeit. Probleme und Methoden der Forschung* (Stuttgart, 1991), pp. 11–50; Rudolf Vierhaus (ed.), *Frühe Neuzeit – Frühe Moderne? Forschungen zur Vielschichtigkeit von Übergangsprozessen* (Göttingen 1992); Heinz Schilling, *Die Neue Zeit* (Berlin, 1999), pp. 9–15; Anette Völker-Rasor (ed.), *Frühe Neuzeit* (Munich, 2000), pp. 15–17.

3 Jack A. Goldstone, 'The Problem of the "Early Modern" World', *Journal of the Economic and Social History of the Orient* 43 (1998), pp. 248–84; Samuel Eisenstadt and Wolfgang Schluchter, 'Introduction: Paths to Early Modernities – a Comparative View', in *Daedalus* 127 (1998), pp. 1–18; Randolph Starn, 'The Early Modern Muddle', *Journal of Early Modern History* 6 (2002), pp. 296–307.

4 For example, John O'Malley, *Trent and All That: Renaming Catholicism in the Early Modern Era* (Cambridge, MA, 2000). O'Malley proposes 'early modern Catholicism' as a less charged replacement for 'Counter-Reformation' and other similar terms, while skirting a definition of 'early modern'.

5 Richard Rorty, *The Linguistic Turn* (1967; Chicago, 1992); Völker-Rasor, *Frühe Neuzeit*, pp. 145–237.

6 For example, David Sabean, *Power in the Blood* (Cambridge, 1988); Peter Burke, *Varieties of Cultural History* (Cambridge, 1997); Kathy Stuart, *Defiled Trades and Social Outcasts: Honor and Ritual Pollution in Early Modern Germany* (Cambridge, 2000).

7 Jan-Dirk Müller, 'Literarischer Text und kultureller Text in der frühen Neuzeit am Beispiel des Narrenschiffs von Sebastian Brandt', in Helmut Puff and Christoph Wild (eds), *Zwischen den Disziplinen? Perspektiven der Frühneuzeitforschung* (Göttingen, 2003), pp. 81–101; Catherine Gallagher and Stephen Greenblatt, *Practicing New Historicism* (Chicago, 2000), pp. 20–1; H. Aram Veeser, *The New Historicism Reader* (New York, 1994).

8 Dominik Perler, 'Was ist ein frühneuzeitlicher philosophischer Text? Kritische Überlegungen zum Rationalismus/Empirismus-Schema', in Puff and Wild (eds), *Zwischen den Disziplinen?*, pp. 55–80.

9 Lynn Hunt (ed.), *The New Cultural History* (Berkeley, 1989).

10 See n. 7, above.

11 Different meanings can be associated with each term, depending on the field. In art, 'postmodern' refers to a set of aesthetic sensibilities about the contemporary present, such as those described by Fredric Jameson, who argued that postmodernism corresponds culturally to

late capitalism: *Postmodernism or the Cultural Logic of Late Capitalism* (Durham, NC, 1991).

12 Gerhild Scholz Williams, *Defining Dominion: The Discourses of Magic and Witchcraft in Early Modern France and Germany* (Ann Arbor, 1995), p. 2.

13 See Peter Berger and Thomas Luckmann, *The Social Construction of Reality* (New York, 1966), a work read by an entire generation; John R. Searle, *The Construction of Social Reality* (New York, 1995) and Ian Hacking, *The Social Construction of What?* (Cambridge, MA, 1999); on the relationship between texts and social power, Stephen Greenblatt, *Shakespearean Negotiations: The Circulation of Social Energy in Renaissance England* (Berkeley, 1988), pp. 1–20.

14 On different sorts of discourse analysis, see Stef Slembrouch, 'What is Meant by Discourse Analysis?' at http://bank.rug.ac.be/da/da.htm (accessed February 2005).

15 Michel Foucault, *The Archaeology of Knowledge* (1969; New York, 1972), p. 66.

16 Stephen Greenblatt, *Renaissance Self-Fashioning: From More to Shakespeare* (Chicago, 1980), p. 9.

17 J.G.A. Pocock, *Politics, Language and Time: Essays on Political Thought and History* (Chicago, 1989); James Tully (ed.), *Meaning and Context: Quentin Skinner and his Critics* (Oxford, 1988).

18 Jean-François Lyotard, *The Postmodern Condition: A Report on Knowledge*, trans. Geoff Bennington et al. (Minneapolis, 1984), p. xxiv.

19 Christopher Norris, *What's Wrong with Postmodernism: Critical Theory and the Ends of Philosophy* (Baltimore, 1990), pp. 44–5.

20 For further definitions, s.v. 'deconstruction' in *The Cambridge History of Literary Criticism, vol. 8. From Formalism to Poststructuralism* (Cambridge, 1995); Leonard Orr (ed.), *Dictionary of Critical Theory* (New York, 1991); J.A. Cuddon, *A Dictionary of Literary Terms and Literary Theory* (London, 4th edn, 1998). Deconstruction has been useful in gender history, where it helped to untangle gender from biological categories assumed to be normative. Pathbreaking here were Joan Wallach Scott, *Gender and the Politics of History* (New York, 1988) and Joan Landes, *Women and the Public Sphere in the Age of the French Revolution* (Ithaca, 1988). See also, Merry Wiesner-Hanks, 'Disembodied Theory? Discourses of Sex in Early Modern Germany', in Ulinka Rublack (ed.), *Gender in Early Modern German History* (New York, 2002).

21 Fredric Jameson, *The Prison-house of Language: A Critical Account of Structuralism and Russian Formalism* (Princeton, 1972).

22 Greenblatt, *Renaissance Self-Fashioning*, p. 7.

23 Joyce Appleby et al., *Telling the Truth About History* (New York, 1995).

24 Roland Barthes, 'The Death of the Author', in his *Image, Music, Text* (New York, 1977); Michel Foucault, 'What is an Author?', in Josué

V. Harari (ed.), *Textual Strategies: Perspectives in Post-Structuralist Criticism* (Ithaca, 1979), pp. 141–60.

25 On counterfactuals, see David Hackett Fischer, *Historians' Fallacies: Toward a Logic of Historical Thought* (New York, 1970), pp. 15–21; Gallagher and Greenblatt, *Practicing New Historicism*, pp. 49–74, Michael Stanford, *A Companion to the Study of History* (Oxford, 1994), p. 309; and Martin Bunzl, 'Counterfactual History: A User's Guide', *American Historical Review* 109(3) (2004), pp. 845–58.

26 For one negative assessment, see H.C. Erik Midelfort, 'Madness and Civilization in Early Modern Europe: A Reappraisal of Michel Foucault', in Barbara C. Malamont (ed.), *After the Reformation* (Philadelphia, 1980), pp. 247–66, and his *A History of Madness in Sixteenth-Century Germany* (Stanford, 1999), pp. 7–9. See also Alan Megill, 'The Reception of Foucault by Historians', *Journal of the History of Ideas* 48 (1987), pp. 117–41.

27 Historians critical of Foucault tend to object not so much to his theorizing as to historical inaccuracy or overgeneralization; Megill, 'Reception of Foucault', pp. 132–3. On historical aspects of Foucault's thought: Pamela Major-Poetzl, *Michel Foucault's Archaeology of Western Culture: Toward a New Science of History* (Chapel Hill, 1983); Alan Megill, *Prophets of Extremity: Nietzsche, Heidegger, Foucault, Derrida* (Berkeley, 1985); Jan Goldstein (ed.), *Foucault and the Writing of History* (Cambridge, MA, 1994); Steven Paul Best, *The Politics of Historical Vision: Marx, Foucault and Habermas* (New York, 1995). On the rejection of the 'Great Confinement' idea, see Joel F. Harrington, 'Escape from the Great Confinement: The Genealogy of a German Workhouse', in *Journal of Modern History* 71 (1999), pp. 308–45, esp. 309–15, and Colin Jones and Roy Porter (eds), *Reassessing Foucault: Power, Medicine and the Body* (London, 1994).

28 Michel Foucault, *Discipline and Punish: the Birth of the Prison*, trans. Alan Sheridan (1975; New York, 1977); *Madness and Civilization: a History of Insanity in the Age of Reason*, trans. Richard Howard (1961; New York, 1965); *The Birth of the Clinic: an Archaeology of Medical Perception*, trans. A.M. Sheridan Smith (1963; New York, 1973).

29 Paul Rabinow (ed.), *The Foucault Reader*, 'Introduction' (New York, 1984), p. 7. This book provides an excellent introduction to the 'late' Foucault, but serious students should also read Foucault's earlier works, named above.

30 Michel Foucault, *The Order of Things: an Archaeology of the Human Sciences* [no translator acknowledged] (1966; London, 1970)

31 Lynn Hunt, 'French History in the Last Twenty Years: Rise and Fall of the *Annales* Paradigm', *Journal of Contemporary History* 21 (1986), pp. 209–24.

32 Jean Delumeau, *Sin and Fear: The Emergence of the Western Guilt Culture, 13th–18th Centuries* (1983; Basingstoke, 1990).
33 Emmanuel Le Roy Ladurie, *Montaillou: Cathars and Catholics in a French Village, 1294–1324* (1975; London, 1978); *Carnival in Romans: Mayhem and Massacre in a French City* (New York, 1979).
34 Roger Chartier, 'Intellectual History or Socio-Cultural History? The French Trajectories', in Dominick LaCapra and Steven L. Caplan (eds), *Modern European Intellectual History: Reappraisals and New Perspectives* (Ithaca, 1982), p. 24.
35 Megill, 'Reception of Foucault', p. 125; Peter Burke, *The French Historical Revolution: The* Annales *School, 1929–1989* (Cambridge, 1990), pp. 89–93, 102.
36 On the legacy of the social sciences in historical writing, see Theodore Hamerow, *Reflections on History and Historians* (Madison, 1987) and Peter Novick, *That Noble Dream: The 'Objectivity Question' and the American Historical Profession* (Cambridge, 1988). For an obstreperous assault on the linguistic turn, see Bryan D. Palmer, *Descent into Discourse: The Reification of Language and the Writing of Social History* (Philadelphia, 1990).
37 François Furet, *Interpreting the French Revolution* (1978; Cambridge, 1981).
38 Lynn Hunt, *Revolution and Urban Politics in Provincial France: Troyes and Reims, 1786–1790* (Stanford, 1978) and *Politics, Culture and Class in the French Revolution* (Berkeley, 1984).
39 Roger Chartier, *The Cultural Origins of the French Revolution*, trans. Lydia G. Cochrane (Durham, NC, 1991).
40 Carol Blum, *Rousseau and the Republic of Virtue: The Language of Politics in the French Revolution* (Ithaca, 1986), pp. 16–17.
41 Keith Michael Baker, *Inventing the French Revolution: Essays on French Political Culture in the Eighteenth Century* (Cambridge, 1990), p. 9.
42 See, for example, my review of a traditional textual history of the Reformation at http://www.h-net.org/reviews/showrev.cgi?path=6928850276362 (accessed February 2005).
43 Roger Chartier, *The Cultural Uses of Print in Early Modern Europe*, trans. Lydia Cochrane (Princeton, 1987), pp. 3–5; Barry Reay, *Popular Cultures in England, 1550–1750* (London, 1998), pp. 198–223.
44 For a new approach to this problem in tension with postmodern approaches, see John Jeffries Martin, *Myths of Renaissance Individualism* (New York, 2004).
45 Natalie Zemon Davis, *Fiction in the Archives: Pardon Tales and their Tellers in Sixteenth-Century France* (Stanford, 1987).
46 See also Joanne Ferraro, *Marriage Wars in Late Renaissance Venice* (Oxford, 2001) and Garthine Walker, *Crime, Gender and Social Order in Early Modern England* (Cambridge, 2003).

47 As Georg Iggers has repeatedly noted, the idea of Ranke as a paragon of 'objectivity' is frequently overplayed: see, for example, his 'The Image of Ranke in American and German Historical Thought', *History and Theory* 2 (1962), pp. 17–40.
48 Brad Gregory, *Salvation at Stake: Christian Martyrdom in Early Modern Europe* (Cambridge, MA, 1999), pp. 8–15.
49 R. Po-Chia Hsia, *The Myth of Ritual Murder: Jews and Magic in Reformation Germany* (New Haven, 1988).
50 Sigrid Brauner, *Fearless Wives and Frightened Shrews: The Construction of the Witch in Early Modern Europe* (Amherst, 1995), pp. 23–7.
51 Philip M. Soergel, *Wondrous in his Saints: Counter-Reformation Propaganda in Bavaria* (Berkeley, 1993), pp. 218–19.
52 Fischer, *Historians' Fallacies*, pp. 4–6; Georg Iggers, *The German Conception of History* (2nd edn, Middletown, 1983); Arthur C. Danto, *Analytical Philosophy of History* (New York, 1965), pp. 27–33, 88–111.
53 Lorraine Daston, 'Early Modern History Meets the History of the Scientific Revolution: Thoughts Toward a Rapprochement', in Puff and Wild (eds), *Zwischen den Disziplinen?*, pp. 37–9.
54 Peter Dear, 'Cultural History of Science: An Overview With Reflections', *Science, Technology and Human Values* 20 (1995), p. 159.
55 Daston, 'Early Modern History', pp. 39–48.
56 A. Wolf, *A History of Science, Technology and Philosophy in the 16th and 17th Centuries* (1935; New York, 1959).
57 Jerome J. Langford, *Galileo, Science and the Church*, (3rd edn, Ann Arbor, 1992), pp. 155–8.
58 Mario Biagioli, *Galileo, Courtier: The Practice of Science in the Culture of Absolutism* (Chicago, 1993).
59 Steven Shapin and Steven Shaffer, *Leviathan and the Air Pump: Hobbes, Boyle and the Experimental Life* (Princeton, 1985), pp. 49–69.
60 Steven Shapin, *The Social History of Truth: Civility and Science in Seventeenth-Century England* (Chicago, 1994).
61 Some valuable examples: Peter Burke, *The Fabrication of Louis XIV* (New Haven, 1992); Douglas Biow, *Doctors, Ambassadors, Secretaries: Humanism and Professions in Renaissance Italy* (Chicago, 2002).
62 Fischer, *Historians' Fallacies*, pp. 132–5.
63 Jerzy Topolski, 'A Non-Postmodernist Analysis of Historical Narratives', in his (ed.), *Historiography between Modernism and Postmodernism* (Amsterdam, 1994), pp. 9–86.
64 Greenblatt, *Renaissance Self-Fashioning*, pp. 255–7.
65 Stephen Greenblatt, *Marvelous Possessions: The Wonder of the New World* (Oxford, 1991). The linguistic turn has informed postcolonial and subaltern studies, two important theoretical fields that cannot be considered here.

66 Berel Lang, *Holocaust Representation: Art Within the Limits of History and Ethics* (Baltimore, 2000).

67 Tony Judt, review of Lynn Hunt, *Revolution and Urban Politics in Provincial France: Troyes and Reims, 1786–1790*, in *Social History* 5(3) (1980), p. 470.

68 Examples of critical responses to three books typical of the linguistic turn: on Simon Schama, *Dead Certainties* (New York, 1991), see Louis P. Masur, 'On Parkman's Trail', *William and Mary Quarterly* 49 (1992), pp. 120–32; on Robert Darnton, *The Great Cat Massacre* (New York, 1984), see Philip Stewart in *Eighteenth Century Studies* 19 (1985–86), pp. 260–4; on Natalie Zemon Davis, *The Return of Martin Guerre* (Cambridge, MA, 1983), see Robert Finlay, 'The Refashioning of Martin Guerre', *American Historical Review* 93 (1988), pp. 553–71 and Davis's response, pp. 572–603.

5

Gender

Merry E. Wiesner-Hanks

The notion that gender would be included among distinct theoretical approaches to the early modern period would have been unintelligible to historians in the 1970s. At that point 'gender' was a word used primarily in linguistics, and it was possible to read everything that had been written about women in every country of early modern Europe in a matter of months; most of these were biographies of queens. (Reading every study of men that questioned how their being men shaped their lives would have taken a matter of minutes.)

The women's movement changed that, as it changed so much else. The feminist movement which began in the late 1960s – often termed the 'second wave' to set it apart from the 'first wave' of feminism, which began in the nineteenth century – included a wide range of political beliefs, with various groups working for a broad spectrum of goals, one of which was to understand more about the lives of women in the past. This paralleled a similar rise of interest in women's history, which accompanied the first wave of feminism, from which emerged studies that are still influential, including Alice Clark's *Working Life of Women in the Seventeenth Century* (London, 1919).

Students in history programmes in North America and Western Europe in the late 1960s and early 1970s, most (though not all) of them women, began to focus on women, asserting that any investigation of past oppression or power relationships had to include information on both sexes. Initially these studies were often met with derision or scepticism, not only by more traditional historians who regarded women's history as a fad, but also by some social and Marxist historians, who were unwilling to see gender join class as a key determinant of human experience. This criticism did not quell interest in women's history, and may in fact have stimulated it, as many women who were active in radical or reformist political movements were angered by claims that their own history was trivial, marginal or 'too political'. By the late 1970s, hundreds of colleges and universities in the United States and Canada offered courses in women's history, and many had separate programmes in women's history or women's studies. Universities in Britain were somewhat slower to include lectures and seminars on women, and continental European universities slower still, with women in the 2000s still reporting that investigating the history of women can get them pegged as less than serious and be detrimental to their future careers as historians. Thus an inordinate amount of the work in women's history, including the history of continental women, has been done by English-speaking historians, though prospects for continental Europe look a bit brighter in the early twenty-first century. The head start of Anglophone scholarship, combined with the ability of many students and scholars throughout the world to read English – and the inability of many English-speaking students and scholars to read anything but English – has meant that the exchange of theoretical insights and research results has been largely a one-way street, however.

Building on studies of women, some historians during the 1980s shifted their focus somewhat to ask questions about gender itself, that is, about how past societies fashioned their notions of what it means to be male or female. They differentiated between 'sex', by which they meant physical, morphological and anatomical differences (what are often called 'biological differences') and 'gender', by which they meant a culturally constructed, historically changing and often fluid system of differences. Historians interested in this new perspective asserted that gender was an appropriate category of analysis when looking at *all* historical developments, not simply those involving women or the family. *Every* political, intellectual, religious, economic, social and even military change had an impact on the actions and roles of men and women, and, conversely, a culture's gender structures influenced every other structure or development. Several university presses started book series with 'gender' in their titles – 'gender and culture', 'gender and law' – and scholars in many fields increasingly switched from 'sex' to 'gender' as the acceptable terminology: 'sex roles' became 'gender roles', 'sex distinctions' became 'gender distinctions', and so on. Though most of the books with 'gender' in the title focused on women, historians attuned to gender began to study the construction of masculinity and men's experiences in history *as men*, rather than simply as 'the history of man', without noticing that their subjects were men.

Along with a focus on the gendered nature of both women's and men's experiences, some historians have turned their attention since the 1980s to the history of sexuality. Just as interest in women's history has been part of feminist political movements, interest in the history of sexuality has been part of the gay liberation movement which began in the 1970s. The gay liberation movement encouraged the study of homosexuality in the past and present and the development of gay and lesbian studies programmes, and also made both public and academic discussions of sexual matters more acceptable. Historians have attempted to trace the history of men's and women's sexual experiences – both homosexual and heterosexual – in the past, and, as in women's history, to find new sources which will allow fuller understanding. The history of sexuality has contributed to a new interest in the history of the body, with historians investigating how cultural understandings of the body shaped people's experiences of their own bodies and also studying the ways in which religious, medical and political authorities exerted control over those bodies.

Right at the point that historians and their students were gradually beginning to see the distinction between sex and gender (and an increasing number accepting the importance of gender as a category of analysis), that distinction became contested. Not only were there great debates about where the line should be drawn – were women 'biologically' more peaceful and men 'biologically' more skilful at mathematics, or were such tendencies the result solely of their upbringing? – but some scholars wondered whether social gender and biological sex are so interrelated that any distinction between the two is meaningless.[1] Historians studying gender often used and continue to use theories and methods drawn from sociology, anthropology and literary studies, and emphasize that gender structures are often contradictory, unstable and frequently changing. This instability, combined with an emphasis on differences among women (differences, for instance, among women of different class, race or ethnic backgrounds), has led a few historians to assert that there really is no single category of 'woman' whose meaning is self-evident and unchanging over time.[2] They note that what are usually described as the 'biological' differences between men and women are themselves influenced by ideas about gender, with a single gender polarity (man/woman) so strong in western culture that individuals born with ambiguous genitalia are generally simply assigned to one category or another. In this view, gender determines sex rather than the other way round, or, better said, there is no such thing as true sex difference, only gender difference. Most scholars do not go quite this far, though they recognize that the boundaries between what is understood as 'biological' sex and what is 'cultural' gender are not always clear.

Debates about the distinction between sex and gender emerged just when many historians were changing their basic understanding of the methods and function of history. Under the influence of literary and linguistic theory – often loosely termed 'deconstruction' or 'poststructuralism' – some historians focused their attention on the language used in the past rather than on events, individuals or groups. This trend is usually labelled the 'linguistic turn' or the 'new cultural history' and its focus described as 'discourse' because it incorporates visual materials such as paintings and film along with written texts. The most radical proponents of this point of view argue that the only thing we can know in history is discourse: that is, because historical sources always present a biased and partial picture, we can never fully reconstruct what actually happened. Historical documents and other types of evidence are 'constructed', produced by particular individuals with particular interests and biases that consciously and unconsciously shape their content. They are thus no different from literary texts in their discursive nature and historians should simply analyse them as texts, elucidating their possible meanings. Historians should not be preoccupied with searching for 'reality' in this viewpoint, because to do so demonstrates a naïve 'positivism', a school of thought whose proponents regarded the chief aim of knowledge as the description of phenomena. (Both advocates and critics of positivism often quote the words of the nineteenth-century German historian Leopold von Ranke (1795–1886), who regarded the best history as that which retold events 'as they actually happened'.) Some poststructuralist historians assert that language determines, rather than simply describes, our understanding of the world; the body, for example, is not an objective reality, but changes according to the way people perceive their bodies.[3]

The linguistic turn – which happened in other disciplines along with history – elicited harsh responses from many historians, including many who focused on women and gender.[4] They asserted that it denied women the ability to shape their world – what is usually termed 'agency' – in both past and present, by positing unchangeable linguistic structures. Wasn't it ironic, they noted, that just as women were learning they *had* a history and asserting they were *part* of history, 'history' became just a text and 'women' just a historical construct? For a period it looked as if this disagreement would lead proponents of discourse analysis to lay claim to 'gender' and those who opposed it to avoid 'gender' and stick with 'women'. Because women's history was clearly rooted in the women's rights movement of the 1970s, it also appeared to some to be more political than gender analysis, and programmes and research projects sometimes opted to use 'gender' to downplay this connection with feminism.

In the early twenty-first century, however, it appears that the division is less sharp; gender analysis is increasingly recognized as an outgrowth of women's history, rather than its replacement, and viewed as a related but separate approach. Gender theory is understood to be rooted in feminist theory, for both undertake critical evaluations of gender and challenge traditional assumptions that regarded the male perspective – often unconsciously – as universal. Historians using gender as a category of analysis no longer feel compelled to adopt an extreme poststructuralist approach, but many instead treat their sources as referring to something beyond language, beyond the sources themselves – an author, an event, a physical body – while recognizing that they do not present a perfect reflection. They do tend to use a wider range of literary and artistic sources than did earlier women's and gender history, so that their work is more 'cultural' in that sense. Conversely, scholars of literature and art now pay greater attention to a text's or painting's relationship to a historical location or setting than they did in earlier decades – a movement labelled 'New Historicism' in English literature – and they are beginning to pay more attention to variables that have been central to historical analysis for decades, such as class.

New theoretical perspectives are adding additional complexity and bringing in new questions. One of these is queer theory, a field which began in the 1990s, in some ways as a combination of gay and lesbian studies and poststructuralism.[5] Just as feminist theory did for gender structures and roles, queer theory challenged the assumption that sexual attitudes and practices were 'natural' and unchanging. It built on these challenges and on the doubts about the essential nature of sex, sexuality and gender to highlight the artificial and constructed nature of all oppositional categories: men/women, homosexual/heterosexual, black/white. Some theorists celebrate all efforts at blurring or bending categories, viewing 'identity' – or what in literary and cultural studies is often termed 'subjectivity' – as both false and oppressive. Others have doubts about this (somewhat akin to doubts among many feminists about the merits of deconstruction), wondering whether one can work to end discrimination against homosexuals, women, African-Americans or any other group, if one denies that the group has an essential identity, something that makes its members clearly homosexual or women or African-American.

Related questions about identity, subjectivity and the cultural construction of difference have also emerged from postcolonial theory and 'critical race theory'. Postcolonial history and theory has been particularly associated with South Asian scholars and the book series Subaltern Studies, and initially focused on people who have been subordinated by virtue of their race, class, culture or language.[6] Critical race theory developed in the 1980s as an outgrowth (and critique) of the civil rights movement, combined with ideas derived from 'critical legal studies', a radical group of legal scholars who argued that supposedly neutral legal concepts, such as the individual or meritocracy, actually masked power relationships.[7] Both of these theoretical schools point out that racial, ethnic and other hierarchies are deeply rooted social and cultural principles, not simply aberrations that can be remedied by legal or political change. They note that along with disenfranchising certain groups, such hierarchies privilege certain groups, a phenomenon that is beginning to be analysed under the rubric of critical white studies. (This is a pattern similar to the growth of men's studies, and there is also a parallel within queer theory that is beginning to analyse heterosexuality rather than simply taking it as an unquestioned given.)

Queer theory, postcolonial studies and critical race theory have all been criticized from both inside and outside for falling into the pattern set by traditional history, that is, regarding the male experience as normative and paying insufficient attention to gender differences. Scholars who have pointed this out have also noted that some feminist scholarship suffered from the opposite problem, taking the experiences of heterosexual white women as normative and paying too little attention to differences of race, class, nationality, ethnicity or sexual orientation. They argue that the experiences of women of colour must be recognized as distinctive, and that no one axis of difference (men/women, black/white, rich/poor, gay/straight) should be viewed as sufficient. These criticisms led, in the 1990s, to theoretical perspectives that attempted to recognize multiple lines of difference, such as critical race feminism and postcolonial feminism.[8] Such scholarship has begun to influence many areas of gender studies, even those which do not deal explicitly with race or ethnicity. It appears this cross-fertilization will continue, as issues of difference and identity are clearly key topics for historians in the ever more connected twenty-first-century world.

The issues raised in queer theory or postcolonial feminism may seem to be quite contemporary and have little to do with the early modern period, but early modern scholars have in fact been in the forefront of every development traced here: the growth of women's history, gender history, the history of masculinity and the history of sexuality; debates about the relative importance of gender, class, race and other categories of difference; debates about the centrality of discourse; discussions of the relationship between gender and sex and the sources of ideas about gender. Early modern historians of gender have both incorporated a number of other theoretical perspectives in their work – psychoanalysis, Marxism, postcolonial theory, queer theory – and criticized those perspectives when they appeared insufficiently attuned to gender.

Women's history of the early modern period, as of most periods, began by asking what women contributed to the developments traditionally viewed as central, in a search for what Natalie Zemon Davis (b. 1928) has termed 'women worthies':[9] How were women involved in the Renaissance, the Protestant and Catholic Reformations, the scientific revolution? Who were the great women artists/musicians/scientists/rulers? How did women's work serve capitalist expansion? What was women's role in political movements such as the English Civil War or other seventeenth-century revolts? They unearthed new sources to reveal the experiences of women and used traditional sources in innovative ways.[10] This work began in Western Europe – though often by historians trained or training in the United States – and gradually expanded to Eastern Europe, although there are parts of Europe for which there has still been very little archival or textual research. These studies are generally narrative, and may now seem to be under-theorized and either overly celebratory or overly pessimistic in that they often highlight either women's agency or their oppression. It is important to remember, however, that in the 1970s and 1980s, the simple statements that women *did* preach, paint, work, compose, protest and engage in other forms of public activity in the early modern period were quite novel and sometimes threatening.

(They continue to be novel for areas of Europe in which this basic research is still in its early stages, including most of Eastern Europe.) Those of us engaged in research at that point – most of us young and female, working on our Ph.D. theses – all experienced bafflement, if not hostility, from archivists, colleagues and (sometimes) doctoral advisors: 'But women didn't work in this city in the sixteenth century!' 'Why would you want to study such a minor figure' – like Christine de Pizan (1365–1430), whose published writings critiqued the misogynistic culture of her time and presented a utopian vision of a city inhabited by powerful and educated women, or Artemisia Gentileschi (1593–1652), a successful female artist – 'when you could work on someone important', by which was meant a well-known male essayist or painter like Montaigne (1533–92) or Michelangelo (1475–1564)?

Along with exploring women's actions, scholars also investigated what effects the developments of the early modern period had on women, and how the female experience in such developments differed from the male. (They were thus using gender as a category of analysis without yet conceptualizing it in that way.) Again this line of questioning might seem rather untheoretical, but it resulted in the rethinking of several major historical issues. Joan Kelly, for example, began with a simple question in 1978, 'Did women have a Renaissance?'[11] Her answer, 'No, at least not during the Renaissance', has not only led to more than two decades of intensive historical and literary research, as people have attempted to confirm, refute, modify or nuance her answer, but has also contributed to the broader questioning of the whole notion of historical periodization. If a particular development had little, or indeed a negative, effect on women, can we still call a period a 'golden age', a 'renaissance' or an 'enlightenment'? Can we continue to view the seventeenth century, during which hundreds or perhaps thousands of women were burned as witches on the European continent, as the period of 'the spread of rational thought'?

Kelly's questioning of the term 'Renaissance' has been joined more recently by a questioning of the term 'early modern'. Both historians and literary scholars note that there are problems with this term, as it assumes that there is something that can unambiguously be called 'modernity', which is usually set against 'traditional' and linked with contemporary western society. (Whether 'modernity' is seen as a good thing or a bad thing depends on the commentator's view of contemporary society.) The break between 'medieval' and 'early modern' is generally set at 1500, roughly the time of the voyages of Columbus and the Protestant Reformation, but recently many historians argue that there are more continuities across this line than changes. Some have moved the decisive break earlier – to the Black Death in 1347 or even to the twelfth century – or have rejected the notion of periodization altogether. Women's historians, most prominently Judith Bennett, have been among those questioning the validity of the medieval/modern divide, challenging, in Bennett's words, 'the assumption of a dramatic change in women's lives between 1300 and 1700' and asserting that historians must pay more attention to continuities along with changes.[12] Most historians – myself and the editor of this book included – continue to use the terms 'medieval' and 'early modern', however, though we are more conscious about our decision, and use them more as shorthand for certain periods than as value labels. There is also more scholarship which bridges 1500, though as yet there is no handy label to describe this period, for 'pre-modern' still assumes there is something we all understand as 'modern' and all agree on when it starts.

Both the original lines of questioning in women's history for this period – women's role in general historical developments and the effects of these developments on women – continue, particularly for parts of Europe or groups of women about which we have very little information as yet: Eastern Europe, Jewish women, peasant women in most parts of Europe, women's religious communities. They have been augmented more recently by quite different types of questions, as historians have realized the limitations of simply trying to fit women into historical developments largely derived from the male experience (an approach rather sarcastically described as 'add women and stir'). Such questions often centre on women's physiological experiences – menstruation, pregnancy, motherhood – and the ways in which women gave meaning to these experiences, and on private or domestic matters, such as friendship networks, family devotional practices or unpaid household labour. Because so little of this was documented in public sources during the early modern period, this research has required a great amount of archival digging and the use of literary and artistic sources.

This emphasis on women's private and domestic experiences has been challenged by some historians, who warn of the dangers of equating women's history with the history of the family or of accepting without comment a division between public and private in which women are relegated to the private sphere. They see a primary task of early modern historians as the investigation of how divisions between what was considered 'public' and what was considered 'private' were developed and contested. Some scholars hold that this period is one of the exclusion of women from many areas of public life and power at the very time larger groups of men were given access, though others emphasize that this exclusion was more theoretical than real.[13]

Questions about the boundaries between 'public' and 'private' have also been played out in investigations of the interplay between gender and the economy in the early modern period. This line of research began during the 1980s as explorations of women's work, and primarily looked at the effects of economic change, especially the expansion of commercial capitalism, on women, generally seeing these, as had Alice Clark decades earlier, as negative. This view was challenged by other scholars, first by those who asserted that women's work changed little in this era, but remained, as it had been in the Middle Ages, low status, badly paid and rarely a full-time occupation. They noted that these qualities continued long after the early modern period, into the industrial and post-industrial economies, which indicates that gender structures have been more important determinants of work experience than economic systems or production processes. This debate might in shorthand be termed the battle between capitalism and patriarchy, and it has involved Marxist and non-Marxist scholars on both sides.[14]

A second challenge, or better said, revision, of early studies grew out of a recognition that the basic categories of analysis were not value-free and self-evident, but shaped by gender: what early modern (and all) cultures define as 'work' is highly gendered, with the same tasks regarded as 'work' when done by men deemed to be merely 'assisting', or 'housework' or even not work at all when done by women, particularly when these are done in the household and do not involve pay. The definitions of 'skilled' and 'unskilled' labour are similarly gendered, with tasks done by women, such as making lace or unweaving silk cocoons, not regarded – or paid – as skilled, though they took as much training and dexterity as similar tasks done by men, such as silver-smithing or glass-making. More recent studies have thus explored the gendered meaning of work along with the actual tasks that men and women were doing.[15]

Recent scholarship has also paid more attention to economic activities that do not involve production, such as trade, property ownership and consumption. Studies often based on personal records such as household inventories and wills have demonstrated that western Europeans, including many with moderate incomes, increasingly purchased cheaper and more diverse consumer goods of all types in the early modern period. From Europe's overseas colonies came new food stuffs such as sugar, chocolate, tea and coffee, new types of fabrics, such as calico, and new types of household goods, such as lacquerware and the porcelain which came to be known as 'china'. Trade in such commodities has long been studied by economic historians, who have concentrated on issues of supply and organization. Historians interested in issues of gender put more focus on demand, noting that it was often women who consumed and purchased these new items. Brewing and drinking tea became part of the lives of urban women in some countries, especially England, and even domestic servants bought their own teapots. Servants, and other relatively poor women, chose to spend their income on other 'frivolous' consumer goods as well, such as parasols, fans, hats, hand mirrors and lace. Middle-class women bought more and fancier clothing and home furnishings, paying attention not only to quality and price but also to changing styles, which they learned about through printed works and shop displays. A dramatic increase in the importation of sugar – and its production in tropical colonies – was perhaps the most obvious result of women's changing tastes, but their demands for certain types of decorative objects, garments and foodstuffs – feathers, small tea tables, flowers, curtains, lace collars and cuffs, Chinese tea sets, lighter undergarments, sugared cakes – also shaped the development of trade both within Europe itself and between Europe and the rest of the world. These newer studies are thus cognizant of both the role of gender and the colonial context, paying attention to the way in which trade relationships not only formally linked states, but informally linked women and men.[16]

In economic history, the impact of gender theory has been felt primarily through historicizing the meaning of 'work' and broadening the focus of inquiry, and in cultural history, early modernists have been very involved in historicizing the meaning of 'women' and, more recently, 'men'. The debate about the boundaries between sex and gender originally involved biologists attempting to draw an absolute line between male and female, and anthropologists studying cultures that had more than two genders (the most famous of which are Native American two-spirit people), but historians and literary scholars have also discovered great debates about these boundaries in the Renaissance and early modern period, which can provide material for contemporary theoretical discussions. In both learned and popular works, people were fascinated by hermaphrodites, and discussed whether a person could possibly change from one sex to the other. Woodcuts and engravings of 'manly' women and 'womanly' men were produced by many artists, and people debated whether a woman's having to do tasks normally associated with men might somehow affect her normal female functions. Both in pamphlets and reported gossip, for example, people in England discussed whether Queen Elizabeth (1533–1603) still menstruated and had a normal female anatomy or whether her being both a virgin and a virago (the standard early modern term for a strong woman with manly qualities and manly duties) might have shaped her physiology.[17] The early modern debate about female rule really involved two very modern issues. Can gender be separated from sex? (This issue was conceptualized in the period as whether a queen might be clearly female in her body and sexuality, but still exhibit the masculine qualities regarded as necessary in a ruler because of traits she had inherited or learned.) What is more important, gender or class? (In other words, would a woman's being born into a ruling family allow her to overcome the limitations of being born female?) As Constance Jordan has pointed out, defenders of female rule clearly separated sex from gender, and even approached an idea of androgyny as a desirable state for the public persona of female monarchs.[18]

Early modern sources also provide good examples for analyses of the construction of masculinity, for concepts of masculinity were important determinants of access to political power. The dominant notion of the 'true' man in early modern Europe was that of the married head of household, so that men whose class and age would have normally conferred political power but who remained unmarried did not participate to the same level as their married brothers; in Protestant areas, this link between marriage and authority even included the clergy. Unmarried men were suspect, for they were not living up to what society viewed as their proper place in a gendered social order. Some of these men, such as journeymen in Germany and France, recognized that they could never become heads of household, so created alternative concepts of masculinity and masculine honour clearly distinct from the dominant one. They came to view their unmarried, unattached state, which had originally been forced on them by guild masters, as a positive thing, and emphasized their freedom from political duties rather than their lack of political rights. They regarded loyalty to the all-male journeymen's organization as extremely important, making a 'true' man, for them, one with few contacts with women, who proved his masculinity through drinking and fighting. Masters and journeymen thus had different ideas about masculinity, a split which can be seen in other contexts as well. The English Civil War (1642–49), for example, is often portrayed as a battle between Royalist Cavaliers in their long hair and fancy silk knee-breeches opposing Puritan parliamentarians with their short hair and sombre clothing; as with so many issues, once one starts thinking about gender, it is hard to understand why it took so long to understand that this clearly involved two conflicting notions of masculinity. Parliamentary criticism of the court was often expressed in overtly gendered and sexualized terminology, with frequent veiled or open references to aristocratic weakness and inability to control the passions. Thus ideas about masculinity were to some degree class-specific, defined in relation not only to ideas about femininity, but also to notions of manhood developing among other male groups.[19]

Notions of masculinity were also important symbols in early modern political discussions. Queen Elizabeth was not the only ruler to realize that people expected monarchs to be male, and that qualities judged masculine by her peers – physical bravery, stamina, wisdom, duty – should be emphasized whenever a monarch chose to appear or speak in public. The more successful male rulers recognized this as well, and tried to connect themselves whenever possible with qualities and objects judged male, though sometimes with ironic results. Jeffrey Merrick has demonstrated, for example, that French monarchs and their supporters used the image of a beehive under a 'king bee' as a model of harmony under royal rule and a community whose existence depended on the health of its monarch; even scientists spoke of the beehive in this way, for they regarded nature as the best source of examples for appropriate political structures, which they then termed 'natural'.[20] When the invention of the microscope made it clear the king bee was a queen, both royal propagandists and scientists tried to downplay her sex as long as possible, embarrassed that nature would provide such a demonstration of 'unnatural' female power. (By the eighteenth century the sex of the queen bee was no longer ignored, but her role was now described as totally maternal, a symbol of motherhood rather than monarchy.)

A concern with masculinity, and particularly with demonstrating the autonomy expected of a man, pervades the political writings of Machiavelli (1469–1527), who used 'effeminate' to describe the worst kind of ruler.[21] 'Effeminate' in the sixteenth century carried slightly different connotations than it does today, however, for strong heterosexual passion was not a sign of manliness, but could make one 'effeminate', that is to say, dominated by as well as similar to a woman. English commentators, for example, described Irish men as effeminate and inferior because they let both their wives and their sexual desires influence their actions. Strong same-sex attachments, on the other hand, were often regarded as a sign of virility, as long as they were accompanied by actions judged honourably masculine, such as effective military leadership, and not accompanied by actions judged feminine, such as emotional outbursts.[22] Early modern society thus provides strong evidence of the culturally constructed and historically changing nature of sexual as well as gender categories, and early modern historians and literary scholars have been active in the development of both the history of sexuality and queer theory. Randolph Trumbach, for example, argues that the widely accepted idea that homosexual 'identity' did not emerge until the late nineteenth century needs to be modified, for there were certainly men, and perhaps women, in eighteenth-century England who thought of themselves as having a permanent 'sexual orientation' (another modern term) towards members of the same sex.[23]

Early modern cultural scholars are also involved in exploring issues of identity linked to race and ethnicity as well as sexuality. Because it marked the beginning of Europe's colonial enterprise, the early modern period was a time when Europeans were more concerned with 'racial' differences than they had been earlier, when they were actively engaged in creating social meanings for racial categories. (Because race is socially constructed and so variable historically, most scientists who study the human species as a whole, such as biologists and anthropologists, avoid using the word completely.) They drew on polarities of white and black which had existed in western culture since ancient times to develop a racial hierarchy out of earlier ideas about religious and social difference, all of which were conceptualized as 'blood'. People were regarded as having blood that was Jewish, Muslim or Christian – or, after the Reformation, Protestant or Catholic – noble or commoner; marriages across these groups were often prohibited or regarded as threatening because they involved the mixing of unlike blood. In early modern Spain, 'purity of the blood' – having no Jewish or Muslim ancestors – became an obsession, and throughout Europe children born of religiously mixed Christian marriages were often slightly mistrusted, for one never knew whether their Protestant or Catholic blood would ultimately triumph. Blood was also used to describe national boundaries, with those having 'French blood' distinguished from those having 'German blood', 'English blood' or 'Spanish blood'. As a number of scholars have noted, describing differences as blood naturalized them, making them appear as if they were created by God in nature.[24]

As Europeans developed colonial empires, these notions of blood became a way of conceptualizing race as well as religion, class and nation. In some cases, such as Jews or Jewish converts in Spain and the Spanish Empire or Gaelic-speaking Catholic Irish in Ireland, religious and racial differences were linked, with Judaism and Catholicism being viewed as signs of 'natural' barbarity and racial inferiority in these areas. This was also initially the case in colonial areas outside Europe, where the spread of Christianity was used as a justification for conquest and enslavement. As indigenous peoples converted, however, religion became less useful as a means of differentiation, and skin colour became more important, though this, of course, could be highly variable even among siblings. In addition, in the Spanish and Portuguese colonies racial categories were to some degree arbitrary, with priests and officials granted the power to declare an individual 'white' for the purposes of marriage, entering a convent or becoming a priest, no matter what his or her ancestry.

Racial categories and hierarchies were linked to gender hierarchies in complex ways; this has been most thoroughly analysed by historians of the later British Empire, but it has also increasingly been a focus of early modern scholarship.[25] European explorers and colonizers described their conquests in sexualized terms, portraying territory and its peoples as feminized, weak and passive and themselves as virile, powerful and masculine. They also passed laws regulating intermarriage and other intergroup sexual relations (which would, of course, erase 'racial' differences if they became common enough), and increasingly described interracial boundaries as even more 'natural' than those of class or religion, making any crossing, particularly a sexual one, unnatural or even demonic. In learned treatises and popular literature, they debated the relationship between hierarchies of race and hierarchies of gender. Was it easier for a woman to be 'manly' or for a non-white man? If social class could outweigh gender as a determinant of social role for a woman like Queen Elizabeth, could gender outweigh race for a man like Shakespeare's Othello? Analysing the debates about such questions allows contemporary scholars to bring together the insights of feminist, postcolonial and queer theory, and still ground their research thoroughly in issues that were central in the early modern period.

It is clear from this essay that I see the most interesting aspects of gender theory as the ways in which it has intersected with other theoretical directions to grow, change and pose new types of questions. The notion of 'intersection' has been key in women's history and other feminist scholarship for a long time – most commonly used in the phrase 'the intersection of race, class and gender' – which highlights the ways various categories of difference overlap and connect, but also conflict with and complicate one another. Thus gender theory has been in some ways totalizing – it has argued that gender is an appropriate category of analysis for every political, intellectual, religious, economic, social and even military development and every basic historical conceptualization and paradigm – but it has also been self-critical.

This discussion of scholarly trends may make it appear as if focusing on women or using gender as a category of analysis has swept early modern history, with scholars simply choosing the approach or topic they prefer. This is far from the actual situation. Though investigating gender may seem self-evident to most younger historians and graduate students, there are also many historians who continue to view this as a passing fad – or, as one put it recently, a 'cancer' – despite the fact that such judgements become more difficult to maintain as the decades pass. Books that survey early modern history – generally the way students are introduced to the field – vary in their coverage, with some giving whole chapters to gender roles and issues, others including information on women and sexuality throughout, and others (particularly those conceptualized as surveys of the Renaissance or Reformation) mentioning only the same queens that surveys of 30 years ago would have. But surveys and textbooks are often the last element of a field to change. A better indication of the wider impact of gender studies might be the fact that of the 28 books published in 2001 submitted for the Roland Bainton prize in early modern history (of which I happened to be a judge), seven focus on women and/or gender, and many of the rest include some discussion of gender issues. We are perhaps not yet at the point in early modern history at which thinking about the impact of gender is as automatic and self-evident (particularly if one is studying a man or men) as thinking about whether one's subjects were English or French, noble or peasant, Protestant or Catholic, but we may be soon.

Guide to further reading

Laura Lee Downs, *Writing Gender History* (London, 2004).

Suzanne J. Kessler and Wendy McKenna, *Gender: An Ethnomethodological Approach* (New York, 1978).

Teresa A. Meade and Merry E. Wiesner-Hanks (eds), *A Companion to Gender History* (Oxford, 2003).

Joan W. Scott, 'Gender: A Useful Category of Historical Analysis', *American Historical Review* 91(5) (1986), pp. 1053–75, and widely reprinted.

Merry E. Wiesner, *Women and Gender in Early Modern Europe* (Cambridge, 2nd edn, 2000).

Merry E. Wiesner-Hanks, *Gender in History* (Oxford, 2001).

Notes

1 The best place to begin in considering the socially constructed nature of gender is still Suzanne J. Kessler and Wendy McKenna, *Gender: An Ethnomethodological Approach* (New York, 1978). More recent works that expand on this include: Sylvia Walby, *Theorizing Patriarchy* (Oxford, 1990); Judith Butler, *Gender Trouble: Feminism and the Subversion of Identity* (New York, 1990); Judith Lorber, *Paradoxes of Gender* (New Haven, 1994). For additional readings on this and other issues involved in gender theory, see the chapter bibliographies in Merry E. Wiesner-Hanks, *Gender in History* (London, 2001) and many of the chapters in Teresa A. Meade and Merry E. Wiesner-Hanks (eds), *A Companion to Gender History* (Malden, MA, 2004).

2 Doubts about the value of 'women' as an analytical category were conveyed most forcefully in Denise Riley, *'Am I That Name?' Feminism and the Category of 'Women' in History* (London and Minneapolis, 1988), though they have been associated primarily with the work of Joan Scott, especially her 'Gender: A Useful Category of Historical Analysis', *American Historical Review* 91(5) (1986), pp. 1053–75 and other essays in her *Gender and the Politics of History* (New York, 1988).

3 See chapter 4 in this volume for a fuller discussion of the linguistic turn.

4 For different perspectives in this debate, see Linda Nicholson (ed.), *Feminism/Postmodernism* (New York, 1990).

5 For queer theory, good places to begin are the aptly titled books by Annamarie Jagose, *Queer Theory: An Introduction* (New York, 1996) and Nikki Sullivan, *A Critical Introduction to Queer Theory* (New York, 2003). For essays linking feminist and queer theory, see Elizabeth Weed and Naomi Schor (eds), *Feminism Meets Queer Theory* (Bloomington, 1997), and for a work that focuses on history, see Scott Bravman, *Queer Fictions of the Past: History, Culture and Difference* (Cambridge and New York, 1997).

6 Two collections that include articles by many major postcolonial scholars are Bill Ashcroft, Gareth Griffiths and Helen Tiffin (eds), *The Postcolonial Studies Reader* (London, 1995) and Henry Schwarz and Sangeeta Ray (eds), *A Companion to Postcolonial Studies* (Malden, MA, 2000). The work of the Subaltern Studies group may best be seen in its ongoing series of essay collections, *Subaltern Studies*, which began publication in 1982 in New Delhi.

7 For an introduction to 'critical race theory', see Kimberlé Crenshaw et al. (eds), *Critical Race Theory: The Key Writings that Formed the Movement* (New York, 1995). For the new field of critical white studies, see Ruth Frankenberg, *White Women, Race Matters: The Social Construction of Whiteness* (Minneapolis, 1993) and Richard Delgado and Jean Stefancic (eds), *Critical White Studies* (Philadelphia, 1997).

8 Two articles are especially helpful for understanding links between gender and race in history, and have been widely reprinted in various collections: Tessie Liu, 'Teaching the Differences Among Women from a Historical Perspective: Rethinking Race and Gender as Social Categories', *Women's Studies International Forum* 14 (1991), pp. 265–76 and Evelyn Brooks Higginbotham, 'African-American Women's History and the Metalanguage of Race', *Signs* 17 (1992), pp. 251–74. Adrien Katherine Wing has edited two important anthologies, *Critical Race Feminism: A Reader* (1997, 2nd edn, New York, 2003) and *Global Critical Race Feminism: An International Reader* (New York, 2000). Another useful collection is Nancy E. Dowd and Michelle S. Jacobs (eds), *Feminist Legal Theory: An Anti-essentialist Reader* (New York, 2003). Works that bring together feminist and postcolonial theory include: Trin T. Minh-ha, *Woman, Native, Other: Writing Postcoloniality and Feminism* (Bloomington, 1989); Anne McClintock, Aamir Mufti and Ella Shoalt (eds), *Dangerous Liaisons: Gender, Nation and Postcolonial Perspectives* (Minneapolis, 1997); Uma Narayan and Sandra Harding, *Decentering the Center: Philosophy for a Multicultural, Postcolonial, and Feminist World* (Bloomington, 2000); Reina Lewis and Sara Mills (eds), *Feminist Postcolonial Theory: A Reader* (New York, 2003).

9 Natalie Zemon Davis's survey of the writing of European women's history and suggestions for future research directions is still useful and provocative: '"Women's History" in Transition: the European Case', *Feminist Studies* 3 (1975/76), pp. 83–103. For other analyses of the development of women's and gender history, see Judith M. Bennett, 'Feminism and History', *Gender and History* 1 (1989), pp. 251–72; Gisela Bock, 'Women's History and Gender History: Aspects of an International Debate', *Gender and History* 1 (1989), pp. 7–30; Sonya Rose et al., 'Gender History/Women's History: is Feminist Scholarship Losing its Critical Edge?', *Journal of Women's History* 5 (1993), pp. 89–128; Joan Wallach Scott (ed.), *Women's Studies on the Edge*, special issue of *differences: a Journal of Feminist Cultural Studies* 9(3) (1997); Joan W. Scott, Afsaneh Najmabadi and Evelynn M. Hammonds, 'The Future of Women's History: Feminism's History', *Journal of Women's History* 16 (2004), pp. 10–39.

10 Hundreds of studies that investigate all aspects of women's lives can be found in the chapter bibliographies of Merry E. Wiesner, *Women and Gender in Early Modern Europe* (1993; 2nd edn, Cambridge, 2000).

11 Joan Kelly, 'Did Women Have a Renaissance?', first published in Renate Bridenthal and Claudia Koonz (eds), *Becoming Visible: Women in European History* (Boston, 1978), pp. 137–64, and widely reprinted.

12 Judith Bennett, 'Medieval Women, Modern Women: Across the Great Divide', in Ann-Louise Shapiro (ed.), *Feminists Revision History* (New Brunswick, 1994), pp. 47–72; Judith Bennett, 'Confronting

Continuity', *Journal of Women's History* 9 (1997), pp. 73–95 (with responses by Sandra E. Greene, Karen Offen and Gerda Lerner). See also Gianna Pomata, 'History, Particular and Universal: On Reading Some Recent Women's History Textbooks', *Feminist Studies* 19 (1993), pp. 7–50.

13 One of the strongest voices arguing for the inclusion of issues involving women in political and intellectual, as well as social history, has been Hilda Smith. See, for example, the introduction to her *Women Writers and the Early Modern British Political Tradition* (Cambridge, 1998). Joan Landes has edited a very helpful collection of essays on issues surrounding the public/private dichotomy: *Feminism, the Public and the Private* (Oxford, 1998). For discussions of women and the public sphere in the early modern period, see: Carole Pateman, *The Sexual Contract* (Stanford, 1988); Christine Fauré, *Democracy Without Women: Feminism and the Rise of Liberalism in France* (Indianapolis, 1991); Joan Landes, *Women and the Public Sphere in the Age of the French Revolution* (Ithaca, 1988); Susan Cerasano and Marion Wynne-Davies (eds), *Gloriana's Face: Women, Public and Private in the English Renaissance* (Detroit, 1992); Hilda Smith, *All Men and Both Sexes: Gender, Politics, and the False Universal in England 1640–1832* (College Park, PA, 2002); Ulrike Strasser, *State of Virginity: Gender, Religion, and Politics in an Early Modern Catholic State* (Ann Arbor, 2004).

14 In terms of theoretical underpinnings, the feminist critique of Marxist analysis, which began during the 1970s, is particularly important, especially in its explorations of the relations between gender and class hierarchies in economic matters. See, for example, Roberta Hamilton, *The Liberation of Women: A Study of Patriarchy and Capitalism* (London, 1978); Heide Hartmann, 'The Unhappy Marriage of Marxism and Feminism: Towards a More Progressive Union', *Capital and Class* 8 (1979), pp. 1–33. More recent considerations of these issues include: Wally Seccombe, *A Millennium of Family Change: Feudalism to Capitalism in Northwestern Europe* (London, 1992); Leonore Davidoff, *Worlds Between: Historical Perspectives on Gender and Class* (New York, 1995); Mary Murray, *The Law of the Father: Patriarchy in the Transition from Feudalism to Capitalism* (London, 1995).

15 See, for example, Patrick Joyce (ed.), *The Historical Meanings of Work* (Cambridge, 1987); Judith Bennett, *Ale, Beer, and Brewsters in England: Women's Work in a Changing World, 1300–1600* (New York, 1996); Pamela Sharpe, *Adapting to Capitalism: Working Women in the English Economy, 1700–1850* (New York, 1996); Sheilagh Ogilvie, *A Bitter Living: Women, Markets, and Social Capital in Early Modern Germany* (Oxford, 2003).

16 Carole Shammas, *The Pre-industrial Consumer in England and America* (Oxford, 1990); John Brewer and Roy Porter (eds), *Consumption and the*

World of Goods (London, 1993); Marcia Pointon, *Strategies for Showing: Women, Possession, and Representation in English Visual Culture, 1665–1800* (Oxford, 1998); Clair Haru Crowston, *Fabricating Women: The Seamstresses of Old Regime France, 1675–1791* (Durham, NC, 2001).

17 The best study of issues of gender surrounding Queen Elizabeth is Carole Levin, *The Heart and Stomach of a King: Elizabeth I and the Politics of Sex and Power* (Philadelphia, 1994).

18 Constance Jordan, *Renaissance Feminism: Literary Texts and Political Models* (Ithaca, 1990).

19 Merry E. Wiesner, '*Wandervogels* and Women: Journeymen's Concepts of Masculinity in Early Modern Germany', *Journal of Social History* 24 (1991), pp. 767–82; Susan D. Amussen, ' "The Part of a Christian Man": the Cultural Politics of Manhood in Early Modern England', in Susan D. Amussen and Mark Kishlansky (eds), *Political Culture and Cultural Politics in Early Modern England: Essays Presented to David Underdown* (Manchester, 1995), pp. 213–33; Lyndal Roper, "Blood and Codpieces: Masculinity in the Early Modern German Town', in her *Oedipus and the Devil: Witchcraft, Religion, and Sexuality in Early Modern Europe* (London, 1996), pp. 107–24; Mark Breitenberg, *Anxious Masculinity in Early Modern England* (Cambridge, 1996); Elizabeth Foyster, *Manhood in Early Modern England: Honour, Sex and Marriage* (London, 1999); Kathleen P. Long (ed.), *High Anxiety: Masculinity in Crisis in Early Modern France* (Kirksville, MO, 2002). A study that combines the history of masculinity and the history of consumption is David Kuchta, *The Three-piece Suit and Modern Masculinity: England, 1550–1850* (Berkeley, 2002).

20 Jeffrey Merrick, 'Royal Bees: the Gender Politics of the Beehive in Early Modern Europe', *Studies in Eighteenth-Century Culture* 18 (1988), pp. 7–37; see also his 'Fathers and Kings: Patriarchalism and Absolutism in Eighteenth-Century French Politics', *Studies on Voltaire and the Eighteenth Century* 308 (1993), pp. 281–303.

21 Hannah Pitkin, *Fortune is a Woman: Gender and Politics in the Thought of Niccolò Machiavelli* (Berkeley, 1984).

22 Jean Howard, 'The Theatre, Cross-Dressing and Gender Struggle in Early Modern England', *Shakespeare Quarterly* 39 (1988), pp. 418–40.

23 Randolph Trumbach, *Sex and the Gender Revolution, Vol. 1: Heterosexuality and the Third Gender in Enlightenment London* (Chicaqo, 1999). See also Emma Donoghue, *Passions Between Women: British Lesbian Culture, 1688–1801* (London, 1993) and the essays in Jonathan Goldberg (ed.), *Queering the Renaissance* (Durham, NC, 1994) and Josiah Blackmore and Gregory S. Hutcheson (eds), *Queer Iberia: Sexualities, Cultures, and Crossings from the Middle Ages to the Renaissance* (Durham, NC, 1999); Valerie Traub, *The Renaissance of*

Lesbianism in Early Modern England (Cambridge, 2002); Helmut Puff, *Sodomy in Reformation Germany and Switzerland, 1400–1600* (Chicago, 2003). For an extensive collection of sources, see Kenneth Borris (ed.), *Same-sex Desire in the English Renaissance: A Sourcebook of Texts, 1470–1650* (New York, 2004).

24 The best discussion of these issues is Liu, 'Teaching the Differences'. See also Deirdre Keenan, 'Race, Gender, and Other Differences in Feminist Theory', in Meade and Wiesner-Hanks (eds), *Companion to Gender History.*

25 Margo Hendricks and Patricia Parker (eds), *Women, 'Race' and Writing in the Early Modern Period* (London, 1994); Kim F. Hall, *Things of Darkness: Economies of Race and Gender in Early Modern England* (Ithaca, 1995); Felicity A. Nussbaum, *The Limits of the Human: Fictions of Anomaly, Race, and Gender in the Long Eighteenth Century* (Cambridge, 2003). For links between conquest and sodomy, see Richard Trexler, *Sex and Conquest: Gendered Violence, Political Order, and the European Conquest of the Americas* (Ithaca, 1995), though Trexler's conclusions have been hotly debated. For further readings, see the bibliographies in Merry Wiesner-Hanks, *Christianity and Sexuality in the Early Modern World: Regulating Desire, Reforming Practice* (London, 2000).

6

Psychoanalysis

Diane Purkiss

To write of the practice of psychoanalysis in early modern history is in some respects to address an ongoing absence. Psychoanalysis is not the theoretical framework to which most early modern historians naturally turn. Few of the great events of sixteenth- and seventeenth-century history – the Renaissance, the Reformation, civil wars in Britain and Europe – have received any specifically psychoanalytic attention. Only in the sphere of psychobiography, beginning with Erik Erikson's 1958 biography of the German reformer Martin Luther (1483–1546), and in studies of the supernatural, particularly studies of beliefs lying outside religion, has much attention been paid to psychoanalysis.[1]

This situation is not unique to early modern history; Anglophone history has generally eschewed the possibilities of psychoanalysis. Of the ten or so recently published books on 'history and theory' that I plucked at random from a shelf, only one had devoted a chapter to psychoanalysis. Some work in nineteenth- and twentieth-century history has been more willing to experiment with psychoanalysis. Even there, though, the full resources of psychoanalysis as a way of thinking about historical questions and the full extent of its challenge to conventional historiography have seldom been explored.

The reasons for this marginalization are many and complex. Most obviously, perhaps, there is scepticism about psychoanalysis itself. However, my business here is not to try to convert those who think the entire body of theory erroneous. I am addressing instead the perceived gap between psychoanalysis and history as valid disciplines, and the possibility of conversation between them. When this is done it is evident that there are perfectly genuine difficulties about marrying the empirical historical method, so recently defended by all and sundry against what are taken to be the assaults of poststructuralism, with a method which in many of its forms asks questions that are not the ones empiricism might wish to ask. It would nevertheless be wrong to speak of psychoanalysis *and* history as entities, systems of thought, or practices which have had nothing to do with each other. More accurately, there have been several kinds of relationship between them, with one perhaps outnumbering all the others put together. Psychoanalysis *and* history – type it into Google and you will end up with a list of sites on the history *of* psychoanalysis. In Google's eyes, peaceful coexistence is replaced by domination. For the history of psychoanalysis is not the same as psychoanalysis *in* history, let alone the psychoanalysis *of* history. While the history of psychoanalysis is a valid project, it sometimes seems to block any alternative uses of psychoanalysis as itself a way for historians to understand the nuances of topics otherwise difficult to manage or interpret.

Why? If Erik Erikson is correct to assert that psychoanalysis and history are engaged in the same process, why are historians uncomfortable with psychoanalysis, even hostile to it?[2] Is it perhaps because of a fear that psychoanalysis will put history on the couch, obliterate it except as part of itself? A fear that the integrity of history will be lost so that it becomes nothing but a reiteration of psychoanalysis? The fear that history will be lost is certainly expressed often. There is also another kind of fear nested inside the first one, and it is the fear of losing a direct relationship with the evidence – the archive, perhaps. Losing the power to be surprised. Losing the (entirely proper) wish to let the evidence be paramount. Losing discovery in formula; as Jacques Barzun put it, 'events and agents lose their individuality and become illustration of certain automatisms'.[3]

Another kind of fear might be generated by a nervousness about which aspects of the subject are emphasized in psychoanalysis. In her germinal review of gender theory and its historical uses, Joan Scott wrote of Lacanian psychoanalysis that 'I am troubled by the exclusive fixation on the individual subject'. One form of this fear is expressed by feminist historian Carolyn Steedman, who points to the way a certain kind of biographical narrative of (usually sexual) revelation privileges some kinds of life-writing and marginalizes others, so that a woman like the suffragette Margaret McMillan (1860–1931) cannot be written about, because what was *historically* significant about her was not her individual and personal relationships or her fantasies, but her public and political importance.[4] One might make exactly the same kind of case for noble and royal early modern women; haring off after the personal in their lives and writings can and has on occasion entirely obscured their public motives and familial loyalties. However, this is not really a problem with psychoanalysis per se, but a problem with how it is generally applied to history, the way it is assumed to work. In historiography, psychoanalysis is normally understood as a way of reading what is silent, or private, or uncomfortably or pathologically feminine (not the same as female). As a result, psychoanalysis (and the psyche, including the unconscious) is evacuated from the public realm, which is populated exclusively by rational, masculine subjects. Consequently, psychoanalysis *in* history is seen to dictate a series of questions (mostly about secrets, lies and pathologies) rather than another series of questions – questions which might seem pressing – about, for example, large-scale historical changes, such as regicide or revolution, and the part the psyche may play in them.

Historians tend to invoke psychoanalysis at the point where we believe that people are behaving irrationally, or to account for acts or events that seem to be inexplicable rationally. The rational subject is therefore, as it were, the default subject for historians, and the psychoanalytic subject in all its strangeness is only invoked when we already find strangeness present. Obviously, this is both a limiting and a risky procedure: limiting because it means that psychoanalysis will only be applied to a very small range of historical issues, and risky because it depends on the notion that we can easily judge a past society and determine what requires non-rational explanation.

It is a central theme of this essay that historical psychoanalysis's chosen focus on moments of aberrance or crisis neglects much of history while confining psychoanalysis to realms designated feminine. I am really addressing one large and three small questions – the large one is why psychoanalysis has been so underused in early modern history, and the small ones (which I think provide the answer to the large one) are whether the psyche has a history (that is, can we just go on assuming Charles I had a castration complex?), whether psychoanalysis has to be about the private realm, and, if not, what else it could be about, and whether anything other than individuals has a psyche (people, histories, representations). I see these as the impasses that have kept psychoanalysis and history apart, so to speak.

This essay will review some psychoanalytic work on the early modern period and identify its strengths and weaknesses in the light of what I see as the superior achievements of those working in the continental historiographic tradition. Central to this work is the concept of fantasy. In psychoanalysis this means more than the mental image of a desired object; not just a breast, a mouth, but a *mise-en-scène* in which those things have meaning. In fantasy, too, one can be both breast and mouth. I will contrast the ideas of fantasy in studies of witchcraft and dreaming with Slavoj Žižek's theory of fantasy as an act where the private individual engages in a representation of his or her place in wider culture. I shall ask whether Žižek's thesis offers a way of understanding issues normally understood as irrelevant to psychoanalysis, issues coded as masculine rather than feminine, issues from the public realm of history.

Witches

It is worth going back to Alex Owen's brilliant study of the mediums of nineteenth-century Britain, *The Darkened Room* (1989), because Owen was the first to point out that psychoanalysis offered a way to talk about what had been hidden from history:

> It was clear to me that the central concern of investigators old and new – is the medium genuine, and by extension, are the spirits real? – has had the effect of closing down the discussion and occluding wider issues involving the question of what spiritualism signified for those who did not doubt the reality of the spirits . . . I am presupposing the existence of a motivational unconscious and suggesting that mediums were capable of self-induced and self-regulated forms of psychological dissociation.[5]

Of course, Owen does not mean that facts are irrelevant to the historian or that facts can somehow be brushed aside with the broom of psychoanalysis. She is, however, drawing attention to the way ontologically problematic areas of historical enquiry might be unwontedly silenced by a passion for the wrong *kind* of truth, the scientific truth that disproves fancy rather than the psychic or historical truth about belief that she is seeking. Owen is reasonably questioning the extent to which areas such as the supernatural are dominated by scientific rather than person- or story-centred enquiries, and suggesting that psychoanalysis can help to elucidate what is happening *inside* the person rather than an unhealthy focus on what may or may not occur *around* the person. This, then, is a case where psychoanalysis is especially applicable to the historical problem posed, and it draws our attention to the possibility that there may be particular historical problems which it is best placed to solve.

Owen's basic insight has been taken up by others who work on the supernatural, notably some of the best witchcraft historians, including Robin Briggs and Lyndal Roper. Roper's work on child-witches aptly illustrates what kinds of historical processes might result from a sophisticated engagement with psychoanalysis in history.[6] She tells the story of Augsburg children in 1723 believed to have been seduced by the devil. Child-witches tend to appear towards the end of a witch-hunting period; hence Roper's goal is to link the history of witchcraft with the history of childhood, arguing that late child-witch accusations exemplify a move from one set of symbolic organizations of childhood to another. The eighteenth century saw the rise of the cult of childhood; an end of swaddling, belief in a child's freedom of movement, a decline in beating, the cult of breastfeeding; the perception of childhood as a separate state and children as needing protection.

Much of Roper's analysis is straightforward microhistory as psychobiography: she reads the children's fantasies about dirt as an attack on the parents. What Roper identifies as 'anal themes', or issues to do with the phase in which a child is preoccupied with excretion and hence with dirt and cleanness, are symbolically manifested as 'lice and mice', mobile dirt or excrement, in accordance with traditional psychoanalytic theory wherein satisfaction in the 'anal' stage of infant development is associated with excretary functions. Diabolic power is transmuted from a symbol of adult fears and fantasies to the preoccupations of early childhood. As Roper writes,

> It is as if the latent content of the witchcraft fantasy had been stripped of its mythic overlay to reveal the crudest primary structure of infant psychology underneath. The children seem to be using bodily products, excrement-like material and sharp cutting objects as harmful substances with which to attack God and injure their parents.[7]

More generally, Roper pinpoints an attack on parental sexuality as an aspect of the children's reported behaviour.

Roper also reports, however, on a larger series of society-wide phenomena, which involve changes in the perception of the figure of the witch and therefore impact on the way a witch-trial operated to release psychic anxiety. For Roper, the prosecutors' identification with the child-victims had the paradoxical effect of annihilating any separate identity for child-victims and accusers. But this identification was problematic because of the children's aggressive behaviours, particularly their interest in adult sexuality. Though Roper sees this as a moment on the cusp of a historical change in the roles of children in adult fantasy, she also individuates the case: 'Something', Roper writes,

> seems to have gone seriously awry in these parents' relationships with their children, making them, too, unable to deal with childish aggression: instead, they seem to have become sucked into their children's imaginative worlds, responding by becoming ill from the dirty objects in their beds, beating their children to excess, and in one case starving them to death to drive out the devil.[8]

This is still a private, parental pathology, and its relation to the social changes identified is not always clear and may not be historically identifiable.

More macrohistorical is the authorities' conversion of an interest in children's bodies to an interest in the children's masturbation. For Roper, this case signifies a move away from the pathologization of the adult woman as carrier of the psychopathologies of childhood, towards a more naked revelation of children's actual desires and fears, together with a specularization of the *child* instead of the woman as point of contact with desire and with the supernatural.[9] The psychic fantasies involved are the familiar ones of love and hate, but they have assumed a different symbolic form. Unlike many readings of psychoanalysis and history, Roper considers the possibility that both psychic expression and society may be subject to historical change. This particular witch-trial draws on the same psychoanalytic literature as others, but it is anything but a stale reiteration of the same mother-child plots. It explains how we can share the *plots*, but not their cultural expression; it points us towards the historicization of the psyche, the principal task (still) awaiting psychoanalytic historians.

Dreams

By contrast to Roper's connection of personal narrative with larger historical changes, two essays on dreams perhaps exemplify Steedman's fear that psychobiography can only tell a story of sexual revelation. Charles Carlton's achievements in psychobiography, and in bringing a psychoanalytic agenda to bear on early modern politics, are remarkable.[10] Nevertheless, his work on the dreams of William Laud, Charles I's Archbishop of Canterbury from 1633 to 1645, though fascinating, is problematic. He sensibly, and with caution, analyses the dreams that Laud recorded in his diary, pointing out that some are so abstruse that it would be foolhardy to try to fathom them, while others are open to obvious interpretations. Carlton rejects the classical psychoanalytic stance of Sigmund Freud (1856–1939) in favour of understanding dreams as dealing with generalized anxieties, including obvious ones like the fear of death. Carlton is also interested in the dreaming mind's struggle to express what cannot ordinarily be said, particularly unconscious desires that can only be expressed painfully in dreams.[11]

Arguably, this is so general, so vague, that it is barely psychoanalysis at all.[12] Carlton correctly points out that Laud himself would have recognized the category of wish-fulfilling dreams from the work of Plato, and symbolic, anxiety and day-residue dreams from the ancient Greek physician Artemidorus of Daldis, whose *Oneirocritica* was the most popular dreambook in early modern Europe. Laud's recorded dreams were mostly unpleasant, but the pleasant ones concerned his mother: 'I dreamed that my mother, long since dead stood by my bed and looked pleasantly upon me, and that I was glad to see her with so merry an aspect', he wrote in January 1627. By contrast, Laud's reflections on death were usually grim. All his life Laud had plenty to be anxious about. By 1642, his life's work in creating an Arminian Anglican Church was being destroyed by his enemies. While a prisoner in the Tower in November 1642, he dreamed 'that parliament was removed to Oxford, the church undone, some old courtiers came to see me and jeered. I went to St John's and found the roof of the old college ready to fall down. God be merciful'.

Now, this is such an obvious *anxiety* dream that Carlton does not elucidate it, and here we see the limitations of his lively and vibrant common-sense approach. The entire article is actually a kind of systematic *evasion* of psychoanalysis in alternative, more palatable explanations. Elucidation of Laud's anxiety dream through psychoanalysis is not entirely out of order, given Laud's waking preoccupation with mother figures as well as their oneiric appearance. His concern for the physical *body* of his college, his alma mater, has significance; indeed I argue elsewhere that it is part of a wider socio-pathology which partially explains the emotional importance of the Civil War.[13] In the context of the upbringing of early modern boys, a conflation of the body of the alma mater with the longed-for but erased body of the mother was entirely natural.

What interests Carlton much more, as predicted, perhaps, by Steedman's model, are the sexual revelations encoded in Laud's dreams. Laud had, for example, a significant dream about Buckingham:

> That night, in my sleep, it seemed to me that the Duke of Buckingham came into bed with me; where he behaved himself with great kindness towards me, after the rest, wherewith wearied persons are apt to solace themselves. Many seemed to me to enter the chamber who saw this.

When the Puritan William Prynne published this dream in his *Breviate of the Life of William Laud, Archbishop of Canterbury*, extracted from the diary, in 1644, he suggested Laud was guilty of 'the sin of uncleanness'. Laud replied angrily that 'there was never fastn'd on me the least suspicion of this sin in all my life'. But in reality matters were not so simple. Laud's diary is full of cryptic references to his 'unfortunateness' with T, SS, PB, EM, AD and EB. The pronouns show all of them were male. But none have been identified. 'Towards the morning [4 August 1635] I dreamed that LMSt came to see me the next day, and showed me all the kindness I could ask for'. 'I dreamed that KB sent to me in Westminster Church that he was desirous to see me'. Laud 'went with joy', but 'met another'. Like other diary references to KB, this one is enigmatic, but points to an intense and troubled relationship. Laud also expressed guilt and terror in a letter to Sir John Scudamore, 'One thing there is which I have many times feared, and still do, and yet I doubt it will fall upon me. I cannot trust my letters, but if it come I will take my solemn leave of all contentment. But in that way shall ever rest your loving friend'.[14] This may simply be part of the consciousness of sin that endeared Laud even to his godly foes. Yet all this information – if it is information – tells us little about Laud's *psychic* investment in the homoerotic.

Carlton does, however, relate his findings on Laud to the historical questions invited by his actions. Concluding that 'all this explains why Laud was such a peppery little man, whose excessive character, more than anything else, brought about his downfall', he argues that far from being 'one of those public figures without private lives', as Hugh Trevor-Roper put it, his private life 'may do much to explain his failure as a public figure . . . a little nocturnal colour that illuminates his daily humanity may not be so bad an ingredient after all'.[15] This is entirely fair, but would be still *more* illuminating if Laud's dreams could be analysed in more detail, with more attention paid to the problem of the mother figure. Why is Laud especially haunted by her and by substitutes for her? Does this have any significance for *specific* decisions he makes? And does it partially explain his relations with Charles I, whom Carlton argues elsewhere is also a figure whose character is shaped by a biographically specific maternal deprivation that turns him into a melancholic? One of the few genuine attempts to suggest a historical specificity for the early modern psyche is Valerie Fildes's suggestion that the prevalence of melancholia among the upper classes might be caused by the practice of abrupt weaning from a wetnurse.[16]

In a different account of early modern dreams, Patricia Crawford tackles the difficulties presented by psychoanalysis more directly than Carlton.[17] First, she is rightly suspicious of dream texts. Accounts of women's dreams, Crawford notes correctly (unlike Carlton), have been shaped by memory, language and narrative form. On psychoanalysis, she writes nervously: 'Initially I thought that Freud's explanations of the meaning of dreams would provide no assistance, because the meaning seemed so often to lie in events in the individual's life history to which we historians had no or very limited access'.[18] This pragmatic objection is united with theoretical concerns. Crawford registers that psychoanalysis is not fully historical: 'the Freudian paradigm of dream interpretation seemed ahistorical, taking insufficient account of historical difference'. However, she also points out that there are similarities as well as differences between ourselves and early modern people. Freud's theory, she writes, that dreaming is about a longing for the early state of union with the mother, offers us an insight into the dreams of Anne Bathurst, a London widow in the later seventeenth century, who was a member of the mystical Philadelphian society, and who recorded her visions of oneness with God: 'O, a fountain seal'd, breasts full of consolation. I am as pent milk in the breast, ready to be poured forth and dilated into Thee, from whom my fullness flows with such fulness and plenitude and pleas'd when eased.'[19] The trouble is that this is not a dream at all (though that is no reason not to psychoanalyse it). It is a *vision*, and this illustrates the need, which Crawford herself points out, to look first at literary protocols and conventions. Later, still more visionaries are identified with dreamers, blurring categories rather problematically; this is only acceptable because early modern women themselves did not always distinguish sharply between dream and vision. Bathurst's language here clearly follows the doctrines of German mystic and theosophist Jacob Behme (1575–1624) and it strongly resembles that of her near-contemporary mystic Jane Lead (1624–1704).[20] Nevertheless, Crawford's analysis is excellent; she shows that Bathurst identifies not with the needy infant, but with the nursing mother. Crawford points to the universality of the experience, and also to the historical variability of its interpretation. This is a perfectly valid and responsible historical enterprise.

However, there is an almost insuperable difficulty here, for Crawford's approach actually divorces rather than marries psychoanalysis and history; for her, psychoanalysis can only talk about the ahistorical parts of women's experience (maternal lactation), not the way they are understood historically by female subjects (religion). Is there any way to bring psychoanalysis into apposition with the historical subject, not the transhistorical subject? Or rather, what if we understand the psyche as at work upon the materials of history in order to construct (say) sanctity? Then there might be a way to talk about Bathurst engaging in a process of choosing and then psychically refashioning the Behmenist text. We can find a clue in a discussion of the relation between the lactating body and God. Bathurst is not, or not entirely, the lactating mother, so much as the milk itself, and the milk is to be 'diluted into thee'. It might seem surprising to imagine God as a baby, but it may make more sense in a world in which prayers are a crucial part of household government; God, though he does not have needs, might nonetheless represent a need that has to be met by the mother.

Other women also use this image of breastfeeding, but it is more usual to see God as the nursing mother, sought by the baby, though these images are still wont to depend on the *experience* of breastfeeding, with a strong focus on the breast's need for the baby.[21] This emphasis too is cultural, not universal: in a pre-antibiotic era, early modern women particularly dreaded mastitis and abscess, and it was part of early modern medicine to be anxious about the build-up of any bodily substance.[22] (By contrast, twenty-first-century mothers worry that they will not have *enough* milk.) If we think about the *psychoanalytic* implications of this idea of the breast's need for the baby, we can see that it may modify hitherto universal notions of the Kleinian breast and encourage us to see our task as historicizing the psyche. Object-relations theorist Melanie Klein's (1882–1960) idea depends upon and is a way of discussing a culture of scarcity, rationing of the breast – timed feedings, maternal commitments – so that mother and baby are both perceived to be restlessly seeking food in a world where breasts are perceived as a frighteningly over-abundant source of food, likely to flood or perhaps even poison mother and baby with their largesse. In that case, the other fear that Klein identifies, the fear of being overwhelmed, might normally be uppermost, and this might be associated with God. Arguably, mystical visionaries like Bathurst use the complex mixture of feelings evoked by the overwhelming breast – love, fear – to express their feelings about God.

Crawford is also concerned that 'psychoanalysis itself seemed to depend upon a different notion of selfhood from that common in medieval and early modern times', a concern she derives from the writings of 'new historicist' literary critic Stephen Greenblatt.[23] Greenblatt argues that individual subjectivity in the sixteenth century may have depended more on relations with others than it did at the end of the nineteenth century. Thus he suggests that the sixteenth-century

French peasant Arnaud du Tilh, who took on the identity of Martin Guerre, was able to do so because 'concepts of owning an individual identity were established not by the individual himself but by evidence as judged in court about his place in society'.[24] The problem with Greenblatt's analysis, as Natalie Zemon Davis (b. 1928) has pointed out, is its lack of interest in Bertrande, Martin Guerre's wife, whose testimony in the court case to establish which of the two men was the true Martin was crucial relationally. For Greenblatt, Bertrande's subjectivity seems not to matter. Yet the identity of the individual in her bed was (very precisely) what was supposed to be crucial for a wife's reputation and chastity.[25]

Arguably, however, Davis's own narrative might be equally problematic for a different reason, and that is its improvisational character. Her story of Bertrande, enjoying Arnaud's prowess and thus needing to defend her sexual reputation by insisting that he *was* her husband, is based, she claimed, on general sources about French peasant women rather than sources especially about Bertrande. Richard Evans concedes that such inferences are drawn all the time, even in traditional history writing. Indeed, one might argue that all attempts to write about the inner life of historical figures are problematically dependent on speculation, and should be left alone. Yet if we make no attempt to explain human choices and human actions, history becomes rather empty. Perhaps part of the resistance to psychoanalysis is resistance, some of it quite proper, to this opening out of the human interior as an improper subject for history, because any such opening out must be partly speculative (in both senses – intrusive and poorly grounded).[26]

One way forward might be to explore more fully and self-consciously the resources of fiction. While some British Civil War historians, notably Kevin Sharpe and Blair Worden, are now comfortable analysing the historical fictions of others, fewer early modern historians are at ease openly incorporating the techniques of fiction into their own work.[27] However, there are a few interesting experiments, which could be much extended if it were possible to talk about their subjects other than rationally. Gillian Tindall's biography of Bohemian engraver Wenceslaus Hollar (1607–77) openly uses fiction to extend what can be said historically. Marjorie Becker, for a later period, uses techniques drawn from fiction to draw readers into the symbolic world of historical figures and the historian herself, in writing a history that is 'empathetic rather than the more purely critical'.[28] One might begin to imagine what this kind of historical work might be like – a conversation between, say, Lucy Hay, Countess of Carlisle (mistress to leading royalist and parliamentarian men and actively involved in political intrigues before and during the civil wars), Matthew Hopkins (the mid-seventeenth-century Puritan English 'witch-finder general') and Edward Hyde (the royalist Earl of Clarendon who wrote the first historical account of the civil wars). This is not just a matter of presentation – to write such a conversation well, the historian would need a very strong sense of what each person might meaningfully say. Conventional history, by focusing on external evidence, by adopting an impersonal third-person perspective in search of a kind of objectivity, and by employing narrative techniques such as the third-person omniscient narrator, often leaves out the felt, the experienced, the lived-through – not only as sources of historical curiosity, but of what makes those in the past human and enriching for our own lives. As Becker says, 'the histories that concern me go down very deep, are at times composed of longing and tenderness'.[29]

The question is, at what point does such an experiment cease to be history, or cease to be valid history rather than an ungrounded model of the past? Is it sensible – or even safe – to blur the boundaries between history and fiction in this manner? While Becker and Tindall clearly signal to the reader the point *within* their work at which invention takes flight, others (Natalie Davis) do not – indeed Becker, at least, might want to argue that there are such points, unacknowledged, in the work of most historians. What about the stretched point, abounding in (let's say) Claire Tomalin's much-lauded biography of Samuel Pepys: 'Sam must have wondered when his turn was coming, the more so since his own health was not good'.[30] Usually signalled by the use of the phrase 'must have', this is really speculation – probably valid speculation, since it refers to the death of four of Pepys's siblings, but speculation nonetheless, acceptable only when signposted clearly and unequivocally as such. The trouble is that the signposts are apt to get in the way of the very evocation of feeling which is aimed at. If Tomalin had written 'It seems likely that Sam wondered' then there would have been a considerable loss of immediacy.

What has this to do with psychoanalysis? Everything, because a lot of psychoanalytic history uses the 'Sam must have wondered' formulation. To speculate means to open to examination, to look into. There is something impertinent about the word. Biographers constantly ask themselves when it is acceptable to speculate – in this expanded sense – to open up their subjects to a public scrutiny that few may have welcomed in life. Diane Wood Middlebrook's biography of the twentieth-century poet Anne Sexton is a case in point. Middlebrook was given access to transcripts of Sexton's sessions with her analyst, including her affair with him. Even though Sexton was dead by this time, some thought this a bridge too far.[31] In another sense, the 2003 teleplay, film and novel about the life of Sylvia Plath raise the issue of how far *fiction* is entitled to go in the service of the truth.[32] Is it acceptable to write, sell and market a novel largely on the grounds that it offers biographical or historical truth, even – put more sordidly – an 'insider's' view? Does the mere passage of time or the public importance of the figure so analysed make any difference to the ethical dilemmas? Is it acceptable to write (imaginatively) about Churchill's depression because he was a wartime national leader and it had an impact on events, but not on Plath's because it was in every way a private matter? Or is probing into Churchill's interior equally problematic?

Does it involve little more than extrapolating likely feelings and ideas using a very general and worryingly common-sense-based and hence untested model of what someone is likely to feel in given circumstances?

Early modern psychobiographers are unlikely to be embarrassed by the wealth of evidence at their disposal, but they may be tempted – as Davis was – to extrapolate from known models to particular cases, and psychoanalysis offers a way of doing this. For all we know, Samuel Pepys Junior might have relished seeing his siblings melt away, allowing him increased attention. Psychic allohistories (that is, counterfactual histories) present the same kinds of issues as other allohistories, but are less frequently explored; indeed, psychic history is generally more rigidly determinist than other forms of history, insisting on the inflexibility of psychic structures not subject to conscious alteration. If the psyche determines action beyond power of choice, then of course history is not and cannot be anything other than determined. This is doubtless one reason why psychohistory deals better with topics of broad social evolution and belief, rather than with single events.

It is possible to imagine that one might want to make out a psychobiographical argument for, say, the decision to execute Charles I or Charles's wish to negotiate with the Irish, but in fact most historians assume that the historical actor is making the best possible stab at rationality of which he is capable, even if he is conspicuously failing. However, there are events in history which seem to require some explanation from outside rationality, such as Charles I's arguably fatal decision to abandon London in 1642 and flee to Hampton Court. Again, however, this was a classic *blunder*, so that, once more, psychoanalysis can help only with the pathological. Could one just as plausibly make out a psychoanalytic argument for a *correct* decision – for parliamentary commander Oliver Cromwell's (1599–1658) actions at the battles of Naseby and Dunbar? Heavily equipped with the wisdom of hindsight, it seems impossible that such choices were irrational. We do not feel prompted to invoke the psyche to explain rationality. But perhaps we should, the more so because in writing about the Civil War and the English Republic we are dealing with some of the finest political thinkers and canonical writers in Anglophone history, and also with some of the Civil War's most prominent political actors. In suggesting that they are not immune to fear and fantasy and desire, psychoanalytic history is not devaluing their ideas, but pointing out that beneath and alongside them lie complex fantasies and imaginings about aspects of the self with which the political discourses of the seventeenth century were not equipped to deal. There has been a tendency on the part of political historians and the literary critics who follow in their wake to write of rational subjects, self-identical and unitary, makers of equally self-identical texts. Similarly, the political criticism of Civil War texts which has flourished in recent years often understands the authors and the texts as active, if ambiguous, political agents; whether the outcome is the battle of Naseby or Andrew Marvell's (1621–78) poem to parliamentary general Lord Fairfax, 'Upon Appleton House', the results involved are assumed to be part of the history of ideas: bright shiny surfaces, fissured only by the intractabilities of language, genre or the political situation itself. Literary critics have fared little better. The standard method involved in analysing Civil War texts picks up a figure, examines all possible sources and positions available to the author and then shows which he or she chose. It goes without saying that this is often illuminating. But it, too, assumes a rational liberal subject. Indeed, literary critics who work on the Civil War frequently do so because they are drawn to the notion of liberal subjectivity politically. The analyses provided by these methods are perfectly adequate on their own terms, but they erase a great deal about the conflict by ignoring the areas of excess and the gaps and silences where unreason flourishes. Our fantasy is that the war was fought by rational actors making a conscious difference to history; to some extent it really was, but if we stress conscious decision making at the expense of unconscious investments, if we stress rational choice at the expense of the irrational fantasies which were also present, then we miss the phantasmagoria, the fantasy of fear and desire, that was also present, also active, and that sometimes governed those choices.

What psychoanalysis knows is that political actors, like social actors, are not unified rational subjects, but fissured and split, the *telos* of ideologies that operate on the unconscious and also the split subjects produced by identity formation itself. Like us, early modern men and women carried about with them an irrational part, an unconscious they could never fully know, one that produced fantasies and dreams and desires. Nor was this alien part of themselves fully separable from the rational self. Rather, its fears and desires infiltrated what might otherwise pass for rationality. The jokes, dreams, longings and terrors of men and women in the Civil War years were opportunities for some of this unconscious desire to find relief, so that resources like ballads, pamphlets, jestbooks and comic interludes give us important information about where the fissures and fractures lie that may determine large events.

One might even argue that one reason it is important to keep psychoanalysis on the table, so to speak, is that it asks us at least to pause and reflect on what our basis is for interpreting sources about behaviour in the way that we do. Why, for example, should we see sex as vital to Bertrande's desires, or to Laud's? If we are to bring fiction and its techniques into the archives to make them more accessible, we need to begin to think carefully about the mode in which we choose to recast the characters of the past. This might be true even when we are not fictionalizing. Kevin Sharpe's analysis of the character of Charles I in his magisterial *The Personal Rule of Charles I* (1992) also depends on certain assumptions, assumptions that might be opened to question by a discussion of psychoanalysis, including the assumption that Charles was in control of his own representations, a notion which Sharpe might now be among those to call into question.

Finally, Crawford is less successful than Carlton in using the logic of psychoanalysis to make a bridge from individual character to public affairs. If we take, for example, the early modern belief that dreams could be oracular, prompted by God and the devil, then how might that lead us to psychoanalyse the dream of Yorkshire gentlewoman Alice Thornton (1627–1707), who recorded in her autobiography her dream of the arrival of a bailiff who was to attempt to repossess some of her property. Alice was prepared for him when he arrived the next day. For Thornton, the case against the bailiff was bound up with a gendered struggle over her dead husband's property; Alice was trying to retain control over the property given to her by her own father. In her dream, the God who sent the dream might stand in for that father, protecting her property.

Similarly, Eleanor Davies (1590–1652) had a tragically prophetic dream of a child's head cut off, and women trying to comfort the head as it cried.[33] Shortly afterwards, her much-loved daughter Lucy wrote to her, telling her of the death of her son. Davies reports this dream as part of a series of events correctly foreseen by her, including the death of her husband Sir John Davies; for her, its significance – at any rate, the significance she attaches to it in her own letter on the subject – is as authentication of her prophetic abilities. Yet the dream is about horror and above all helplessness – it is about women who stand by and cannot save the child they try to comfort. What does this spectacle of maternal passivity tell us? In Davies's case, it may tell us less about her *private* responses to maternity than about her *public* circumstances. The child's severed head is strikingly reminiscent of the apparitions conjured from the cauldron in *Macbeth*, which are usually interpreted as speaking about succession and rule and authority. An aristocratic family's loss of a son in early modern England, too, was a public as well as a private event, and this would have been especially true for Davies's, keen as she was on the aristocracy and fervent as she was in the struggle against what she and some others saw as the swelling power of the monarchy. We also need to consider the form taken by the dead child. A severed head – a head literally cut off – is not merely and drearily a castration metaphor, but also a symbol of what castration represents; loss of a place in patriarchal and patrilineal society. Decapitation – a traitor's death, characteristically – symbolically cuts off the single identity from the identity of the body politic. The head of the traitor was displayed on London Bridge Bar, while the body was buried privately. The idea of a head speaking oracularly without its body is also common in folklore, most conspicuously in the tale of Friar Bacon and Friar Bungay and the brazen head. All these ideas point towards a public rather than a private dimension to Davies's dream, but this public significance is firmly grounded in the private loss and the maternal grief to which the dream also testifies.

In different ways, then, Charles Carlton, Patricia Crawford and Eleanor Davies demand that we ask the question, does the unconscious have a history? Moreover, there might be two ways of understanding the history of the unconscious. First, we might want to note the difference made by social arrangements: does it matter that most early modern women used wetnurses? What kind of role did the splitting of the mother function have? How can we think this through in relation to the early modern period's own anxieties about maternal lactation? Though the *need* to do this work is registered by everyone, the work is not often done; indeed, historical biographies of Charles I, on the one hand, and Jane Austen, on the other, assume that their subjects are shaped by being sent away to wetnurses and then abruptly removed from them, without considering the possibility that such practices may either have pathologized the entire culture or, alternatively, have been absorbed by it through psychic and social strategies (hypothetically, the role of religion comes to mind). In the absence of such considerations, the drift away from history and into the privatization of lives in biography is all too apparent, and psychoanalysis becomes a way of stepping round the past rather than a way into it.

Second, we might want to make a larger and more complex argument for a kind of social unconscious, a dumping ground for repressed social and cultural practices that then resurface in fragments, neuroses or jokes. Russian literary theorist Mikhail Bakhtin (1895–1975), for example, in his book *Rabelais and his World* (1965), makes a sustained argument for the cultural obviation of carnival and the carnival body of pleasure, phenomena which, for Bakhtin, are pushed into a kind of social unconscious (though Bakhtin does not use this term), from which they reappear in displaced, disguised forms (the novel, principally). In their work on witchcraft, French feminist philosophers Hélène Cixous (b. 1937) and Catherine Clément (b. 1939) argue that hysteria is itself a history of sorts – that upon the tormented and writhing or paralysed body of the hysteric, unspeakable social memories are acted out. They argue that the hysteric *recalls* or gives voice to the unspeaking figure of the witch.[34]

Whether or not we accept these individual arguments, we might want to accept the general need to think about processes of historical repression in the formation of historical narratives; what is at stake, for example, in feminist narratives of witchcraft persecutions as 'the Burning Times'? When women historians spend years working on a person or an object, what psychic processes are involved? Perhaps one use of psychoanalysis might be to reflect on the historian him- or herself. An early example might be cultural theorist Michel de Certeau's notion of history as a space where the declining religions of the past could be replaced by the nation state. For de Certeau, history 'permits a society to situate itself by giving it a past in language; and it thus opens up to [the society] its own space in the present'.[35] Noting de Certeau's debt ('in language') to the poststructualist psychoanalytic philosopher, Jacques Lacan (1901–81), we could see this moment as precisely the formation of a subject-identity for the individual citizen within a society; the learning of stories about the past (and therefore the repression of other stories) becomes a way for the individual subject to find him- or herself within a language and a culture. It follows, of course, that there may be a degree of *irrational* attachment to particular stories, which does not imply the suspension of categories such as truth and falsehood, but rather exists alongside them. Indeed, it might even be argued that some awareness of our own desires respecting the past might help rather than hinder the pursuit of truth; this is the difference between acting out and working through, as theorists of trauma term these two polarities, a point to which I will return. Most sharply of all, in *The Gender of History: Men, Women and Historical Practice*, Bonnie Smith suggests that the construction of male subjectivity *within* the profession is subject to both irrationality and psychoanalysis.

> No matter what the changes from realism to modernism or modernism to postmodernism, from claims of truth to claims of explanation, masculinity continues to function as it did in the nineteenth century: as part of a flight, a deepening, a broadening, in which the historian ascends, reaches, incises, and conquers to surpass himself and all others. He creates more, a supplement, an extra, beyond what others have done – but does it transcendentally, invisibly, so that while we see powerful historians as men, we also see only truth, pure intelligence, and compelling explanation. The professor's unacknowledged libidinal work – the social ideology that draws us to value male plenitude, power, and self-presentation – is but rarely glimpsed in the mirror of male history.[36]

For Smith, this dynamic will continue in 'acting out' until it is 'worked through' and acknowledged. Whether or not her provocative argument is valid, it is intriguing because it suggests what psychoanalysts have always known; that to be an analyst, one must first be an analysand.

The uses of Žižek

The psychoanalytic writings of Slavoj Žižek (b. 1949) provide a way of thinking about writing a genuinely historical psychoanalysis. Unlike first- and second-wave Lacanians, Žižek's theories are embedded in analyses of cultural practices – or, to put it less rebarbatively, his books are great fun to read because he expounds his theories with references to popular film. What I want to do is to expand on two of Žižek's theories, and then sketch the ways in which they might open up to us aspects of English Civil War history hitherto neglected or unresolved.

For Žižek, what 'confers on the other the dignity of a person is not any universal-symbolic feature but precisely what is "absolutely particular" about him, his fantasy; that part of him that we can be sure we can never share'. For Žižek, fantasy is precisely the moment of individuation. And because fantasy is always particular, 'we can acquire a sense of the dignity of another's fantasy only by assuming a kind of distance towards our own'. For Žižek, the dilemma of psychoanalysis, which threatens the particularity of the subject's fantasy, is the same as the dilemma faced by postmodern philosopher and literary critic Richard Rorty,[37] writing of the difficulty in building a liberal-democratic ethic after the failure of its universal and rational foundations. For Rorty, the only way this can now happen is by resignation to the split between private and public and the clear demarcation of private and public zones; a society that makes possible to individuals and communities 'the different sorts of little things around which they centre their fantasies and their lives' – a society in which the role of social law has been reduced to guarding the freedom of self-creation. The problem with what Žižek calls 'this liberal dream' is that the split between private and public never comes about without what he terms 'a certain remainder', by which he does not mean that the very split private/public is socially constructed. Rather what Žižek wants to show is that the very social law that, as a neutral set of rules should limit our aesthetic self-creation and deprive us of a part of our enjoyment, is always already penetrated by an obscene pathological surplus enjoyment. The point is not that the split public/private is not possible, but that it is only possible on condition that the very domain of public law is 'smeared' by an obscene dimension of 'private' enjoyment; public law draws the energy for the pressure it exerts on the subject from the very enjoyment of which it deprives him or her, by acting as agent of prohibition. This is called the superego, says Žižek, and, as Freud argues, it feeds on the forces of the id (the unconscious), which it suppresses and from which it acquires its obscene, malevolent, sneering quality. The more we obey the superego, the more guilty we feel, for the more enjoyment it accumulates (in indulging its own desires, to rule, to dominate). To be a democratic subject, Žižek opines, requires that individual subjects be emptied of their particularity, even their fantasy, to be understood as democratic; yet this can never be done because (as with the public/private split) there is always a remainder on which the democratic self then depends. This left-over is precisely the particularity which was supposed to be suspended – Žižek focuses on ethnicity, ignoring class and gender, but his argument could well be applied to either – and which therefore returns disruptively, in the form of (say) one nation or its foes, or ethnic cleansing.[38] Of what use is this argument to a historian of the English Civil War, for example? In a seventeenth-century context, the arguable surplus of identity which deforms the polity is religion.

What if we look at Žižek's arguments about the nation state as mother? For Žižek, the images of the nation as motherland or fatherland are not satisfying fantasies, but fantasies destined never to be realized. The perfection of this motherliness or fatherliness is precisely the goal nationalists set themselves to achieve – in so doing, they are struggling to give meaning to their lives. In the nationalist imaginary there is always already an Other in the form of persons (papists, sturdy beggars, rioting apprentices, Puritans) or practices (nobles abandoning their estates, stage plays, church ales) which makes the achievement of the nationalist state as perfect mother or father figure temporarily difficult. This gratifying fountain of sweets is forever deferred, barred off, by these others. Such national threats are always at hand – can we trust our youth, our peers, our king? And they also come from outside – the pope, the Spanish, the Irish, the French. Sometimes figures manage to combine both inside and outside threat, as was the fate of Charles I's wife, Henrietta Maria (1609–69), who also added the particular threat of femininity at the heart of government. What characterizes a nation is crisis where the defensive functions are overwhelming. The good father nation is supposed to protect and secure the availability (from the national subject) of the good breast of the motherland, without undermining its goodness. When its goodness becomes not good enough, when the defensive function starts to take over from the enjoyment function, then there is a collapse.[39]

A final example: Žižek reflected in a lecture on the failure of the British Left to dent the appeal of Margaret Thatcher among the working classes by emphasizing the massive inequalities her policies were generating. This led to a certain amount of random stigmatization of the Thatcherite working classes as irrational morons, tricked by 'ideology'. But for Žižek, the opposition, in its preoccupation with material inequality, neglected Thatcher's ability to redistribute fantasy. 'Fantasy', in Žižek's Lacanese, is the set of subliminal beliefs that individuals hold, which makes them feel that their life has a purpose, that they have a meaningful future.[40] Fantasy can, in this way, override material circumstances. Thatcher's proffered hope was that you could (through inborn British virtue) clamber off the bottom rung of society to the top, so that the pleasures offered at the top were only deferred and not unavailable. Literary critic Jacqueline Rose, in a further analysis of Thatcher's appeal, points to her impossible conjunction of femininity with the resolute and calculating male attitude of control; the identity itself, says Žižek, summarizing Rose's argument, consists in an 'impossible' coincidence of caring law-and-order woman with tough criminality.[41] So, says Žižek, Thatcher's critics' attempts to draw attention to her darker side, her vengefulness and bloodthirstiness, were in fact consolidating her identity.

There might be other forms of identity formation along similar lines. For instance, Charles I's identity was a similarly 'impossible' conjunction of a depriving father, one who took away pleasure, and a worryingly feminized man, one who indulged *himself* in pleasure. That 'impossible' combination initially drove some (though not all, or even most) of the nation into paranoia and dysfunction. Others identified with an abstract principle (monarchy), but Charles was only able to act as a redistributor of hope (and an object of fantasy and desire) when his death, in 1649, made the combination of fatherhood and motherhood no longer impossible but satisfying; from then on, his opponents' attempts to blacken him through critiques of his feminization operated to sustain rather than to undermine his image. This mode of analysis allows us to understand Charles as *both* an active political agent *and* an icon of the nation and of fatherhood and motherhood *at the same time.* It offers one model – but only one among many – of how a truly historical psychoanalysis might illuminate what cannot otherwise be understood.

Guide to further reading

Tim Ashplant, 'Psychoanalysis and Historical Writing', *History Workshop Journal* 26 (1988), pp. 102–19.

Geoffrey Cocks and Travis L. Crosby, *Psycho/History: Readings in the Method of Psychology, Psychoanalysis and History* (New Haven, 1987).

Discussion: *Comparative Studies in Society and History* 35 (1993): Laura Lee Downs, 'If "Woman" Is Just An Empty Category, Then Why Am I Afraid To Walk Alone At Night? Identity Politics Meets the Postmodern Subject', pp. 414–37; Joan W. Scott, 'The Tip of a Volcano', pp. 438–43; Laura Downs, 'Reply to Joan Scott', pp. 444–51.

Diane Purkiss, *The Witch in History: Early Modern and Twentieth-Century Representations* (London, 1996).

Diane Purkiss, *Literature, Gender and Politics in the English Civil War* (Cambridge, forthcoming).

Garthine Walker, 'Psychoanalysis and History', in Stefan Berger, Heiko Feldner and Kevin Passmore (eds), *Writing History: Theory and Practice* (London, 2003), pp. 141–60.

Elizabeth Wright and Edmond Wright (eds), *The Žižek Reader* (Oxford, 1999).

Notes

1 E.H. Erikson, *Young Man Luther: A Study in Psychoanalysis and History* (New York, 1958). Previous surveys of history and psychoanalysis include Peter Gay, *Freud for Historians* (Oxford, 1985), Geoffrey Cocks and Travis L. Crosby, *Psycho/History: Readings in the Method of Psychology, Psychoanalysis and History* (New Haven, 1987), and Tim Ashplant,

'Psychoanalysis and Historical Writing', *History Workshop Journal* 26 (1988), pp. 102–19. For a useful discussion of Lacanian psychoanalysis, see Joan Scott, 'Gender: A Useful Category of Historical Analysis', in *Gender and the Politics of History* (New York, 1988), Laura Lee Downs's critique of Scott, 'If "Woman" Is Just An Empty Category, Then Why Am I Afraid To Walk Alone At Night? Identity Politics Meets the Postmodern Subject' and Scott's reply, 'The Tip of a Volcano', *Comparative Studies in Society and History* 35 (1993), pp. 414–37, 438–43.

2 E.H. Erikson, *Childhood and Society* (1950; London, 1995), p. 48.

3 Jacques Barzun, *Clio and the Doctors: Psychohistory, Quantohistory, and History* (Chicago, 1974), p. 23.

4 Carolyn Steedman, 'La théorie qui n'en est pas une, or, Why Clio Doesn't Care', *History and Theory* 31 (1992), pp. 33–50.

5 Alex Owen, *The Darkened Room: Women, Power and Spiritualism in Late Victorian England* (London, 1989), 'Introduction', unpaginated.

6 Lyndal Roper, '"Evil Imaginings and Fantasies": Child-Witches and the End of the Witch-Craze', *Past and Present* 167 (2000), pp. 107–39. Roper discusses her own use of psychoanalysis in her *Oedipus and the Devil: Witchcraft, Sexuality and Religion in Early Modern Europe* (London, 1994). For a critique of Roper's method, see Garthine Walker, 'Psychoanalysis and History', in Stefan Berger, Heiko Feldner and Kevin Passmore (eds), *Writing History: Theory and Practice* (London, 2003), pp. 141–60. Other historians of witchcraft who draw on psychoanalysis include Robin Briggs, *Witches and Neighbours: the Social and Cultural Context of European Witchcraft* (London, 1996); Diane Purkiss, 'Desire and its Deformities: Fantasies of Witchcraft in the English Civil War', *Journal of Medieval and Early Modern Studies* 27(1) (1996/7), pp. 103–32 and *The Witch in History: Early Modern and Twentieth-Century Representations* (London, 1996); and John Demos, *Entertaining Satan; Witchcraft and the Culture of Early New England* (Oxford, 1982): the last is a fine example of pathologization.

7 Roper, 'Evil Imaginings', p. 116.

8 Roper, 'Evil Imaginings', p. 127.

9 The term 'specularization' is used by feminist philosopher Luce Irigaray (b. 1930) to mean, roughly, the scientific or analytical opening to view of the women, which she likens to being opened by a pelvic speculum during a gynaecological examination. The term is also a pun on speculation, in the sense of knowing nothing after allegedly finding out so much.

10 Charles Carlton, *Charles I: The Personal Monarch* (1983; London, 1995), *Going to the Wars: The Experience of the British Civil Wars 1638–1651* (London, 1992) and *Royal Childhoods* (London, 1986).

11 Charles Carlton, 'The Dream Life of Archbishop Laud', *History Today* 36(12) (1986), pp. 9–14; *William Laud, 1573–1645* (London, 1987).

12 Ironically, Carlton defends psychoanalysis against his critics on the grounds that it offers a precise vocabulary of personality, but unlike Roper he seems reluctant to use that vocabulary himself: *Charles I*, pp. xiv–xv.

13 Diane Purkiss, *Literature, Gender and Politics During the English Civil War* (Cambridge, 2005).

14 Carlton, 'Dream Life', p. 12.

15 Carlton, 'Dream Life', p. 14; H.R. Trevor-Roper, *Archbishop Laud: 1573–1645* (1940; 2nd edn, London, 1962), p. 35.

16 Valerie Fildes, *Breasts, Bottles, and Babies: A History of Infant Feeding* (Edinburgh, 1986), p. 79.

17 Patricia Crawford, 'Women's Dreams in Early Modern England', *History Workshop Journal* 49 (2000), pp. 129–42.

18 Crawford, 'Women's Dreams', p. 130.

19 Cited in Crawford, 'Women's Dreams', p. 131.

20 On Behmenism, see Brian J. Gibbons, *Gender in Mystical and Occult Thought: Behmenism and its Development in England* (Cambridge, 1996).

21 See, for example, Elizabeth Hincks, *The Poor Widows Mite, Cast into the Lords Treasury* (London, 1671), p. 24.

22 Fildes, *Breasts, Bottles, and Babies*, pp. 44 ff.; Audrey Eccles, *Obstetrics and Gynaecology in Tudor and Stuart England* (London, 1982), pp. 49–50; and Gail Kern Paster, *The Body Embarrassed: Drama and the Disciplines of Shame in Early Modern England* (Ithaca, 1993).

23 Crawford, 'Women's Dreams', p. 130.

24 Stephen Greenblatt, 'Psychoanalysis and Renaissance Culture', in Patricia Parker and David Quint (eds), *Literary Theory/Renaissance Text* (Baltimore, 1986), p. 130.

25 Greenblatt, 'Psychoanalysis', pp. 210–24.

26 Natalie Zemon Davis, *The Return of Martin Guerre* (Penguin, 1985). See also Robert Finlay's critique, 'The Refashioning of Martin Guerre' and Davis's reply, 'On the Lame', *American Historical Review* 93 (1988), pp. 553–71, 572–603.

27 Kevin Sharpe, *Remapping Early Modern England: The Culture of Seventeenth-Century Politics* (Cambridge, 2000); Blair Worden, *The Sound of Virtue: Philip Sydney's 'Arcadia' and Elizabethan Politics* (New Haven and London, 1996).

28 Gillian Tindall, *The Man Who Drew London: Wenceslaus Hollar in Reality and Imagination* (London, 2002). Marjorie Becker, 'Talking Back to Frida: Houses of Emotional *Mestizaje*', *History and Theory* 41 (2002), pp. 56–71.

29 Becker, 'Talking Back', p. 59.

30 Claire Tomalin, *Samuel Pepys: The Unequalled Self* (London, 2002), p. 8.

31 Diane Wood Middlebrook, *Anne Sexton: A Biography* (New York, 1992). On Middlebrook's biography and the ethical issues it raises, see Jacqueline Rose, *On Not Being Able to Sleep: Psychoanalysis and the Modern World* (London, 2003), pp. 17–24.
32 The novel is Kate Moses, *Wintering* (London, 2003).
33 Esther Cope, *Handmaid of the Holy Spirit: Dame Eleanor Davies Never Soe Mad a Ladie* (Ann Arbor, 1992), p. 22.
34 Hélène Cixous and Catherine Clément, *The Newly Born Woman*, trans. Betsy Wing (1975; Minneapolis, 1986).
35 Michel de Certeau, *The Writing of History*, trans. Tom Conley (New York, 1988), p. 127.
36 Bonnie Smith, *The Gender of History: Men, Women and Historical Practice* (Cambridge, MA, 1998) p. 239. See also Carolyn Steedman, *Dust* (Manchester, 2001).
37 Richard Rorty, *Achieving Our Country: Leftist Thought in Twentieth Century America* (Cambridge, MA, 1998).
38 Slavoj Žižek, *Looking Awry: An Introduction to Jacques Lacan through Popular Culture* (Cambridge, MA and London, 1998), pp. 154–62. For a slightly different version of this argument, see 'Fantasy as a Political Category: A Lacanian Approach', in Elizabeth Wright and Edmond Wright (eds), *The Žižek Reader* (Oxford, 1999), pp. 87–101.
39 Slavoj Žižek, 'Enjoy Your Nation As Yourself', in his *Tarrying With the Negative: Kant, Hegel, and the Critique of Ideology* (Durham, NC, 1993).
40 Slavoj Žižek, *For They Know Not What They Do: Enjoyment as a Political Factor* (London, 1991), pp. 37–8.
41 Žižek, *For They Know Not*, p. 38; Jacqueline Rose, 'Margaret Thatcher and Ruth Ellis', *New Formations* 6 (1989).

Part 2

7

Religion

Trevor Johnson

An understanding of religion is crucial to any engagement with early modern history. This era saw the Protestant and Catholic Reformations, missionary endeavours by European Christians in the New World overseas after 1492 and the shock to traditional cosmologies occasioned by 'scientific revolution'. A concern with religion is one of the defining characteristics of the age and the Protestant Reformation, in particular, has traditionally been regarded as marking the beginnings of the 'modern world'.[1] Given the centrality of religious belief to the culture, society and politics of early modern Europe, historians have not only explored it extensively, but also have done so for a very long time; indeed, beginning in the sixteenth and seventeenth centuries, when the first chronicles of the contemporary religious reforms were written, a substantial body of more or less scholarly literature on religious history pre-dates the modern historiography with which we are concerned here.[2] Modern historical writing on religion has, of course, been influenced by broader changes in the discipline. In the twentieth century, and particularly since the Second World War, the subject has undergone something of, to use a well-worn word, a revolution. New approaches, methodologies and concepts have drastically altered our perceptions of the period's turbulent religious history. But while general theories, often originally devised with other subjects of enquiry in mind, have enlightened the field, early modern historiography, in particular, including the historiography of religion, has often been at the forefront in developing fresh concepts, testing them and furthering their extension to other periods and themes. Indeed, historians of early modern religion have often been compelled to devise new approaches to its study, which can be (and have been) subsequently transplanted into the study of other topics.

Traditional approaches

Scholars typically divide the topic of 'religion' into three broad categories of belief, practice and experience, although the boundaries between these fields are blurred and often elusive. In the past, a concern with belief, and, in more narrowly defined terms, with 'doctrine', mainly determined approaches to the history of early modern religion. Scholarship on the topic was typically conceived as a branch of intellectual history (the history of 'ideas') or, more narrowly still, of theology. Emphasis was placed on the means by which individuals, chiefly the most prominent 'divines' or religious scholars, arrived at, altered or maintained their doctrines. When looking at the period of the Reformation and Catholic Counter-Reformation, an age characterized by the persecution of religious minorities (Jews and Muslims in fifteenth-century Spain, for example, or Protestants, and then Catholics, in sixteenth-century England, or radical sectarians almost everywhere), the religious historian's primary task was conceived as charting the delimitations of orthodoxy, the rise of new doctrine and the degrees of toleration of heterodox belief. This was approached chiefly through intensive study of the circumstances of the creation of 'confessional' texts, that is to say, manifestos of belief (such as the Lutheran *Confessio augustana* of 1530, the decrees of the Council of Trent of 1563 or the Anabaptist 'Schleitheim Articles' of 1527), alongside studies of the often prodigious writings of leading exponents of religion, such as Desiderius Erasmus (*c.*1466–1536), Martin Luther (1483–1546), and John Calvin (1509– 64), and the writing of their biographies.

The patient reconstruction of the intellectual processes by which novel theological ideas were conceived and traditional ones defended or assaulted remains a potent branch of the historiography of early modern religion. Traditionally, though, this approach has two main flaws. First, it potentially lacked critical distance from the object of study given that, in the past, most writers were 'committed'; that is to say, they wrote as conscious adherents of the same institutions (churches, denominations) whose histories they were reconstructing. Much of this scholarship was therefore partial, frequently apologetic and at times fiercely confessional in tone. Presentation of the key figures associated with the development of particular churches or denominations was often hagiographical or adulatory. Moreover, the discussion of doctrine often tended to be 'presentist', in that it was concerned with justifying past developments in terms of modern preoccupations and needs. For religious institutions, this has tended to mean an endeavour to demonstrate the continuity and the integrity of ideas, especially doctrines, as substantially immune from the historical circumstances in which they were generated, developed, articulated and communicated. Today this has largely given way to more critical and neutral, less partial and more historically aware approaches. Nonetheless, reading some religious history one still gets a whiff of authorial identification and empathy with the sectarian struggles of the sixteenth century. Even when the bias is not explicitly confessional, it can still be evoked by the professional or institutional as well as religious situation in which scholars find themselves. As Professor John O'Malley (himself a Jesuit priest) has written of the complex history of the contested nomenclature of the 'Catholic' or 'Counter'-Reformation, 'the resistance some Catholic historians originally had to "Catholic Reformation" stemmed from anti-Protestant animus, surely, but it suggests the hermeneutical gap between outsiders and insiders investigating any historical phenomenon'.[3]

A second danger, which is perhaps that of traditional intellectual history in general, remains that of insularity: of a preoccupation with a set corpus of ideas to the diminution of interest both in their historical context and in ideas beyond those of an arbitrarily defined mainstream. However, here also the methodological range has expanded, leading to what has inevitably been dubbed the 'new history of ideas', or the 'new intellectual history'. Particularly associated in English-language scholarship with the history of political thought, this approach has advocated the examination of a vastly amplified repertoire of sources and source types, an extension of the range beyond canonical notions and a concern with the embodiment of thought in individuals and its embeddedness in particular contexts. In the words of Steven Shapin, 'historians have in recent years become dissatisfied with the traditional manner of treating ideas as if they floated freely in conceptual space'.[4] A similar approach has underpinned the recent history of religious ideas. Canonical thinkers are still discussed, but generally in more rounded ways. For example, Heiko Oberman's 1982 biography of the German Protestant reformer, Martin Luther, subtitled 'Man between God and the Devil', places the development of Luther's ideas in the context of the apocalyptic climate of his age. Oberman highlights factors that are underrepresented in traditional portrayals, but which are nonetheless crucial to the religious thought which would later be regarded as mainstream. Above all, perhaps, he stresses the sheer 'otherness' of Luther's age from our own. A similar case in point is Thomas Mayer's study of Cardinal Reginald Pole – the English Catholic exile under the Protestant regimes of Henry VIII and Edward VI, Archbishop of Canterbury under the Catholic Mary Tudor and one of the key Catholic religious reformers in Europe at the time of the Council of Trent (1545–63). Mayer used Pole's correspondence and literary as well as theological output to portray his intellectual development, in addition to less obvious material, including such quasi-visual sources as emblems, in order to reconstruct the subtle religious politics of Pole's circle in Italy and even to hint at the nature of his subject's sexuality. The interplay of ideas and personalities, of social, political and intellectual networks, is conveyed in detail.[5]

One older, if never mainstream, approach may be mentioned in this context: that of psychobiography, which has had some success in the twentieth century as an explicit and self-conscious sub-genre. The classic example is Erik Erikson's *Young Man Luther* (1958), which applied a Freudian analysis to the fragmentary information of the Protestant founder's early years. Erikson derived Luther's later development of the doctrine of 'justification by faith', which rested on an acceptance of the arbitrary nature of the divine programme of human salvation, at least in part from the reformer's childhood experience of his own father's chastising temper:

> Here, I think, is the origin of Martin's doubt that the father, when he punishes you, is really guided by love and justice rather than by arbitrariness and malice. This early doubt later was projected on the Father in heaven with such violence that Martin's monastic teachers could not help noticing it. 'God does not hate you, you hate him', one of them said; and it was clear that Martin, searching so desperately for his own justification, was also seeking a formula of eternal justice which would justify God as judge.[6]

That psychobiography remains a current, though far from dominant, approach can be seen from W.W. Meissner's 1992 study of Luther's Catholic counterpart, the founder of the Society of Jesus, St Ignatius Loyola (1491–1556). As Meissner concedes, psychohistory is not only conjectural but also reductive, in that it only focuses on aspects of the life and personality of the subject which can be 'delineated and encompassed in strictly and specifically psychoanalytic terms'. At the same time, the author suggests, it allows us 'to see with more clarity the human side', the subject's 'inner psychic needs and conflicts, his hopes and fears, and the forces that drove him to the extremes of spiritual devotion and the heights of mystical experience'.[7] Early modern religious history perhaps attracts a psychobiographical approach for two reasons: first, the irrational nature of religious belief appears especially inclined to prompt a discussion of subconscious motivation in the subject; second, it was often theological professionals who left self-revelatory sources in the form of table talk, introspective spiritual diaries, autobiographies and a frequently massive literary output.

Besides the growing tendency towards historical contextualization, there has been a move beyond revisiting the lives of mainstream historical figures in order to study those on the fringes of historical memory and, in particular, the religiously idiosyncratic. Such individuals were conventionally either left out or subjected to a more sectarian hagiographic treatment because of the heterodoxy of their ideas, or because they represented 'minority' religious traditions, such as Judaism. Fresh studies, therefore, seek not only to reconstruct the life of an individual, but also to illuminate their intellectual milieu and to reinstate in the foreground of historical consciousness intellectual and religious currents previously neglected or subsumed under the mainstream trends. Historians have turned to biography to illuminate the ideas of previously unknown figures and, through them, to rediscover significant religious subcultures. Perhaps the best example in modern literature is Carlo Ginzburg's (b. 1939) study, published in 1976, of the humble sixteenth-century North Italian miller, Domenico Scandella, known as Menocchio (1532–99). Using the records of the miller's inquisitorial trial, Ginzburg reconstructs Menocchio's highly idiosyncratic religious world-view, showing how it was imaginatively assembled into a meaningful whole from a haphazard collection of written texts and local oral tradition. Menocchio's cosmology, complex, sophisticated, coherent and clearly vital to his own self-perception – including such ideas as that God and the angels emerged from primordial matter in the manner of worms emerging from rotten cheese – seemed shockingly unorthodox to his judges.[8] This broadening of what constitutes religious ideas opens the way for a non-dogmatic history of belief; in Ginzburg's work, this material becomes, additionally, a manifesto for 'microhistory', of which more below.

Traditional approaches to religious history connect ideas with individuals on the one hand and institutions on the other. Most obviously, this is because so many leading early modern religious intellectuals were founders or co-founders of new institutions, whether these were denominations, sects or such organizations within the Church as religious orders. Max Weber's (1864–1920) famous notion of the 'routinization of charisma' – a model of the process whereby a founder's ideals gain permanency through the invention of institutions designed to perpetuate them, but suffer distortion and even subversion along the way – can be observed for the early modern period. The historical study of religious institutions is not new, but in the past an often rather antiquarian approach produced a narrative institutional history without connection to broader historical themes. The 'internalist', or inward-looking, tendency of such scholarship was reflected in its publication in 'house' journals, such as the *Mennonite Quarterly Review*, or historical journals produced under the aegis of the Roman Catholic religious orders, such as the leading Jesuit historical journal, *Archivum Historicum Societatis Iesu*.

As with other approaches, the watchword in intellectual history since the 1990s has been contextualization, implying a broadening of the topics considered and an explicit relating of the history of ecclesiastical institutions to mainstream historical themes and approaches, sometimes drawing upon a variety of disciplines. Such multidisciplinarity is evident, for example, in an important collection of essays on Jesuit science and the arts published in 1999. Here a highly complex, stratified and multifaceted religious institution, the early modern Society of Jesus, is approached and defined, through metaphor, as a 'cultural ecosystem' or, alternatively, as a 'global corporation', bearing comparison with modern multinational enterprises. The analysis of the Jesuits' praxis of communication, and of their role in constructing knowledge (and thereby power), is influenced by Weber, but also by post-structuralist language and concepts.[9] That the study of religious institutions can contribute significantly to the history of ideas (and vice versa) is further exemplified by Simon Ditchfield's groundbreaking 1995 study of Counter-Reformation Catholic intellectual practices. Ditchfield's patient examination of the rewriting of Church history by episcopally mandated revisers of hagiography for the liturgies of local Italian churches shows how a novel and critical, if institutionally driven, historiographical praxis was called into being in the later sixteenth and early seventeenth centuries, prompted by an urgent need to refute Protestant versions of Church history and by the centralizing ideology of papal Rome.[10]

Social and cultural 'turns'

Other approaches to early modern religious history have been less concerned with hierarchical institutions, less Church-minded, as it were. Instead, they are more interested in exploring religion as daily practice and in studying belief, especially popular belief, envisaged as embracing far more than officially sanctioned doctrine. As a result, a social history of religion, often taking the form of a religious 'history from below', has arisen, which exemplifies broader trends in social and cultural history. Marxism, sociology, the *Annales* school, social anthropology and, latterly, poststructuralism have all contributed to this development.

The classical Marxist approach to the history of religion was primarily to identify religious ideas as a reflection of broader social realities and to describe religious conflict as an expression of social (especially class) tensions. In a perhaps less explicitly Marxist fashion, this way of conceptualizing religion continues to bear fruit in studies which seek to relate the success of movements like the Reformation or Counter-Reformation to their appeal to specific social groups, and to show how economic and social group-interests might make particular religious messages more or less attractive, or allow a single message to be read in different ways.[11] This approach might be described as sub-Marxian, but it also owes much to the Weberian tradition of sociological thought. Max Weber's highly influential essay on the Protestant ethic and the spirit of capitalism (first published in 1904–5) sought to show the dynamic connections between early modern Calvinist predestinarian theology and the thrifty bourgeois accumulators who allegedly became its most enthusiastic adherents. A historical approach to religious sociology was also promoted by the French medievalist, Gabriel Le Bras, in the mid-twentieth century. Although Le Bras strongly advocated a structural approach to historical analysis, based on a statistical and quantitative study of French Catholicism, he hoped that such methods would also capture the humanity of his subject. In the process he nudged scholarship, as O'Malley has put it, 'away from "church history" to the history of practising Christians'.[12]

Methodologically, this approach brought Le Bras close to the *Annales* school of French post-war historians, whose development of the concept of a 'history of mentalities' has made perhaps the most important single contribution to the field of early modern religious history. The history of mentalities viewed religious belief not just as a set of doctrines, but also as the fundamental cosmology underlying the cultural framework of society. It also embraced religious practice, in the form of liturgy and ritual, and extended its interest to religious experience.

The *Annales* approach and method have never been confined to one period; indeed traditional periodization has been criticized heavily by the school. However, in practice, many of its adherents have worked on late medieval and early modern Europe. The importance of the *longue durée* emerges in *Annaliste* works on religion: Jean Delumeau's innovative *Annaliste* study of the Counter-Reformation, *Catholicism between Luther and Voltaire* (1971), spans the best part of three centuries.[13] *Annalistes* have also noticeably adopted the quantitative approaches of social and economic history for the history of religion: Michelle Vovelle's study of 'de-Christianization' in Provence, for example, used the statistical analysis of the content of some 20,000 eighteenth-century wills to demonstrate the growing secularization of the component groups of Provençale society under the Old Regime.[14] Quantification and the exploitation of serial sources have became essential tools for social historians of early modern religion, including those who would not necessarily subscribe totally to the *Annaliste* paradigm. Inventories and church wardens' accounts tell much about the economy of local churches and, by implication, the changing 'mentalities' of their parishioners. Testamentary records have been used, as by Vovelle, to gauge the changing levels and patterns of religious allegiance or enthusiasm, by analysing the nature and extent of bequests for pious purposes or the commendation formulae by which testators commended themselves to the deity. Baptismal records have been used to chart changes in patterns of name-giving, from Catholic to Protestant, for example, or to gauge the fluctuating popularity of particular saints' cults. The records of ecclesiastical visitations, the use of which was pioneered by Le Bras, have also been employed, perhaps most controversially by Gerald Strauss in a landmark study which sought to demonstrate that by the later sixteenth century the German Reformation had, at the grass roots, largely failed to meet the high-minded aims of its proponents.[15]

From the start, however, the *Annales* approach included not just quantitative, but also qualitative evaluation of the evidence for cultural change and its social dynamic over the long term. In Anglophone scholarship on late medieval and early modern religion, perhaps the best-known exemplar of this qualitative and hermeneutical approach is John Bossy, although, as an appraisal of his career pointed out in 2001, Bossy's work also displays a rich mix of non-*Annaliste* influences (including Weber) in a highly original combination. In a series of works on such themes as Mass, confession and god-parenthood, Bossy demonstrated the social significance of ecclesiastical ritual, and of the relationship between transformations in liturgical expression and social change in late medieval and early modern Europe.[16]

The *histoire des mentalités* of the *Annales* school has expanded into what has come to be termed the 'new cultural history', which, in Peter Burke's formulation, defines 'culture' as a system of shared meanings, attitudes and values, and the symbolic forms in which they are expressed or embodied.[17] This broad definition of culture encourages an equally generous definition of religion, to include not just formal, official belief, but also the unofficial, unorthodox or non-canonical. The latter is seen as a cultural form in its own right, as evidence of a people making their own religion, and as valid, interesting and deserving of study on its own terms as the canonical theologies and rituals promulgated by learned elites. Thus, much scholarly attention has been devoted to religious idiosyncrasy, as noted above, and to appraisals of early modern religion which naturally include magic, 'superstition' and witchcraft as part of their remit. Here early modernists might have enjoyed one advantage over scholars of other periods. It was precisely the sixteenth and seventeenth centuries which saw sustained and systematic campaigns by elites, first to define and then to reform or eradicate these non-canonical beliefs and practices, a tendency which Max Weber described as the 'disenchantment of the world', and which had its most notorious expression in the 'witchcraze'. Arguably, this horizontal religious schism – between elite and popular religion – was more significant than the vertical split between different religious denominations and constituted one of the period's most salient distinguishing features. Furthermore, it was a campaign which left much documentary evidence in the form of sermons, visitations and, most importantly of all, the records of the court cases heard by state and ecclesiastical tribunals. The existence of such rich source material offers much scope for this 'new cultural history' approach.

Few studies of early modern religion would therefore now exclude discussion of magic, witchcraft and popular religion. David Gentilcore, for example, has described the pattern of religious life in early modern Terra d'Otranto, in the heel of the Italian peninsula, as a 'sacred system'. By this, he means that the religious beliefs and practice of the population encompassed a spectrum, from those beliefs and practices endorsed and promoted by the official ecclesiastical establishment at one end, and those self-consciously unorthodox, as in the widespread recourse to cunning folk and magical practitioners, at the other. Even the Devil, it appears, might be incorporated at the popular level as a not always adversarial player within such a system. Gentilcore reconstructed the local sacred system from trial records of various kinds: inquisitorial trials for heresy, trials in secular criminal courts and 'canonisation trials', in which testimony was proffered to the ecclesiastical hierarchy concerning the lives and miracles of would-be saints. Since too few suitable records survived for quantitative analysis, Gentilcore assessed these sources qualitatively to build up a picture of the texture of religious life over the *longue durée*.

This qualitative approach owes much to the influence of social anthropology and, in particular, the school of functionalism, which stresses the efficiency of particular belief systems and religious codes and institutions as providers of the glue which binds a given society. Keith Thomas (b. 1933) and his student Alan Macfarlane drew on social anthropology in their studies of English witchcraft beliefs, making explicit a claim that comparisons between early modern and modern witch-believing societies can, by imputation, be used to fill some of the gaps in the historical record. The focus is on the social meaning of beliefs in magic. Alongside functionalism, the method of 'thick description' associated with the anthropologist Clifford Geertz (b. 1926) has influenced the new cultural history in general and the history of religion in particular, especially since religious ritual, 'thickly' described, offers plentiful scope for the exploration of social meaning and collective mentalities.[18] In the works of historians of popular religion, such as Bob Scribner, the examination of ritual has not been restricted to official liturgies, but has extended to other expressions of ritualistic behaviour, including para-liturgy and even anti-liturgy. It has been argued that forms of collective behaviour previously regarded as random, such as iconoclasm or interconfessional violence, have a highly ritualized aspect and thus a previously unseen inner logic and coherence. Similarly, the influence of anthropology has led to a new appreciation of the spatial dimension to early modern religion and of Protestantism's reordering of the pre-Reformation sense of sacred and profane space, an interest reflected in a growing number of studies of pilgrimage, processions and religiously contested space.

'Thick description' has been one of the analytic tools employed by the Italian school of 'microhistorians', originally associated with historians at the university of Bologna from the later 1960s, and above all with the work of Carlo Ginzburg. Microhistory has eschewed totalizing theories in favour of penetrating studies of individual events or lives, wherein even the most apparently everyday or trivial details are held to be suggestive of underlying cultural and social structures. Accompanying the above-mentioned *The Cheese and the Worms*, Ginzburg has produced a series of microhistorical studies on the theme of early modern religious culture. In a work first published in 1966 and later translated into English as *The Night Battles*, what appears to be an early modern fertility cult among some North Italian villagers is reconstructed on the basis of the records of inquisitorial trials. The book makes a case for the possible survival, at some level of popular substratum, of extremely ancient beliefs.[19] It also illuminates very powerfully the dynamics of the trial process and the strengths and limitations of the Inquisition as an instrument of ideological and social control. In the course of their interrogations, the accused were coerced into dropping their original stories and admitting to the charge of witchcraft. Paradoxically perhaps, the inquisitors found the confession of witchcraft much easier to handle than the (to them) bizarre heterodoxy of the villagers' original cosmology. Ginzburg's works, like Emmanuel Le Roy Ladurie's (b. 1929) classic study of the village of Montaillou, and the microhistorical approach to both society and religion, raise the problem of typicality. Not all would accept that the everyday, taken-for-granted, unwritten, normative 'grammar' of a society and its beliefs can be illuminated by the detailed study of single examples, especially when these are, perhaps extraordinary, cases of deviance. It might also be objected that a single 'snapshot' of time, an isolated moment, can tell us little about the dynamics of historical change. Paradoxically though, what emerges from Ginzburg's *Night Battles* is precisely a historical dynamic: the enduring, static world of local rural popular religion appears here to be confronted and, to an extent, 'acculturated' by a 'modernizing' force (the Inquisition) bent on its suppression.

As with the larger construct of 'popular culture' of which it may be described as a subset, popular religion as a discrete subject resists easy definition. As Bob Scribner argued, its use as a counterpart to 'elite' religion has a pedigree, by implication, dating back to the early modern period's own classifications, where binary distinctions of learned and lay, orthodox and heretical, 'religious' and 'superstitious' were axiomatic.[20] However, the period's own taxonomies are not as clearly reducible to modern notions of class – pitting the religion of the economically and politically dominant nobles and bourgeois against the religion of the poor – as some historians have assumed. Indeed, in place of an essentialized distinction between elite religion and popular religion as fixed categories, Natalie Zemon Davis (b. 1928) has preferred a more flexible model, in which a variety of overlapping religious cultures coexist. Alternatively, Roger Chartier (b. 1945) has used the term 'cultural appropriation' to describe how the same cultural forms might be appropriated, that is to say adopted, utilized or rendered meaningful, by different social groups.[21]

Likewise, a sensitivity to the nuances of cultural exchange has arisen in relation to the associated concept of 'acculturation': as Chartier puts it, 'so-called popular religion was at once acculturated and acculturating: neither totally controlled nor absolutely free'.[22] The notion of acculturation emerges from the study of one of the period's distinguishing features: the opening up of vast new fields of cultural encounter between Europeans and non-Europeans, through voyages of exploration and the beginnings of colonial conquest and settlement. Hard on the heels of conquerors, settlers and traders came Catholic and Protestant missionaries, whose efforts to spread Christianity among indigenous populations in the Americas or in the East met with varying degrees of success. An older triumphalist or apologetic historiography understood acculturation as the simple displacement of indigenous belief systems by European faith. In contrast, work since the 1980s has tended to centre on three areas: the dynamics of cultural exchange; the creative adaptation of Christianizing messages by the non-European 'Other', and the interactive nature of such cultural transfer. Fernando Cervantes's work on the role of the Devil in colonial Mexico, for example, shows how a religious syncretism arose, in which a superficially orthodox Catholic popular religious culture incorporated elements of pre-Hispanic religion.[23] The concept of 'acculturation' has also been applied by historians to missionary activity back 'home' in Europe. It is striking that not only did early modern Jesuits and other clergy take to referring to their own rural hinterland as 'our Indies', but their missions to the European countryside also borrowed from the techniques of their confrères overseas.[24] But historians have also used acculturation as a way of introducing an element of dynamism into their analyses of the general relationship between elite and popular religion, and of avoiding the relative stasis of anthropological description. Hence, Robert Muchembled depicted the European witchcraze as part of a process of elite acculturation of the rural world, although here at the risk of again reproducing reified categories of elite and popular religion.[25]

Without doubt, the impact of new trends in social and cultural history upon the study of early modern religion has been immense. In their concern to explore religion beyond the utterances of professional theologians, both social and cultural historians have fostered a vast broadening of the primary source base for religious history, as well as the development of sophisticated quantitative and qualitative methods for exploiting such sources. Investigating the religion of ordinary people has required a particularly imaginative approach, since documentary traces from the period are almost exclusively of the elite, who had little interest in describing the faith of their subordinates, except when they found it deficient and tried to suppress it. Social history has nonetheless run the risk of being too reductionist in its reading of religious belief as a mere signifier of economic and social concerns and of failing to understand past societies, especially religious societies, in their own terms. However, cultural history has restored the ideational, taking doctrines and beliefs not necessarily at face value, but more sympathetically, in its stress on the assertion that ideas shape reality, or at least people's perception of reality. Problematically, studies inspired by functionalist anthropology are in danger of limiting themselves to static models, leaving little space for an appreciation of the historical dynamic and favouring the description of an extant 'reality' over the analysis of the 'how' and 'why' of change over time. Moreover, while the profusion of local studies and microhistories has given enormous texture to our picture of religious life in early modern Europe, by definition the microhistorical approach has tended to shy away from relating this new evidence to a more general account, a metanarrative, one might say, of historical change.

Religious change, state formation and confessionalization

A notable feature of the religious history of the early modern period is provided by the varied trajectories taken by national historiographies, despite the pull of shared concepts. Recent approaches to religious history in France have been heavily influenced by the *Annales* school and those in Italy by microhistory. In Germany, the totalizing paradigm of 'confessionalization' has been a dominant framework for conceptualizing religious change. 'Confessionalization', a distinctive application of a species of modernization theory, was developed by Wolfgang Reinhard and Heinz Schilling in the early 1980s, drawing upon foundations laid earlier by Ernst Walter Zeeden and Gerhard Oestreich. This approach saw the Lutheran, Calvinist and Catholic Reformations in Germany as parallel and related movements, as instances of 'confession-building', which, even as they established rival doctrinal systems, did so in markedly similar ways, using similar tools and with similar social and political effects. Alongside accounts of doctrinal definition and the creation of new churches, emphasis was placed on the contribution of religious change to state formation. Historical analysis was therefore refocused onto the period following the Peace of Augsburg (1555), which granted German territorial rulers the right to determine the religious affiliation of their subjects. The imposition of confessional uniformity and the correspondingly enhanced power of the prince over the souls as well as the bodies of his subjects have come to be regarded as key aspects of a broader modernizing process. In these discussions, the phenomenon of 'social disciplining' figures highly. The term 'social disciplining', taken from Oestreich, is used as shorthand for the greater power exercised by early modern German princes over the everyday conduct of their subjects, from religious ritual to sexual mores, a control gained through propaganda and indoctrination, and by means of enhanced regulatory mechanisms and surveillance strategies. Confessionalization also implicitly invokes the notion of 'Christianization' and the concept of acculturation, with its detailing of the suppression of a popular religious culture and its substitution by another in line with the new confessional norms. All told, so the model suggests, the urgencies of religious conflict offered a new legitimation for the prince's grab for greater power over the Church (officially in Protestant states, unofficially but nonetheless significantly in Catholic ones) and, in turn, over society. Futhermore, this legitimation of increased princely power paved the way for the rise of absolute monarchy, and, by degrees, the modern state, with its enhanced means of social control, its expanded fiscal regimes and its rationalized bureaucracies. For historians like Schilling, it was the confessionalization process itself, rather than any single element intrinsic to Reformed or Catholic dogma (such as Weber's 'Protestant ethic'), which produced such 'modernization'.[26]

The confessionalization paradigm has certainly enjoyed immense popularity in German scholarship. One significant result has been a shift in emphasis within German Reformation historiography from the pre-1555 to the post-1555 period, the latter traditionally having been somewhat neglected in favour of interest in early reform. The equivalence of attention (and, implicitly, value) given to all the mainstream confessions, along with the incentive to fit local histories into a broader geographical and comparative framework, have been positive outcomes. Most importantly, perhaps, in linking religion with social, economic and political change and imparting an ideological aspect to state formation, the confessionalization model's totalizing approach has offered an important revision to earlier approaches to the state, as well as reviving the importance of a historical metanarrative.

Such strengths, however, can become weaknesses if pushed too far, as with most (if not all) overarching paradigms. Critics of confessionalization have attacked the model and the approach on several fronts. Some have taken issue with its allegedly reductionist and functionalist approach to its subject, redolent of the social history of religion in general, and its indifference to the nuances of theology and the great differences between the churches in areas of doctrine and spirituality. Others have questioned the strength of the new religious institutions and identities, even in the ostensibly most 'confessionalized' historical contexts, and have highlighted cultural continuities and resistance to social disciplining. Associated with this has been a scepticism in some quarters about the alleged closeness of the relationship between religion and the state. Indeed some historians have sought to underplay the role of religion and to reinstate non-religious factors in promoting modernization. Confessionalization as a model has also been attacked on the grounds that it perpetuates a modernization theory current in the 1970s and seen now as inadequate because of its reliance on teleological assumptions about the 'progressive' character of social and political change.[27] Moreover, if the relevance of the model for the study of religious change in the Holy Roman Empire is problematic, even for the history of the mainstream churches, some would say that it becomes still more so when applied to the experience of minority religions, such as Judaism, or to the history of non-German regions. Scholars of early modern religion in east-central Europe, for example, have questioned the applicability of the model to their regions. There, it seems that early modern elites often valued toleration of religious variety (rather than the imposition of confessional conformity) as the best way of keeping their states together and fostering social control.[28]

Religion, gender and postmodernism

The rise of women's history and gender history in the 1970s and 1980s has had a marked impact on the study of early modern religion. Historians of women and gender have raised long-neglected questions, among which the most fundamental and the most obvious is whether, and to what extent, women and men perceived, experienced and practised their religion differently. In the first instance, the result has been to redirect the focus of discussion from an almost exclusively male traditional cadre of theologians and ecclesiastics and their public utterances and acts, towards more private activities and spaces, including the domestic sphere, and to the sites of expression of individual and communal female spirituality. To an extent, this has also involved paying fresh attention to minority religious groups, where, in contrast to the mainstream churches, women could sometimes find an authoritative voice, as in the orbit of the early sixteenth-century Spanish Alumbrados or among some Anabaptist communities. The experience of women in the religious mainstream has, however, been the primary focus. Here, it has been traditionally more common to highlight the constraints imposed by male elites in the name of religion upon women's lives generally and their spiritual expression in particular. For Protestant Europe, the effects of the 'social disciplining' fostered by Reformation elites have been extensively explored: while the general principles of godly obedience were common to both sexes, the Reformation's reassertion of patriarchal values and its renewed emphasis upon marriage as the cornerstone of Christian society meant that, in practice, it was women's roles which were the more restricted. A similar resurgence of patriarchy has been noted in Counter-Reformation contexts as well. In Catholic Europe, however, there existed communities of female religious, whose individual and institutional records bear testimony to a vigorous and, in some respects, distinctive spiritual life, despite their subjection to stricter regimentation after the Council of Trent. Historians have sought to infiltrate the enclosures of convents and explore the religious experience of their inhabitants. Judith Brown's 1986 study of the sixteenth-century convent mystic, Sister Benedetta Carlini, may be subtitled the 'Life of a Lesbian Nun in Renaissance Italy', but, although non-normative eroticism is one of the book's themes, it is equalled in importance by the author's patient dissection of the reasons why one woman's claims to sanctity were not vindicated by broader approval. The gendered norms of behaviour, in particular the controlled deportment and linguistic modesty expected of segregated female religious, are thereby highlighted.[29] Nuns, indeed, have been one of the success stories of recent historiography, with plentiful studies of convent life, sometimes analysed through surprisingly voluminous first-hand documentary testimony. One influential study of the best-known sixteenth-century Spanish mystic, St Teresa of Ávila, has focused precisely on the rhetorical strategies chosen by its subject in order to secure both patronage and acceptance from the male ecclesiastical establishment, which seems in some respects to have treated her, ironically enough, as an honorary man![30]

Another line of approach has been to investigate the shifting fortunes of the gendered religious symbols shared by men and women. Perhaps the most important of these is the figure of the Virgin Mary, crucial to the devotional culture of Catholic and Orthodox Christians, but also occupying a place (albeit a contested one) within early modern Protestantism. Based on an examination of printed sermon literature from sixteenth- and seventeenth-century Catholic Europe, one study published in 2001 has charted a shift in emphasis in the public portrayal of the Virgin; specifically a movement away from medieval glorification of Mary's shared flesh with her son. By the later sixteenth century new sensibilities, formed against the backdrop of changing attitudes to women, as well as the impact of humanism and the Reformation, preferred to stress Mary's role as Christ's spiritual mother, united to him more closely by shared will and affection than by flesh, and to present her as silent, distant, passive and obedient.[31] In such an approach, religious symbolism provides an indicator of social change and, by the same token, the social context becomes a key to accounting for change in the symbolism. At the opposite end of the spiritual spectrum, sensitivity to the gendered nature of symbolic archetypes has also been evident in accounts of the witchcraze, especially in those influenced by women's history and gender history. How the stereotype of the witch came to occupy a significant place in the religious imagination of early modern Europeans and why witchcraft was a gender-related crime are questions more easily posed than answered. In one suggestive approach, Lyndal Roper draws on the psychoanalytic theories of Melanie Klein in order to explore the psychic dimension and inner logic of 'irrational' witchcraft fantasies and the origin of (some) accusations in the emotionally charged physical circumstances of child-birth and motherhood.[32]

The construction of masculinity has yet to find as great a resonance in the literature on early modern religion. While studies of men and of male religious institutions and communities naturally abound, few explore whether, or in what ways, their experience was distinctively masculine. Nonetheless, historians of gender have opened up new possibilities for religious history. Admittedly, while the Protestant and Catholic Reformations have been associated with what Roper has called a 'crisis of gender relations' in sixteenth-century Europe, the precise nature of this association and of the chain of causation is harder to define. It may reasonably be asked whether there were secular cultural, social, political and economic factors, unconnected (or only minimally connected) with religious values and practices, which can account for changes in the social position of women and in the relationship between the sexes. How important, in short, was religion to this story?

Lyndal Roper's reassertion of the somatic or bodily elements of experience (including religious experience) can be seen, in part at least, as a response to the influence of postmodernism. The 'new cultural history' discussed above owes much to the postmodernist or, more specifically, poststructuralist 'linguistic turn', with its alleged tendency to reduce 'reality' to discourse. Similarly, the emphasis on 'social disciplining' is clearly determined (in part, although not exclusively) by the work of the influential French poststructuralist theorist, Michel Foucault (1926–94). However, it is arguable that the poststructuralist challenge to conventional positivist historical writing has had less impact on religious history than it has in some other fields. Scholars of early modern religion have, after all, long paid close attention to the nuances of language, for their basic subject matter is primarily a discursive construct. Indeed, one could argue that there seems little need for a linguistic turn away from 'experience', given that the category of experience has itself traditionally taken second place to the language of belief, and that the role of (religious) ideology in creating and maintaining relationships of power has also been long recognized. Nonetheless, a postmodern tone can be detected in many recent applications of the approaches mentioned above. A general climate of intellectual 'subversion' has assisted that broadening of the field of enquiry away from the mainstream institutions which the social history of religion had already initiated. Postmodernism's fracture of monolithic constructs and sceptical approach to metanarratives (such as 'reform' or 'secularization') have had a ready appeal among those scholars wishing to diminish the singularity of, say, the Protestant Reformation or the compulsion to find the roots of secularization in the religious changes of the sixteenth century. Consequently, while textbooks do continue to be written on 'the Reformation' with the title in the singular, the plural, 'reformations', has become increasingly common, and it is rare for new textbooks of Reformation history not to include at least one chapter on Catholic reform. Postmodernism's emphasis on multiple perspectives has also encouraged approaches to religious history which focus more on the popular than on the elite, but at the same time less on collectivities than on individual instances.

Conclusion

What has been the net effect of the approaches to early modern religious history considered above? In the first instance, religious changes such as the Protestant Reformation are no longer seen as automatically coterminous with 'progress' or 'modernity', a shift which reflects the decline in importance of such historical grand narratives. Historians have, by contrast, been more anxious to point to continuities than to sharp ruptures and to stress the varied and uneven impact of change. Second, this has been accompanied by a substantial broadening of the definition of religion as a subject of historical analysis. The latter now spans a spectrum from formal doctrine, institutions and worship to magic, witchcraft and what at different times and places was regarded as 'superstition'. These linked but distinct phenomena are approached through the analysis of varied media, including a vast range of textual genres as well as objects of material culture, visual images and music. The history of religion may be approached as a history of ideas, but equally as a branch of a social history which concentrates on the study of a variety of religious experiences and practices and is sensitive to distinctions of place, age, class and gender.

One problem, above all, seems to emerge as a result of this broadening of the conceptual and methodological base: that of reducing religious questions to the interplay of economic and social forces and motivations and to the dynamics of class conflict or the struggle for political power. As Simon Ditchfield has written (apropos of the tendency of some modern historians to see papal canonization policy in purely 'political' terms):

> It is rather that the claim to understand the true motivations of people for whom religious belief constituted social and personal identity, embracing and informing as it did so all other aspects of their understanding of life and death, commits a serious anachronism (and category error) by assuming the existence of a deeper, 'truer' level of motivation which can only be revealed by stripping the religious mask off the faces of early modern Christians.[33]

Just as the 'new military history' is sometimes criticized for leaving out war, so the new history of religion can sometimes end up by failing to engage with the very subject which defines its field. As Euan Cameron has written, 'one needs a "social history of belief" in which the role of ideas is neither assumed, nor ignored, but *analysed*'.[34] Achieving such integration remains the primary challenge facing historians of early modern religion in the early twenty-first century.

Guide to further reading

James E. Bradley and Richard A. Muller, *Church History: An Introduction to Research, Reference Works and Methods* (Grand Rapids, 1995).

Stuart Clark, *Thinking with Demons. The Idea of Witchcraft in Early Modern Europe* (Oxford, 1997).

A.G. Dickens and John M. Tonkin, *The Reformation in Historical Thought* (Oxford, 1985).

Bruce Gordon and Peter Marshall (eds), *The Place of the Dead. Death and Remembrance in Late Medieval and Early Modern Europe* (Cambridge, 2000).

Alister McGrath, *Reformation Thought: An Introduction* (Oxford, 1988).

Edward Muir, *Ritual in Early Modern Europe* (Cambridge, 1997).

Helen Parish and William G. Naphy (eds), *Religion and Superstition in Reformation Europe* (Manchester, 2002).

Lyndal Roper, *Oedipus and the Devil: Witchcraft, Sexuality and Religion in Early Modern Europe* (London, 1994).

Keith Thomas, *Religion and the Decline of Magic* (London, 1971).

Notes

1 This view is traceable back at least to Leopold von Ranke, *Deutsche Geschichte im Zeitalter der Reformation* (Berlin, 1839–47). The debate on sixteenth-century religious changes and 'modernity' has been particularly pronounced in German scholarship. See T. Nipperdey, 'The Reformation and the Modern World', in E.I. Kouri and Tom Scott (eds), *Politics and Society in Reformation Europe: Essays for Sir Geoffrey Elton on his Sixty-Fifth Birthday* (Basingstoke, 1987), pp. 535–52.

2 A.G. Dickens and John M. Tonkin, *The Reformation in Historical Thought* (Oxford, 1985).

3 John W. O'Malley, *Trent and All That: Renaming Catholicism in the Early Modern Era* (Cambridge, MA, 2000), p. 121.

4 Steven Shapin, *The Scientific Revolution* (Chicago and London, 1996), Introduction.

5 Thomas F. Mayer, *Reginald Pole: Prince and Prophet* (Cambridge, 2000).

6 Erik H. Erikson, *Young Man Luther: A Study in Psychoanalysis and History* (1958; London, 1972), p. 54.

7 W.W. Meissner, SJ, *Ignatius of Loyola: The Psychology of a Saint* (New Haven and London, 1992), Introduction.

8 Carlo Ginzburg, *The Cheese and the Worms: The Cosmos of a Sixteenth-Century Miller*, trans. John Tedeschi and Anne Tedeschi (Baltimore, 1980).

9 John W. O'Malley, SJ, Gauvin Alexander Bailey, Steven J. Harris and T. Frank Kennedy, SJ (eds), *The Jesuits: Cultures, Sciences, and the Arts, 1540–1773* (Toronto, Buffalo, NY and London, 1999).

10 Simon Ditchfield, *Liturgy, Sanctity and History in Tridentine Italy: Pietro Maria Campi and the Preservation of the Particular* (Cambridge, 1995).

11 The social location of religion has been important in the work of a number of leading Reformation historians, including Bob Scribner for early modern Germany and Natalie Zemon Davis for early modern France: R.W. Scribner, *Popular Culture and Popular Movements in Reformation Germany* (London, 1987); Natalie Zemon Davis, *Society and Culture in Early Modern France* (London, 1975).

12 O'Malley, *Trent and All That*, p. 99.

13 Jean Delumeau, *Catholicism between Luther and Voltaire: A New View of the Counter-Reformation*, trans. Jeremy Moiser (1971; London, 1977).
14 Michelle Vovelle, *Piété baroque et déchristianisation en Provence au XVIIIe siècle* (Paris, 1973).
15 Gerald Strauss, *Luther's House of Learning* (Baltimore, 1978).
16 John Bossy, *Christianity in the West, 1400–1700* (Oxford, 1985); Simon Ditchfield (ed.), *Christianity and Community in the West: Essays for John Bossy* (Aldershot, 2001), Introduction.
17 Peter Burke, *Popular Culture in Early Modern Europe* (London, 1978), Prologue.
18 See, for example, Peter Burke, 'Sacred Rulers, Royal Priests: Rituals of the Early Modern Popes', in his *The Historical Anthropology of Early Modern Italy: Essays on Perception and Communication* (Cambridge, 1987), pp. 168–82.
19 Carlo Ginzburg, *The Night Battles: Witchcraft and Agrarian Cults in the Sixteenth and Seventeenth Centuries*, trans. John and Anne Tedeschi (London, 1983).
20 Bob Scribner and Trevor Johnson (eds), *Popular Religion in Germany and Central Europe, 1400–1800* (Basingstoke, 1996), Introduction.
21 Roger Chartier, 'Culture as Appropriation: Popular Cultural Uses in Early Modern France', in S. Kaplan (ed.), *Understanding Popular Culture* (Berlin, New York and Amsterdam, 1984), pp. 229–53.
22 Roger Chartier, 'Texts, Printing, Readings', in Lynn Hunt (ed.), *The New Cultural History* (Berkeley, Los Angeles and London, 1989), pp. 154–75, at p. 172.
23 Fernando Cervantes, *The Devil in the New World* (New Haven, 1994). See also Inga Clendinnen, 'Franciscan Missionaries in Sixteenth-Century Mexico', in Jim Obelkevich, Lyndal Roper and Raphael Samuel (eds), *Disciplines of Faith: Studies in Religion, Politics and Patriarchy* (London, 1987), pp. 229–45.
24 Louis Châtellier, *The Religion of the Poor: Rural Missions in Europe and the Formation of Modern Catholicism, c.1500–1800*, trans. Brian Pearce (1993; Cambridge, 1997).
25 Robert Muchembled, 'The Witches of the Cambresis: the Acculturation of the Rural World in the Sixteenth Century', in J. Obelkevich (ed.), *Religion and the People, 800–1700* (Chapel Hill, 1979), pp. 221–76.
26 R. Po-Chia Hsia, *Social Discipline in the Reformation: Central Europe, 1550-1750* (London, 1989).
27 For a discussion of these critiques, see Ute Lotz-Heumann, 'The Concept of "Confessionalization": a Historiographical Paradigm in Dispute', *Memoria y Civilización* 4 (2001), pp. 93–114.
28 Maria Crăciun, Ovidiu Ghitta and Graeme Murdock (eds), *Confessional Identity in East-Central Europe* (Aldershot, 2002).

29 Judith C. Brown, *Immodest Acts: The Life of a Lesbian Nun in Renaissance Italy* (Oxford, 1986).
30 Alison Weber, *Teresa of Avila and the Rhetoric of Femininity* (Princeton, 1990). For case studies of the pressure on Catholic women in the Hispanic world in the Counter-Reformation, see Mary E. Giles (ed.), *Women in the Inquisition: Spain and the New World* (Baltimore and London, 1998).
31 Donna Spivey Ellington, *From Sacred Body to Angelic Soul: Understanding Mary in Late Medieval and Early Modern Europe* (Washington, DC, 2001).
32 Lyndal Roper, *Oedipus and the Devil: Witchcraft, Sexuality and Religion in Early Modern Europe* (London, 1994), pp. 199–225.
33 Simon Ditchfield, ' "In Search of Local Knowledge". Rewriting Early Modern Italian Religious History', *Cristianesimo nella storia* 19 (1998), p. 265.
34 Euan Cameron, *The European Reformation* (Oxford, 1991), p. 3.

8

Economy and material life

Clare Haru Crowston

Scholars have long treated the economy and material life as central issues in early modern history. Indeed, the distinction between 'early modern' and 'modern' itself derived from an understanding of the economic changes that were supposed to have brought the pre-modern period to a close and ushered in the modern era. Up to the mid-1970s at least, the watershed that created the 'modern' for many historians was the Industrial Revolution and the birth of capitalism. Europe thus became modern as property relations changed, as a new class system emerged from the old caste hierarchies and as politics were recast to give prominence to the new bourgeois elite. In this Marxian view, the source of the modern world lay in a great economic transformation that in turn produced that world historical event par excellence, the French Revolution.

After 20 years of revolt against the Marxist model, we find a historiographical context in which economic production per se has been discredited as the catalyst of historical change. The French Revolution has in many ways retained its status as a transformative event, but now the transformation is seen in political and cultural terms, set loose from economic determinism.[1] However, even in this new context, economic and material life continues to hold a decisive sway over many historians' understanding of the transition from the early modern to the modern era. On the one hand, the Industrial Revolution is still seen by most historians as a crucial turning point in European and indeed world history; on the other, a rival literature on the 'consumer revolution' of the eighteenth century has developed since the 1980s and is still thriving. This literature asserts that the emergence of a consumer culture in this period essentially created the modern world as we know it, with an abundance of finished goods available to all social classes and individual identity developed and expressed through selective consumption of commodities.[2]

This chapter examines the role played by different theoretical frameworks in these historiographies. To what extent have historians drawn on theories from the discipline of economics to understand the early modern economy and material life? What other theoretical frameworks have they used? What insights have historians gained from their engagement with theory and what limitations may we identify? The first issue to be addressed in answering these questions is the gap that exists between economic historians per se and other types of historians who devote attention to economics and material life. In general, communication between those who define themselves as economic historians and those who do not is sorely lacking. Economic historians are often lodged in economics departments and are thus institutionally and intellectually isolated from developments in the wider discipline. For their part, historians who work on issues touching the economy and material life (labour historians, historians of consumption, social historians, historians of women and gender, and so on) seldom read the work of economic historians and consider their work to be of an essentially different nature.

The metanarratives of Marx and Malthus

One result of the observation noted above is that the implicit and explicit theoretical frameworks sustaining works on the early modern economy rarely derive from the discipline of economics itself. Historians of early modern Europe have been distrustful of economics as a discipline and, by extension, of economic theory. They have tended to assume that economic theory evolved – from British economists Adam Smith (1723–90) through David Ricardo (1772–1828), Alfred Marshall (1842–1924) and John Maynard Keynes (1883–1946) – in conjunction with industrial capitalism and that it served as an implicit ideological justification for that economic system and the political regimes that uphold it. They have believed that economic theory assumes an individual, rational, economic actor engaged with a perfect market system and that it is thus profoundly ahistorical in nature. For historians concerned with treating the past as a foreign country and understanding the mentalities and values of historical actors on their own terms, economic theory seemed to demand from the outset eliminating major areas of historical change and interest. Therefore, instead of making use of economic theories used by economists themselves, they often adopted theories from scholars in the social sciences, who viewed economic questions through the lens of society and culture.

A second result is that the theorists most heavily used derived their perspectives precisely from an engagement with early modern European history itself. Indeed, their theoretical projects consisted primarily of explaining how and why the modern world arose from the pre-modern.[3] This offered the advantage of providing historians with theories that were built on the specific period they wished to understand. It also presented the disadvantage, however, of building a teleological reading of the early modern period into the very framework adopted to understand that history. Because they relied on theorists whose main goal was to explain the birth of modernity, historians accepted that there was a fundamental difference between the modern world and what preceded it. As a result, a set of prefabricated assumptions – about historical change, periodization and progress – underpinned much historical writing about the early modern period.

Marx

Karl Marx (1818–83) is the obvious starting point in this discussion. Marx has been and in many ways remains the most influential thinker for historians interested in how economics shaped early modern Europe.[4] According to Marx, the transition from feudalism to capitalism began in the early modern period. England represented the ideal type for this transition. Through enclosure of common land, large landowners created ever bigger and more efficient farms, acting as prototypical capitalists. Rising agricultural production freed peasants to become wage labourers in the cities. The Glorious Revolution (1688–89), wherein the Catholic James II was replaced by the Protestant William III and Mary II on the English throne, enshrined the political power of capitalist landowners and great merchants by giving them control over the constitutional monarchy. By contrast, France was a case of stalled development. The stubborn traditionalism of French peasants and their successful resistance to enclosure led to stagnant agricultural production. Commerce and manufacturing suffered from guild regulations and resistance to innovation. The French Revolution transferred power to bourgeois capitalists, but France remained economically backward compared to England.

Marx's theory has profoundly impacted early modern historical research regarding periodization, class formation, economic growth and industrialization, politics and the emergence of modern nation states. Historians like Eric Hobsbawm (b. 1917) drew on Marx to explain Britain's successful, rapid path toward industrialization and its basis in the enclosure movement, entrepreneurial capitalism and early and rapid mechanization. Historians also sought signs of class formation and working-class consciousness in the late eighteenth and early nineteenth centuries, as the first urban proletariat emerged from the industrialization process. For France, *Annales* historian Ernest Labrousse's (1895–1986) massive study of eighteenth-century price movements established an 'economic crisis' in the late 1780s that explained the origins of the Revolution. Emphasizing this backdrop of economic and therefore social crisis, Georges Lefebvre (1874–1959), another *Annaliste*, identified 'bourgeois' characteristics of major actors in the Revolution and the 'proletarian' ideals of the more radical figures, like the sans-culottes (groups of poor Parisians who became mobilized during the Revolution).[5] For the German states, Marx's work led historians to locate an explanation for the failure to develop adequate bourgeois, liberal foundations in the crushing weight of feudal privileges, the impoverished and suppressed peasantry and the too fledgling commercial and urban sector.[6]

The large-scale framework of Marxist analysis has been sharply criticized in recent decades. For example, economic determinism has been discredited as a means to understand the political and social movements of seventeenth- and eighteenth-century Europe. It is now clear that political positions cannot be mapped neatly onto objective social classes, nor can the birth of capitalism be credited with catalysing political change.[7] The usefulness of Marxist analysis for understanding social life is also in question. The cultural turn in history has sharpened the critique of the notion of class, leading many to see it as formed through cultural discourse rather than the collective experience of a certain relation to the means of production.[8]

In economic terms, historians have elaborated and challenged Marx's explanation of how, when and why industrialization took place. Franklin Mendels contributed the notion of 'proto-industrialization', arguing that cottage industry in rural areas was not a pre-industrial activity, but in fact constituted the first stages of the industrialization process. Thus, industrialization did not emerge as a sudden break in the late eighteenth century, but had long roots in the early modern period. In a series of books and articles, Peter Kriedte, Hans Medick and Jürgen Schlumbohm have elaborated on Mendels's initial contribution. They have defined proto-industry as production for export – most often in the textile industries – that used simple technology and drew industry from urban areas to profit from the low wages and work hunger of poor rural populations. In addition to fostering a symbiotic relationship between cottage workers and merchants, proto-industrialization allowed poor peasants to embark on marriage and procreation earlier in life, thereby transforming traditional demographic behaviour and contributing to a rise in population. Kriedte, Medick and Schlumbohm also asserted that proto-industrialization led to proletarianization among rural workers, thereby easing the path for urban industrialization.[9]

The 'proto-industrialization' model has generated significant debate among historians, some of whom deny the central importance it has been accorded in the rise of capitalism. The most recent literature on proto-industrialization stresses the variety of forms of proto-industry across types of product, wealth and family strategies of workers.[10] As the original theorists of proto-industrialization were inspired by contemporary debates about growth in developing countries, the model has in turn been important for scholars of the pre-modern non-West, intent on identifying autonomous, non-western paths to industrialization. The advantage of proto-industrial theory for them is that it provides a theoretical explanation for the indigenous growth of capitalism and thereby frees non-western countries from their assumed reliance on imported models and practices.[11]

Malthus

While the Marxist model of the French Revolution was the guiding framework of revolutionary historians like Georges Lefebvre and Albert Soboul (1913–82), other important twentieth-century works of French social and economic history drew on the ideas of an earlier theorist. Robert Thomas Malthus (1766–1834) was a political economist who argued that population had the natural tendency to grow until checked by the limits of the available food supply. The Malthusian model was crucial for the *Annales* school, which dominated French historiography from the 1930s to the 1980s. A pessimistic Malthusian perspective lay at the heart of *Annales* historians' interpretation of the early modern period. Technological constraints meant that the food supply was always limited and vulnerable to bad weather, crop disease and other natural disasters. The Malthusian scissors thus opened as the gap expanded between the demands on resources and the available supply of them, and brutally closed in the form of disease, death and decreased fertility until equilibrium was reached once more. Across Europe, population thus stagnated – with a few significant fluctuations. Only in the mid-eighteenth century did the decline of disease, better weather conditions and shifting mentalities allow for agricultural improvement and significant growth in population. The Malthusian dilemma was eased even more at the turn of the nineteenth century as contraceptive techniques became widespread. Henceforth population growth would be controlled primarily through fertility, not death.

A corollary of demographic and economic stagnation was the conviction that society and culture also remained largely static, particularly in the countryside. *Annales* historians such as Marc Bloch (1886–1944), Fernand Braudel (1902–85) and Emmanuel Le Roy Ladurie (b. 1929) thus identified a long period of 'traditional' or 'immobile' society emerging after the Black Death in the fourteenth century, continuing unchanged to the mid-eighteenth century and persisting, in some ways, up to World War I. For centuries, they claimed, social relations and values in the peasant village remained as untouched as agricultural techniques. Indeed, in the *Annales* view, cultural fears of risk taking and resistance to change, forged by the Malthusian dilemma, played a decisive role in obstructing economic growth. As Le Roy Ladurie argued in *The Peasants of Languedoc* (1966), technological stagnation was 'the result of a whole series of cultural stumbling blocks' resulting from 'the customs, the way of life, the mentality of the people'.[12] For him, as for other *Annalistes*, the 'economy was servant not master, dictated to not dictator. Importantly as it loomed in the early stages of our studies, in the last analysis the economy seems to have been fairly obedient to the great forces of life and death'.[13] For the early modern period, at least, demography was the driving force of history.[14]

The Malthusian framework of the *Annales* model has received harsh criticism from economic historians, who question the immobility of traditional society and the assumption that technological limitations and cultural backwardness were the factors inhibiting growth. Phillip Hoffman argues that this view does not hold up against the mounting evidence produced by his and other historians' research, which shows, he asserts, that peasants did in fact trade in markets, reap the benefits of technological advances and employ economic strategies to advance their interests. Transaction costs, not resistance to change, played the major role in inhibiting economic growth: 'the real obstacles to growth lie elsewhere: with politics, with institutions, and with the rest of the economy – in particular, with the economy's ability to provide human and physical capital and opportunities for trade'.[15] Thus, Hoffman credits peasants with a rational approach to economic questions and the capacity to make choices within the constraints of the imperfect markets they faced.

Exchange, reciprocity and the moral economy

Historians looked to the social sciences, primarily anthropology and sociology, to develop insight beyond Marxian or Malthusian metanarratives. There they found emphasis on pre-modern societies as collectivities, where exchange functioned to form and maintain reciprocal social ties rather than to further individual interests. Economic concerns were embedded in wider social values; a moral economy predated the market economy. Anthropologist Marcel Mauss's (1872–1950) *The Gift* (1925) has informed the work of many early modernists. Drawing on ethnographic studies of the north-west coast of North America and the Pacific Islands, Mauss argued that in pre-market societies the central mode of exchange was gift giving.[16] The shared practice of gift giving was a means of building social ties. Each gift – be it an object, person or service – called for another gift in return, creating an interwoven and ongoing network of reciprocal relations. In turn, the gift-giving system shaped cultural values; generosity and largesse were prized, while individual accumulation was shunned as an antisocial behaviour.[17]

Mauss's view of historical change was ambiguous. He asserted that Roman law instituted an opposition between people and objects, thus marking a decisive step away from the gift economy for western society. Mauss also believed, however, that a long transitional period followed this break, with the gift system persisting in many ways, until the emergence of market society and money finally displaced it. Even in modern European societies, he noted, traces of the gift economy lingered in Christmas and birthday gifts. Historians of early modern Europe have tended to use Mauss's work not to understand economic life per se but to clarify the rituals governing social and political life and the central role of reciprocal exchange in such rituals.

In *The Gift in Sixteenth-Century France* (2000), Natalie Zemon Davis (b. 1928) downplays the evolutionary side of Mauss, stressing instead elements of continuity and interaction among different forms of exchange. For Davis, gift giving coexisted with the market-based economy in sixteenth-century France. Because monetary transactions normally ended after payment, gifts were used to personalize and extend mutually beneficial relationships. Gift giving was practised across many social and political forms, including noble patron–client relations, in intellectual circles, between the king and his subjects and between God and believers. Davis uses her study to argue the wider point that historians must stop thinking in linear terms and accept the coexistence and interaction of multiple systems of thought and practice.

Despite emphasizing historical continuity, Davis argues that the gift system was profoundly implicated in two crucial transitions. In the sixteenth century, French subjects' exchange of gifts with their king during royal entries still displayed elements of reciprocity. By the late seventeenth century, the rise of royal power under Louis XIV (1638–1715) had eliminated any pretence of reciprocity between subjects and king. In the religious arena, Davis portrays the Protestant Reformation as bound up with a fundamental change in notions of gift giving and reciprocity. Calvin rejected in Catholicism the idea of the possibility of reciprocal exchange with God. Belief in the efficacy of good works and the sacrifice of the mass implied that humans could give God gifts that carried obligations on divine grace. Calvin replaced this idea with an image of God as a transcendent giver and humans as humble receivers. Thus, while the gift economy did not *cause* Absolutism or the Reformation, it did act as the vehicle through which profound concerns about relations of authority and exchange were experienced and expressed. With the abandonment of the mutually obliging relationships fostered by the gift economy, the French had taken decisive steps towards 'modern' conceptions of political power and religious authority and freed the individual to become a capitalist economic actor.[18] It seems that an evolutionary model remains at the heart of Davis's use of Mauss, despite her claim to the contrary.

The birth of the capitalist spirit: Max Weber and the Protestant Reformation

Another influential social scientist was the sociologist Max Weber (1864–1920). In *The Protestant Ethic and the Spirit of Capitalism* (1904) Weber argued that the theology of the Protestant Reformation contained elements particularly conducive to the development of capitalism. The idea of vocation, the emphasis on the here and now and, especially, the doctrine of predestination all made converts to Protestantism more likely to become good capitalist subjects. Predestination mattered because it made people strive for the exemplary (honest, hard-working, self-disciplined and austere) conduct that would prove they were chosen for salvation. Rich and successful entrepreneurs could thus congratulate themselves on possessing tangible proof of God's grace.

Weber directly challenged the Marxist notion that economic conditions created culture, positing that a 'capitalist spirit' pre-dated capitalism itself and was a necessary precursor to it.[19] This capitalist spirit dictated that: 'Man is dominated by the making of money, by acquisition as the ultimate purpose of his life. Economic acquisition is no longer subordinated to man as the means for the satisfaction of his material needs'.[20] The accumulation of capital and its investment in commercial or industrial enterprises did not themselves create capitalism; instead, it was a product of entrepreneurs possessed of the capitalist spirit who went out and acquired the necessary capital for their ventures. Protestantism – and Calvinism, in particular – played a crucial role in shaping and propagating the capitalist spirit.

Weber rejected the notion of an inevitable march towards capitalism in which Protestantism played a merely functional role, viewing capitalism's rise as a result of historically contingent circumstances. Yet he shared with Marx the notion of a radical split between the pre-capitalist, 'traditionalist' world and the modern capitalist one. Although Weber did not define traditionalism, he provided several examples of the confrontation between traditionalist mentalities and the new capitalist spirit: among agricultural pieceworkers, female workers and cottage workers in the textile industry.[21] By inference, Weber's 'traditionalism' consists of a suspicion of the profit motive, an unsystematic approach to work and earning, the desire to live and work according to established traditions rather than rational principles, and a valuing of non-economic over economic values. The result of the introduction of capitalist rationalism, according to Weber, was always the same: 'those who would not follow suit had to go out of business'.[22] The spread of the capitalist spirit – and the rise of capitalism itself – thus destroyed the traditional world in the West and the 'natural' embeddedness of the economy within culture and society.

Weber's thesis has sparked a long debate among historians and social scientists.[23] Marxian historians resisted the priority he accorded to cultural factors.[24] Others shared Weber's search for a cultural explanation for capitalism, yet differed in their interpretation of the effects of culture. Simon Schama in 1987 offered a reading of Dutch Calvinist culture deeply engaged with the Weberian model, but critical of it. Schama agreed with Weber in rejecting materialism and seeking an explanation for Dutch economic activity in a particular set of cultural traits. However, he ultimately rejected the notion that Calvinism itself produced individuals more likely to accumulate wealth for investment and seek signs of their predestined salvation in worldly success. Indeed, he underlined the comfortable and even luxurious lifestyles the Dutch enjoyed, against their preachers' strident protests. Yet far from feeling reassured by his wealth, a successful merchant was as likely to worry that he was straying into sin and tempting fate. For Schama, a paradoxical combination of civic pride and dread of disaster characterized the Dutch, who had achieved so much so quickly in the face of Spanish oppression and the incursion of the sea. The charity and good works that distinguished Dutch society were thus one way of soothing the 'embarrassment of riches'. Calvinism profoundly shaped Dutch commercial culture not by creating ascetic, self-denying entrepreneurs, but by producing an ambiguous mixture of comfort, ambition and constant anxiety.[25]

Consumption and material culture

In the 1980s and 1990s, early modern historians have increasingly shifted their focus away from production and towards changes in consumption. This shift was intended to challenge the previous concentration on production and the search to explain the rapid growth of production in the Industrial Revolution. Consumer-oriented history was pioneered by British historians Neil McKendrick, John Brewer and Roy Porter, and, for France, by Daniel Roche.[26] Together, they have argued that a 'consumer revolution' occurred across the eighteenth century. Through an examination of printed sources and probate inventories, these historians and their successors have documented the spread of consumer goods across wide sectors of the population. From clothing to porcelain, to food, water and heat, Western Europeans made significant gains in consumption that cut across class lines. Not only did the comfort of everyday life improve; for the first time, ordinary people could aspire to choose from among superfluous commodities.

An important element of this research has been a focus on gendered patterns of consumption. Research on France and Britain has shown that women were central participants in the consumer revolution. For example, in France, Roche noted: 'In all social categories, it was women who were chiefly responsible for circulating the new objects [of dress] and the new values of a commercialized fashion and superfluous consumption'.[27] In turn, Roche's discovery of women's dominant role in the consumption of clothing has been linked to women's large-scale entry to the garment trades.[28] In an accelerating cycle, female participation in paid labour – largely in the needle trades – gave women the income and the taste for fashionable dress. Attempting to reconcile the pessimism of social historians' accounts of stagnant wages and falling living standards with the optimism of consumer historians, Jan de Vries has argued for a late seventeenth-century 'industrious revolution'. This revolution witnessed the large-scale entry of women and girls to the paid labour market, as part of a conscious strategy to achieve greater consumption of market goods. According to de Vries, this new orientation to labour and consumer markets was the necessary prerequisite for industrial revolution.[29]

Beyond women's empirical participation in purchasing items of consumption, historians have also argued that eighteenth-century observers ascribed consumption itself with feminine characteristics. Like women, the new modes of consumption based on fashion and individual desire were capricious, superficial, vain and self-indulgent (as opposed to the more sober and austere consumption of traditional society). The creation of a modern consumer society thus coincided with the emergence of a gendered split between a private feminized sphere of consumption and a public masculinized sphere of political and economic activity.[30] As this example suggests, the shift in historians' focus from production to consumption was often paralleled by a shift from socio-economic to cultural history. Increasingly, historians have focused on the 'meaning' of consumption and how European men and women experienced their relationship to the expanded variety of goods available to them. In this cultural turn, they have echoed broader trends in the historical discipline.

Research on consumption is one area where the most important theorists have not been those who dwelt on the early modern period itself. The economist Thorstein Veblen (1857–1929), who analysed the growth of a leisure class in late nineteenth-century America, is perhaps the most important theorist for historians of consumption.[31] His notion of social emulation – where conspicuous consumption is driven by the desire of lower social classes to emulate their superiors and the subsequent flight of superiors to new styles in order to maintain their prestige – has been used frequently to explain the dynamic behind early modern consumption patterns.[32] As Neil McKendrick argued, 'Spurred on by social emulation and class competition, men and women surrendered eagerly to the pursuit of novelty, the hypnotic effects of fashion, and the enticements of persuasive commercial propaganda'.[33] This argument has drawn strenuous critiques from some historians, who point out that evidence for the model is largely drawn from statements by social elites and based on elites' limited understanding of the behaviour of other social groups.[34] The suspicious and self-congratulatory nature of elite perceptions notwithstanding, imitation is not necessarily emulation. The same style may have had different meanings and messages for different social groups.

Studies of early modern consumption have offered new perspectives on the catalysts for growth and the significance of economic change. They have also brought welcome new attention to women's relationship to the market and the gendered effects of economic transition and consumption. This literature, nonetheless, in large part continues the paradigm of a momentous shift from early modern to modern that was at the heart of the earlier literature. The consumer revolution displaces the Industrial (or the French) Revolution, but the framework of revolution remains in place. Like the earlier forms of revolution, the consumer revolution is credited with creating the modern world. According to this literature, pre-modern consumption was for the most part collective, traditional, unchanging and unreflective. The modern world emerged when the consumer revolution allowed men and women to become individuals through the development of taste and style in the choice of their clothing and food. At stake in the birth of a consumer society was the birth of individuality, self-expression and a new relationship between private and public, all hallmarks of the modern world.[35]

Another noteworthy aspect of this historiography is the light it sheds on a glaring theoretical absence in the study of the early modern economy and material life: the lack of engagement with postcolonial or transnational theories. This does not mean that attention to the transnational *contexts* of European economics has been lacking. Since the eighteenth-century origins of political economy itself, accounts of European economic life have frequently emphasized the crucial context of empire for trade and commerce.[36] In this area, however, we have – in striking contrast with trends in the larger historical discipline –witnessed a move away from emphasizing colonial affairs. Recent work in British economic history has tended to downplay the importance of the colonies, arguing that colonial trade did not play the decisive economic role that earlier historians had imagined.[37]

Debates among economic historians about the relative weight of colonial trade will no doubt continue. What is more striking is the ways in which historians of consumption and material life, who have argued for a cultural approach to history and for attention to previously neglected topics such as women and gender, should have paid so little attention to the growing scholarship on western representations of foreign 'others' and the powerful effects such representations have had on colonized peoples abroad and colonizers at home. Studies of consumption have discussed the colonial origins of products like tea, coffee and chocolate and they have often emphasized the fashion for the 'exotic' and the 'oriental' that drove so much of elite consumption in this period.[38] Few studies, however, place such issues at the centre of their concerns and bring to bear the theoretical apparatus of postcolonialism or transnational studies.[39] We have considerable empirical material, for example, on trade in textiles between Europe and South and East Asia, but we have few studies that address in a sustained or sophisticated manner the cultural significance of such ties or the passion for 'oriental' dress styles through the eighteenth century. Given the substantial scholarship on such questions for the period of high imperialism, we may expect this situation to change in the coming years.

The newer economic history

If most social and cultural approaches to the early modern economy and material life continue to rely tacitly on the framework of a fundamental divide between the pre-modern and the modern, a stringent critique of this framework comes from the field of economic history itself. It arises, in particular, from what has been called the 'newer economic history'. Due to the division that exists between economic history and the rest of the discipline, these criticisms have received little attention outside the field and deserve some elucidation here. The newer economic history continues to look to economic theory, yet to a discipline that has moved beyond neoclassical assumptions of unfettered rationality operating in perfect markets. Practitioners of the newer economic history have adopted a number of theoretical tools from current work in economics. Whether or not they use mathematical models (and some do not), they have introduced concepts that considerably complicate the neoclassical model. These include transaction costs, information asymmetries and bounded rationality. Transaction costs is a blanket term that refers to myriad expenses and obstacles involved in bringing goods to exchange.[40] 'Information asymmetries' are the limited and partial knowledge that actors bring to their market activities. Following this, the concept of bounded rationality acknowledges that individuals' 'rational' choices will always be shaped by their limited and partial understanding of available opportunities and constraints. Following current trends in economics, practitioners of economic history tend to focus on a micro-analysis of markets and their operation, rather than attempting macro-level explanations for the birth of capitalism or the Industrial Revolution.[41]

Philip Hoffman, Jean-Laurent Rosenthal and Gilles Postel-Vinay have been among the most active proponents of a renewed dialogue between economic theory and history. These historians object to the continuing hold of the transitional model of early modern history. In their eyes, this view has wrongly persuaded historians that economic theory cannot be used for pre-modern – by definition 'non-economic' – societies. They also argue that prior certainties about what produces economic growth have led historians to focus only on elements of pre-modern society that have survived and thrived in the modern financial world. These assumptions thus limit the tools historians can use to approach the early modern world and pre-determine which elements of it were historically significant. Overall, 'The traditional story . . . obscures the workings of pre-modern economies by making economic behaviour in the pre-modern world seem stranger than it really was'.[42]

In a series of books and articles, Hoffman, Rosenthal and Postel-Vinay have used models drawn from economic theory to re-examine the economy and society of early modern France. In economic terms, the major contribution of Hoffman's *Growth in a Traditional Society* (2000) is its reassessment of French agricultural productivity. Given the lack of firm data on agricultural production, Hoffman focuses on the 'total factor productivity' of agriculture. He uses information on land rent and wages, on the one hand, and food prices, on the other, to compare the total cost of inputs into agriculture and the cost of outputs. His assumption is that a rise in the ratio of rents to food prices signals a rise in productivity, because if farmers are willing and able to pay more for land that they will use to produce goods sold at the same price, they must be producing more goods.[43] This indirect means of calculation is vulnerable to critique, yet economic historians on the whole have approved Hoffman's method and the results it produced.[44] Having sampled a number of regions across France, he finds that growth was tremendously variable according to region and across time. The area around Paris performed as well as the vaunted English model, but most other regions showed little sustained progress. Farm size had little effect on productivity, thus disproving the old assumption that the enclosure movement enabled superior production. Peasants were capable of innovation and of fostering significant growth in agricultural production. They were heavily and often successfully involved in market transactions, to which they brought calculation and strategy. The impetus and results of their strategizing were more often conflict and discord than they were the collective, harmonious values assumed by the notion of moral economy.

For England, Hoffman's findings are backed by the work of Robert C. Allen. Allen also used the total factor productivity model, which showed that growth in agricultural production in England occurred primarily in the second half of the seventeenth century, that is, in a period when legal restrictions prevented enclosure. According to Allen it was British yeomen – small farm-owning peasants – who produced this growth through innovation, hard work and sound calculation. A second, smaller period of growth did occur during the eighteenth century as a result of enclosure. Measurable growth in total factor productivity, however, was not due to an actual increase in productivity of the land, but to a decline in employment on large farms. Landowners benefited from rising rents and prices, but the situation of most rural dwellers declined. As Allen declares: 'The conclusion is unavoidable – most English men and women would have been better off if the landlords' revolution never occurred'.[45]

Economic historians have also challenged traditional views of the Industrial Revolution. For England, N.F.R. Crafts and C.K. Harley have criticized the standard view that technological innovations in manufacturing created a sudden boom in productivity from 1780 to 1830. Instead, they argue, 'New estimates of national income per caput identify a longer period of transition. Growth had probably begun to accelerate by the early eighteenth century but modern economic growth only became fully established in Britain in the railway age'.[46] The period prior to 1760 was more industrial than we have believed and the latter part of the century experienced less sudden and significant growth. Crafts and Harley are careful to acknowledge, in response to criticism from fellow economic historians, that an Industrial Revolution did occur, which gave Britain a unique position in manufacturing and external trade; it is the timing and the pace of the revolution they question.[47]

For France, which was supposed to represent the negative counter-example to England, we now understand that its economic trajectory was not dysfunctional, just different. Given French market niches in luxury trades, it made sense for French industry to focus on high-quality production in small workshops.

Apart from its challenges to assumptions about the timing and pace of growth, one of the most provocative contributions of the newer economic history as practised by Hoffman and his colleagues is its way of understanding historical actors. As we have seen, Philip Hoffman's study relies on assumptions about the (bounded) rationality of peasants in seeking their interests. He also rejects notions of a 'transcendent group interest' dictating their actions and the assumption that exchange serves to cement collective values and community. The economist's perspective, he claims, allows more room not only for individual choice and strategy, but for strife and conflict in communities as well.[48]

Hoffman's understanding of early modern rationality is not solely drawn from economic theory. He also draws on the perspective of Italian microhistorian, Giovanni Levi. In his microhistorical reconstruction of a Piedmont village, Levi argues that the economic actor of neoclassical theory is a myth:

> A man who makes his decisions with a well-defined utility function, who chooses among well-defined alternatives, who has a solid image of the probability distribution of all future events, and who maximizes the expected value of this utility function is in large measure a theoretical fiction, even in contemporary societies.

He also contends, however, that previous generations of historians built up their own image of the early modern actor in opposition to that model: 'as a man at the mercy of the elements, of tradition, and of uncertainty, and incapable of active or strategic behaviour'.[49]

His alternative to these extremes is to accord early modern peasants a bounded rationality and strategic agency. Peasants were confronted by a series of rules and norms generated by a variety of institutions, but they maintained the ability to negotiate among the demands of competing institutions. Similar to the newer economic historians' emphasis on imperfect markets and information asymmetries, Levi underlines that the rules were ambiguous and inconsistent and information incomplete and often distorted. Peasant society was painfully aware of the limits on information, but it was not 'paralyzed by insecurity, however, nor was it hostile to all risk taking, passive, or entrenched for protection behind the bastions of immobile values'.[50] Instead, peasants constantly sought to improve the predictability of their environment, most often by mobilizing extended kin networks. Economic advancement was a secondary goal compared to the primary importance of diminishing uncertainty and vulnerability.

Given this new emphasis on bounded rationality and strategic choices among peasants, the question becomes: how did they make choices and what criteria did they employ? Where Levi focuses on the importance of family ties, Hoffman emphasizes the key role of reputation for transactions that took place beyond the family. In making loans, renting land or exchanging goods, what mattered was an individual's reputation for honesty and trustworthiness and his prior record in keeping his word. Relying on reputation was not a backward or uneconomic practice, it was a workable 'solution to the problem of trust – or, in the jargon of economics, moral hazard – inherent in extending credit'.[51] According to Hoffman, reputation was not simply a concern of the lowly, but was as important for the tenant farmer seeking to rent land as it was for the landlord renting it.

As we now know, reputation was equally crucial in urban settings. In a co-authored study of urban financial markets, Hoffman, Postel-Vinay and Rosenthal take on another sacred assumption of the older visions of history, that France was economically backward in developing credit due to its lack of autonomous financial institutions. They show that in fact an enormous amount of credit was generated in eighteenth-century Paris through the mediation of notaries, who drafted and certified contracts, deeds, and so on. Since notaries had personal knowledge of their clients – who tended to use the same notary for multiple transactions – they were well placed to judge the financial situation and trustworthiness of potential lenders and borrowers. In a study of credit in early modern England, Craig Muldrew similarly underlines the key role of reputation, reminding us of the double meaning of credit in economic and social terms. As he states, 'the early modern economy was a system of cultural, as well as material, exchanges in which the central mediating factor was credit or trust'.[52] Although Muldrew is often critical of economic theory and its applications in history, his findings offer striking echoes with the themes of the newer economic history.

As this example suggests, current work in economic history intersects in exciting ways with insights historians are drawing from other disciplines and theories. For example, Philippe Minard offers new perspectives on French economic regulation informed by work in the sociology of conventions. He begins with a paradox: why did manufacturers in the textile industry demand that the government enforce detailed and restrictive regulations over their production practices? Eighteenth-century liberals castigated such demands as backward and ignorant, arguing that merchants should understand that free markets would be more efficient for their own interests and for French economic development as a whole. Historians have largely followed suit. Against these views, Minard argues that regulation served to foster 'the social organization of confidence' among producers, intermediaries and buyers in the textile industries.[53] Because cloth was sold in tightly bound rolls, often to buyers who were not physically present for the sale, confidence in the quality of the goods was a serious problem. The government seal of approval allowed buyers to be confident about the goods they were receiving. Manufacturers demanding regulation were therefore not guilty of a traditional or backward mentality, but were acting to eliminate a major obstacle to trade. Minard's larger argument is that historians should pay attention to what historical actors claim as their own motivations and seek the rationale of their actions, rather than dismissing them as belonging to an inherently irrational, pre-modern mentality.

These arguments change our understanding of the economic life of early modern Europe. It now appears that the Industrial Revolution was not one period of sharp change but a much longer and varied process. It is clear that there was not one proper path to development but several. The basis of the Industrial Revolution in an earlier Agricultural Revolution brought about by enclosure by enterprising capitalist landowners is also in doubt. Moreover, given the intense regional variation scholars have found and the blurring of once familiar national distinctions, one must question the usefulness of the national framework. Ordinary people engaged in markets in many different ways throughout the early modern period, not just in the cities – as Fernand Braudel implied – but in the countryside as well. Urban–rural connections were dynamic and complex in ways that require continued attention.[54]

Beyond economic history per se, these results have important implications for the broader questions in social, cultural and political history that have long fascinated historians. First of all, the assumption that the period 1780–1815 represents a sharp turning point between the pre-modern and the modern must be seriously questioned. Our 'gut feeling' that this is the key transitional moment does not always hold up to the latest scholarship.[55] It would be understandable if early modernists were reluctant to follow this path, for it means abandoning our claim to outstanding historical significance, one that is not easy to maintain in a discipline increasingly weighted towards contemporary history.

Apart from this general point, taking seriously early modern people's engagement with markets and the notion of transaction costs calls for new ways of viewing the state, society and culture. For example, it changes our understanding of the state's relationship to the economy. Rather than thinking about the state's regulation of industry as part of an overall (and misguided) mercantilist project to increase production and decrease reliance on imports, we should think about the state's activities in removing or increasing transaction costs and their impact on a local and national level. The notion of transaction costs and work in the sociology of conventions together urge a new emphasis on the importance of reputation and confidence. In a world where people are engaged with markets but lack formal institutions regulating them, confidence and reputation are key factors that allow people to exchange. Strategies for building confidence and establishing reputations (as well as for demolishing them) take on new importance in understanding village and neighbourhood life. Familiar players like notaries and state inspectors take on a new meaning in this perspective. One has to wonder where women and their reputation would fit into this picture. The ever-present problem of sexual reputation and the challenges of public self-presentation must have rendered women's multiple dealings with credit – in the market place, in their own mercantile activities – particularly complex.

Another fascinating contribution of these historians is the new way they encourage us to understand human behaviour and motivation. Rather than seeing early modern people as ruled by collective mentalities, we can now imagine them as possessed of a bounded rationality that sought the best possible solutions in situations of imperfect access to knowledge and resources. By lossening the bonds of mentality or discourse, we can imagine early modern actors as strategists who possessed limited but real agency to assess possibilities, devise strategies and make choices. Having shed ourselves of the teleological burden of modernization narratives, we can wonder about the strategies that did not work or were only partially successful, and which have faded from historical recollection.

These achievements are open to doubts from historians in social and cultural history, who may find that the newer economic history has insufficiently distanced itself from the neoclassical model. We can identify at least four potential areas of concern. First, the notion of power, so important to both social and cultural history, is not developed as an explicit theme in the newer economic history. Reintroducing the notion of power might require us to complicate the notion of 'reputation'. For example, if the personal nature of early modern markets calls on economic agents to be concerned with their reputation, what about people – like nobles – whose social and economic standing carries a pre-established and persuasive reputation? Surely there were individuals whose social and economic standing allowed them to get what they wanted regardless of what others thought of them. Second, the emphasis on choice is also sure to elicit criticism from historians wary of the very notion of free exchange. They might ask how well the term 'choice' describes the experience of exchange partners whose very inequality rendered the stakes and open-endedness of the transaction completely different. As William Reddy noted precisely with regard to tenancy agreements: 'However freely both parties entered into the transaction, the owner had only inconvenience at stake; the tenant feared destitution. The rich can afford to be capricious; the poor must therefore be careful'.[56]

A third potential area of concern is the lack of attention to discourse, a central theme of the new cultural history.[57] In the context of current historiographical trends, it is striking that Hoffman's world is one where no one appears to say anything. Our primary access to what early modern people thought and believed are the records noting what they did. Little time is spent examining their categories of thought or their representations of the physical and social worlds they inhabited. In this respect, Hoffman differs little from Le Roy Ladurie (at a certain period in his career), who claimed: 'when it comes to words, I am rather like the semiliterate of the nineteenth century . . . I have had my work cut out learning to count, never mind learning to read as well!'[58] Moreover, Hoffman asserts that the perfect market did not exist, but he pays little attention to those who were busy proclaiming that it should and were trying to bring it into existence. One wonders how he would fit these writings into a wider picture of economic change and strategic action. One also wonders what insight into human ideas and motivations this model offers. How much can we learn about what inspired actors to exchange or what they understood about their exchange activities by simply assuming a bounded rationality and examining the choices it makes?

A final, and related, area of concern is the focus on individuals. In the newer economic history (as in its earlier forms) it is largely individuals who make choices in terms of their own perceived best interests. While it seems clear that throwing individuals back into the primordial stew of 'mentalities' is not the answer, simply freeing individuals from collective values and interaction seems an inadequate alternative. Hoffman dismisses this objection simply by saying that a Foucauldian negation of all human agency is not a historical approach he can accept.[59] Surely there is room for compromise between an absolute negation of human agency and a sole focus on individuals. A great deal of historical interest lies precisely at the intersection between individual and group, a hinge that the newer economic approach does not seem able to pry open.

As these questions suggest, the solution to earlier problems with the application of theory in early modern historical writing is probably not a wholesale switch to models drawn from economic history. The tools of economic history offer a powerful complement to, not a replacement of, those of social, cultural and political history. This field has nonetheless generated important contributions that all early modern historians should take into account. In particular, we need to come to terms with the impact new findings in economic history have for old and new assumptions in social, cultural and political history. The stakes of this re-evaluation are higher than they may initially appear, for the new cultural history – for all its criticism of metanarratives and overarching theories – has largely adopted the 'revolution' framework and its teleological notion of periodization. Thus, the editors of a recent collection argue for a reassessment of the period from 1750 to 1820 as an age of 'cultural revolution'. As they state, 'It is as though the revolutionary arch over this period is being re-erected even while its content is changing before our eyes'.[60] The drift of the revolutionary model into cultural history demonstrates how tenacious the model is and how difficult it will be to achieve a new synthesis that takes account of the findings of a generation of economic historians.

As always, the best way forward will lie in a combination of different approaches and a greater mutual sharing of ideas among historians in different fields. Recent publications in mainstream and specialized journals suggest that this is underway. The current interest in literary studies in reuniting 'culture' and 'economy' is a promising model for historians.[61] We can look forward to the fruits of this new exchange and, some day, to the disappearance or radical reshaping of the very categories of 'early modern' and 'modern' Europe.

Guide to further reading

Fernand Braudel, *Civilization and Capitalism, 15th–18th Century*, 3 vols, trans. Siân Reynolds (New York, 1982–84).

John Brewer and Roy Porter (eds), *Consumption and the World of Goods* (London, 1993).

Natalie Zemon Davis, *The Gift in Sixteenth-Century France* (Madison and Oxford, 2000).

Victoria de Grazia (ed.), *The Sex of Things: Gender and Consumption in Historical Perspective* (Berkeley and Los Angeles, 1996).

Philip T. Hoffman, Gilles Postel-Vinay, Jean-Laurent Rosenthal, *Priceless Markets: The Political Economy of Credit in Paris, 1660–1870* (Chicago, 2001).

Pat Hudson, 'Economic History', in Stefan Berger, Heiko Feldner and Kevin Passmore (eds), *Writing History: Theory and Practice* (London, 2003), pp. 223–42.

Karl Marx, *Pre-Capitalist Economic Formations*, trans. Jack Cohen, ed. E.J. Hobsbawm (New York, 1964).

Thorstein Veblen, *The Theory of the Leisure Class* (1899; New York, 1994).

Max Weber, *The Protestant Ethic and the Spirit of Capitalism*, trans. Talcott Parsons (1904–5; London, 1976).

Notes

1 Thanks to Philippe Minard, Laura Lee Downs, Antoinette Burton and the members of the 'History Workshop' at the University of Illinois at Urbana-Champaign for their helpful comments. On the continued assumption that the French Revolution marked the birth of modernity and the implicit Marxism involved see Rebecca L. Spang, 'Paradigms and Paranoia: How Modern Is the French Revolution', *American Historical Review* 108(1) (2003), pp. 119–47.

2 Neil McKendrick, John Brewer and J.H. Plumb (eds), *The Birth of a Consumer Society: The Commercialization of Eighteenth-Century England* (Bloomington, 1982); John Brewer and Roy Porter (eds), *Consumption and the World of Goods* (London, 1993); Daniel Roche, *The Culture of Clothing: Dress and Fashion in the 'Ancien Régime'*, trans. Jean Birrell (1989; Cambridge, 1994); Daniel Roche, *A History of Everyday Things: The Birth of Consumption in France, 1600–1800*, trans. Brian Pearce (1997; Cambridge, 2000); Annik Pardaihlé-Galabrun, *The Birth of Intimacy: Privacy and Domestic Life in Early Modern Paris*, trans. Jocelyn Phelps (1998; Philadelphia, 1991).

3 The same is true of other influential theorists such as Michel Foucault, Norbert Elias, and Jürgen Habermas.

4 For an accessible introduction to Marx's account of history, see Karl Marx, *Pre-Capitalist Economic Formations*, trans. Jack Cohen, ed. E.J. Hobsbawm (New York, 1964).

5 Georges Lefebvre, *The Coming of the French Revolution*, trans. R.R. Palmer (1939; Princeton, 1947); *The French Revolution*, trans. Elizabeth Moss Evanson, John Hall Stewart and James Friguglietti, 2 vols (revised edn, 1951; New York, 1964–65).

6 See William Reddy, *Money and Liberty in Modern Europe: A Critique of Historical Understanding* (Cambridge, 1987) for Marxism's influence on European historiography.

7 Alfred Cobban, *The Social Interpretation of the French Revolution* (Cambridge, 1964); George V. Taylor, 'Noncapitalist Wealth and the Origins of the French Revolution', *American Historical Review* 72 (1967), pp. 469–96; William Doyle, *Origins of the French Revolution* (Oxford, 1980). For the 'revisionist' school, see François Furet, *Interpreting the French Revolution*, trans. Elborg Forster (Cambridge, 1981).

8 E.P. Thompson, *The Making of the English Working Class* (New York, 1966); Patrick Joyce, *Class* (Oxford, 1995); Reddy, *Money and Liberty*; William Sewell, *Work and Revolution in France: The Language of Labor from the Old Regime to 1848* (Cambridge, 1980).

9 Franklin Mendels, 'Proto-industrialization: the First Phase of the Industrialization Process', *Journal of Economic History* 32 (1972), pp. 241–61; Peter Kriedte, Hans Medick and Jürgen Schlumbohm, *Industrialization Before Industrialization: Rural Industry in the Genesis of Capitalism* (Cambridge, 1981).

10 Jürgen Schlumbohm, 'Labour in Proto-industrialization', in Maarten Prak (ed.), *Early Modern Capitalism: Economic and Social Change in Europe, 1400–1800* (London and New York, 2000), p. 126.

11 Immanuel Wallerstein (b. 1930) offered his own modification of Marxist economic theory by insisting on the global dimensions of capitalism: *The Modern World System*, 3 vols (New York, 1974–89); *The Capitalist World Economy: Essays by Immanuel Wallerstein* (Cambridge, 1979).

12 Emmanuel Le Roy Ladurie, *The Peasants of Languedoc*, trans. John Day (1966; Urbana, 1974), p. 298.
13 Emmanuel Le Roy Ladurie, 'History That Stands Still', in his *The Mind and Method of the Historian*, trans. Siân and Ben Reynolds (1973; Chicago, 1981), pp. 3–4.
14 Fernand Braudel offered a more nuanced version of immobile history. In his celebrated three-volume examination of *Civilization and Capitalism*, Braudel divided the economy into three tiers: material civilization, market exchange and capitalism. Braudel acknowledged that markets had existed since time immemorial and even suggested that capitalism – which he relegated to a small group of individuals involved in international finance – had a long history before industrialization. Markets and capitalists were mostly consigned to the city, however; Braudel shared the notion that the material life of most Europeans living in small peasant villages hardly altered over the course of centuries. Fernand Braudel, *The Structures of Everyday Life: The Limits of the Possible*, trans. Siân Reynolds (Berkeley and Los Angeles, 1979), vol 1 of *Civilization and Capitalism*, p. 27.
15 Philip T. Hoffman, *Growth in a Traditional Society: The French Countryside, 1450–1815* (Princeton, 1996), p. 19.
16 He relied, in particular, on Bronislav Malinowski's work on the Trobriand Islanders. Bronislav Malinowski, *Argonauts of the Western Pacific* (1922; Prospect Heights, IL, 1984).
17 Marcel Mauss, *The Gift: The Form and Reason for Exchange in Archaic Societies*, trans. W.D. Halls (1950; New York and London, 2000) Another important figure is Karl Polanyi, a Hungarian economist and economic historian, who argued passionately against the use of modern economic models for pre-industrial society. Karl Polanyi, *The Great Transformation: The Political and Economic Origins of Our Time* (1944; Boston, 2001).
18 Natalie Zemon Davis, *The Gift in Sixteenth-Century France* (Madison, 2000). Davis argues that the sixteenth-century Protestant 'ideal type' was an individual who did not locate exchange in collectivist perspective. She does not evoke Weber, but her arguments fit into the Weberian thesis.
19 He states, 'we must free ourselves from the idea that it is possible to deduce the Reformation, as a historically necessary result, from certain economic changes'. Max Weber, *The Protestant Ethic and the Spirit of Capitalism*, trans. Talcott Parsons (1904–5; London, 1976), pp. 90–1.
20 Weber, *Protestant Ethic*, p. 53.
21 Weber, *Protestant Ethic*, pp. 36, 59–63, 65–7.
22 Weber, *Protestant Ethic*, p. 68.
23 See Anthony Giddens's introduction to Weber's *Protestant Ethic*, pp. 8–12.

24 R.H. Tawney and Christopher Hill both accepted Weber's thesis of a special affiliation between Protestantism and capitalism, but ultimately gave causal priority to capitalism; Margaret C. Jacob and Matthew Kadane, 'Missing Now Found in the Eighteenth Century: Weber's Protestant Capitalist', *American Historical Review* 108 (2003), pp. 46–8.
25 Simon Schama, *The Embarrassment of Riches: An Interpretation of Dutch Culture in the Golden Age* (New York, 1987).
26 See note 2, above.
27 Roche, *Culture of Clothing*, p. 504.
28 Clare Haru Crowston, *Fabricating Women: The Seamstresses of Old Regime France, 1675–1791* (Durham, NC, 2001).
29 Jan de Vries, 'Between Purchasing Power and the World of Goods: Understanding the Household Economy in Early Modern Europe', in Brewer and Porter (eds), *Consumption and the World of Goods*.
30 On women's relationship to consumption, see Victoria de Grazia (ed.), *The Sex of Things: Gender and Consumption in Historical Perspective* (Berkeley, 1996); Amanda Vickery, 'Women and the World of Goods: a Lancashire Consumer and her Possessions, 1751–81', in Brewer and Porter (eds), *Consumption and the World of Goods*.
31 Also important is Pierre Bourdieu, *Distinction: A Social Critique of the Judgment of Taste* (Cambridge, MA, 1984).
32 Thorstein Veblen, *The Theory of the Leisure Class: An Economic Study of Institutions* (1899; New York, 1994).
33 Neil McKendrick, 'The Consumer Revolution', in McKendrick, Brewer and Plumb (eds), *Birth of a Consumer Society*, p. 11.
34 Grant McCracken, *Culture and Consumption: New Approaches to the Symbolic Character of Consumer Goods and Activities* (Bloomington, 1988); Colin Campbell, *The Romantic Ethic and the Spirit of Modern Consumerism* (Oxford, 1989).
35 See McKendrick, Brewer and Plumb (eds), *Birth of a Consumer Society*, esp. Introduction; Roche, *Culture of Clothing*, esp. Conclusion.
36 James D. Tracy (ed.), *The Political Economy of Merchant Empires: State Power and World Trade, 1350–1750* (Cambridge, 1992); James D. Tracy, *The Rise of Merchant Empires: Long-Distance Trade in the Early Modern World, 1850–1750* (Cambridge, 1990); Philip D. Curtin, *Cross-Cultural Trade in World History* (Cambridge, 1984).
37 For the strongest critic of the role ascribed to the colonies, see Patrick O'Brien, 'European Economic Development: The Contribution of the Periphery', *Economic History Review* 35 (1982), pp. 1–18. See also John J. McCusker and Kenneth Morgan (eds), *The Early Modern Atlantic Economy* (Cambridge, 2001); David Cannadine, 'The Empire Strikes Back', *Past & Present* 147 (1995), pp. 180–94.
38 Carolyn Sargentson, *Merchants and Luxury Markets: The Marchands Merciers in Eighteenth-Century Paris* (London, 1996); Maxine Berg and

Helen Clifford (eds), *Consumers and Luxury: Consumer Culture in Europe, 1650–1850* (Manchester, 1999).

39 For an exception, Benjamin Schmidt, 'Inventing Exoticism: The Project of Dutch Geography and the Marketing of the World, circa 1700', in Pamela H. Smith and Paula Findlen (eds), *Merchants and Marvels: Commerce, Science, and Art* (New York and London, 2002).

40 Philip T. Hoffman and Jean-Laurent Rosenthal, 'New Work in French Economic History', *French Historical Studies* 23(3) (2000), p. 447.

41 James R. Farr, 'Introduction' to 'Forum: New Directions in French Economic History', *French Historical Studies* 23(3) (2000), p. 418.

42 Philip T. Hoffman, Gilles Postel-Vinay and Jean-Laurent Rosenthal, 'Information and Economic History: How the Credit Market in Old Regime Paris Forces Us to Rethink the Transition to Capitalism', *American Historical Review* 104(1) (1999), p. 70.

43 Philip Hoffman, *Growth in a Traditional Society: the French Countryside, 1450–1815* (Princeton, 2000).

44 George Grantham, 'The French Agricultural Productivity Paradox: Measuring the Unmeasurable', *Historical Methods* 33(1) (2000), pp. 36–46.

45 Robert C. Allen, *Enclosure and the Yeoman* (Oxford, 1992), p. 21.

46 N.F.R. Crafts and C.K. Harley, 'Output Growth and the British Industrial Revolution: A Restatement of the Crafts-Harley View', *Economic History Review* 45(4) (1992), p. 705.

47 Maxine Berg and Pat Hudson, 'Rehabilitating the Industrial Revolution', *Economic History Review* 45(1) (1992), pp. 24–50; Julian Hoppit, 'Counting the Industrial Revolution', *Economic History Review* 43(2) (1990), pp. 173–93; R.V. Jackson, 'Rates of Industrial Growth During the Industrial Revolution', *Economic History Review* 45(1) (1992), pp. 1–23. See Crafts and Harley's responses in 'Output Growth and the British Industrial Revolution'.

48 Hoffman, *Growth in a Traditional Society*, pp. 76–7.

49 Giovanni Levi, *Inheriting Power: the Story of an Exorcist*, trans. Lydia G. Cochrane (1985; Chicago, 1988), p. 44.

50 Levi, *Inheriting Power*, p. xv.

51 Hoffman, *Growth in a Traditional Society*, p. 78.

52 Craig Muldrew, *The Economy of Obligation: The Culture of Credit and Social Relations in Early Modern England* (London and New York, 1998), p. 2.

53 Philippe Minard, 'Colbertism Continued: The Inspectorate of Manufactures and Strategies of Exchange in Eighteenth-Century France', *French Historical Studies* 23(3) (2000), p. 488; Philippe Minard, *La Fortune du colbertisme: Etat et industrie dans la France des Lumières* (Paris, 1998).

54 Gilles Postel-Vinay, *La Terre et l'argent* (Paris, 1998).

55 The 'gut feeling' belongs to Colin Jones and Dror Wahrman, 'An Age of Cultural Revolutions?' in Jones and Wahrman (eds), *The Age of Cultural Revolutions: Britain and France, 1780–1820* (Berkeley and Los Angeles, 2002), p. 2.

56 Reddy, *Money and Liberty*, p. 66.

57 See, for example, Gareth Stedman Jones, 'The New Social History in France', in Jones and Wahrman (eds), *Age of Cultural Revolutions*.

58 Le Roy Ladurie, 'History That Stands Still', pp. 3–4.

59 Phillip Hoffman, *Growth in a Traditional Society*, p. 274, n. 15.

60 Jones and Wahrman, 'An Age of Cultural Revolutions?' in Jones and Wahrman (eds), *The Age of Cultural Revolutions*, p. 2.

61 Erin Mackie, *Market à la Mode: Fashion, Commodity, and Gender in* The Tatler *and* The Spectator (Baltimore and London, 1997); Liz Bellamy, *Commerce, Morality and the Eighteenth-Century Novel* (Cambridge, 1998); Geoffrey Clark, *Betting on Lives: The Culture of Life Insurance in England, 1695–1775* (Manchester, 1999); Catherine Ingrassia, *Authorship, Commerce, and Gender in Early Eighteenth-Century England: A Culture of Paper Credit* (Cambridge, 1998).

9

Politics

Lloyd Bowen

The definitions of what constitutes 'the political' in early modern history are legion. For some, 'political history' is self-evidently the study of the actions of monarchs, ministers and MPs; others have stressed the need to see politics essentially as a product of socio-economic changes; yet others have sought to locate politics within the parish and the household, seeking to uncover the manner in which it structured power relations at these more prosaic levels. Such differences of approach not only are functions of divergences in historians' perspectives, but also reflect the deeper influences of the context within which historians have worked and the presumptions and theoretical underpinnings they bring to bear upon the broadly defined early modern period. This chapter endeavours to explore this fractionation in the writing of early modern political history and to illustrate some of the ways in which this can be related to the prejudices, predilections and politics of its authors. We shall see how 'political history', once considered solely as the machinations of monarchs, statesmen and parliaments, has transmuted into a more pliable and socially diverse category in recent accounts. The chapter focuses particularly on British historiography of the seventeenth century, one of the most contested and fruitful in terms of conflicting interpretations of its political processes and significance.

'Our master interpreter': Gardiner, Ranke and the writing of political history in the late nineteenth century

The early modern period has long been a principal focus for political historians in Britain, largely because of the seismic developments, principally the Reformation, Civil War and Glorious Revolution, which were believed to have played a central role in shaping 'modern' society and the values upon which it was constructed. English historians in particular have looked to the sixteenth and seventeenth centuries as the crucible within which the essential elements of modern liberal parliamentary democracy were first extracted and refined. The political world of the nineteenth century was in many ways structured by reference to the history of the early modern period and the linear and progressive path which had led, inexorably, to the acme of imperial grandeur under Queen Victoria in the nineteenth century. The seventeenth century, and particularly the convulsions of the civil wars of the 1640s and 1650s, had attracted the attention of men like Thomas Carlyle (1795–1881), who used history to lament the problems of the present; importing moral lessons from the lives of great men like England's Lord Protector Oliver Cromwell (1599–1658). In the 1840s, Carlyle bemoaned how England had 'wandered very far' from the guiding ideas of the seventeenth century and 'must endeavour to return, and connect ourselves therewith again!'[1] However, his grieving over the loss of Christian principles which he believed to have animated men like Cromwell had less influence in the fledgling English historical academy of the nineteenth century than the method of the German historian Leopold von Ranke (1795–1886).

Ranke rejected the idea of studying history for its moral messages and advocated the examination and presentation of past societies in their own terms rather than refracted through present-minded agendas. The Rankean ideal, with its emphasis on objectivity and 'scientific' accuracy, has had an enormous influence in configuring perceptions of the historian's role and his or her relationship with the period s/he studies. This is true of the writing of early modern political history also, influenced in no small measure, perhaps, by the fact that Ranke's own study of the English people concentrated on the seventeenth century.[2] His method was revered by contemporaries as the 'correct' approach for studying political developments in early modern society, and perhaps the most influential of his acolytes was Samuel Rawson Gardiner (1829–1902), who wrote his mammoth *History of England* between 1856 and 1901.

Gardiner's massively detailed and meticulously researched project on British politics from 1603, with the accession of James I to the English throne (he had been King of Scotland since 1567), to the middle of the Protectorate, in 1656, has been hugely influential in establishing the narrative framework for interpreting this disturbed period and for identifying the principal characters and institutions which would form its primary focus. Gardiner was a forthright advocate of Rankean precepts, calling Ranke the 'father of modern historical research' and writing a laudatory essay on this paragon of historical objectivity in 1886.[3] He eschewed importing contemporary political prejudices into the interpretation of the convulsions of seventeenth-century England, claiming that mapping the attributes and perspectives of Whig and Tory, Liberal and Conservative onto the royalists and parliamentarians of the 1640s was wholly misplaced. He asserted that the continued evaluation of the past by comparison with the present was 'altogether destructive of real historical knowledge', and advocated rather the 'scientific study of history as a whole'. Gardiner's works were written in Rankean ink and in them he endeavoured to reconstruct the politics of the seventeenth century in its own terms, 'for the mere sake of understanding them'. In order to achieve this almost hermetic objectivity in the evaluation of the political events of the seventeenth century, Gardiner adopted a remarkable commitment to chronology. He determined to restrict his research by examining only those sources relevant to the particular short period he was examining at any given time; it was even said that he would refuse to examine a source for 1654 until he had finished writing a section on 1653. Gardiner adopted this approach in the belief that it would insulate him from prejudging the outcome of events and so restrict to a minimum the bias of hindsight in his work. Here was the Rankean ideal of examining historical societies within their own contexts writ large, and Gardiner's method was deemed as one of the most praiseworthy elements in this new 'scientific' approach to political history.

The form and content of Gardiner's *History* have served as the template for much of the political history subsequently written on early modern England. In Gardiner's *magnum opus*, narrative, chronological development was emphatically the form within which the true political nature of England could emerge. This narrative revolved around the politics of princes and parliaments, of struggles over the development of the English constitution, of the great battles and set pieces of the Civil Wars and the personalities of King Charles I (1600–49) and Oliver Cromwell. Gardiner emphasized the animating force of religion, especially puritanism, and its influence within the House of Commons. His work set the agenda for the study of seventeenth-century political history for decades, with an emphasis on 'high' politics, the 'political class' of the gentry and the great leaders of the 'opposition' to Charles I, particularly the parliamentarian and Puritan John Pym (1583–1643). His story revealed how parliament threw off the shackles of its Tudor subjugation to the monarchy and moved towards its rightful place at the centre of the English constitutional system.

For all the claims to empirical objectivity made for Gardiner's work, his narrative is suffused with the assumptions and partialities of the intellectual, political and religious milieu within which he operated.[4] He was a lapsed member of the millenarian Irvingite Church, which he abandoned in favour of Darwinian evolutionism. He was descended from Oliver Cromwell's daughter, although he claimed that this did not influence his attitude to the Lord Protector. He became a convinced and active Liberal, who viewed the leader of his party and twice prime minister, William Gladstone, with something approaching reverence, and clothed his leading historical players and early Stuart England's polity in a distinctively

Victorian-Liberal fabric. He described, for example, the Committee of Both Kingdoms, established in the 1640s to direct parliament's war effort and to coordinate the English and Scottish armies' military strategy, as 'the first germ of the modern Cabinet system', while Cromwell's proposals to Charles I in November 1648, he asserted, anticipated 'in all essential points, the system which prevails in the reign of Victoria'. Despite an adherence to chronology, throughout Gardiner's *History* the English parliament and men like Cromwell emerge as vessels of political *progress*, pitted against an obstructionist and reactionary Tudor governmental system. These progressive, forward-looking agencies naturally formed the focus of his interpretation of the period's political history, as they embodied the values and ideals which had triumphed by the nineteenth century. In a Darwinian schema, Gardiner identified those elements of the English polity which were strongest and best suited to survive, and which consequently embodied best the Liberal values of post-reform England. In many senses, the seventeenth century was viewed for its role in the *evolution* of English parliamentary democracy. He stated that 'it was here [England] that religious and political liberty was ultimately adopted', and he determined to 'tell the story at least of the earlier stages of the process of the discovery of that situation'. The criterion against which political values and institutions were measured, against which they succeeded or failed, was the degree to which they agreed with the national character of the English people. Although Gardiner pioneered a type of history which examined the interconnectedness of the three kingdoms of early modern Britain, England, London and the House of Commons very much occupied centre stage. His was a national political history. Consequently, intertwined with an extended exegesis of the 'laws by which the progress of human society is governed', was an amorphous but pervasive idea of a 'national will' which could assert itself in unfolding political events. Charles I was defeated in part because of his 'positive antagonism to the national spirit', while the republican governments of the 1650s failed because, although they had removed 'obstacles from the natural development of a nation', namely, Charles I and his ministers, their illiberal (il-Liberal?) agendas ensured that they too would be swept away in turn.[5] Gardiner's 'Whiggish' interpretation, then, was predicated upon ideas of progress and evolution, with a fixed end of a liberal parliamentary democracy in sight, an end which needed explanation through the structures of history.

Despite the acknowledgement by later generations that the purity of his objectivity and commitment to a 'scientific' and wholly objective approach were flawed, Gardiner's work has proven immensely important in establishing the basic narrative of seventeenth-century English political history and its principal *dramatis personae*. The writings of associates and followers like Charles Firth (1857–1936) and Godfrey Davies (1892–1957) helped ensure the continued influence of Gardiner's work, despite the emergence of new approaches to the study of politics. The British academic Austin Woolrych (1918–2004) produced an 800-page narrative history of the Civil Wars in 2002 which immediately brings to mind Gardiner's *History*.[6] Like most of his contemporaries, Woolrych's high political narrative acknowledges its debt to 'the great Samuel Rawson Gardiner', whose approach had been defended through periods of historiographical flux by scholars like Davies. In some senses Gardiner's claim to represent the pinnacle of 'objective' and 'correct' early modern political history endures to the present day.

We shall now examine how this focus on high political narrative has remained central to the writing of early modern political history throughout the twentieth century, before turning to some of the challenges it faced from historians who instead emphasized the role of social and economic forces in understanding early modern politics.

G.R. Elton and the defence of political history

One of the most prominent and influential intellectual heirs of the Rankean tradition, refracted through the challenges to narrative history posed by the social sciences and Marxism discussed below, was Geoffrey Elton (1921–94). Elton was a Cambridge academic and émigré from Nazi Germany, whose principal interest was in the high politics of the Tudor period, especially the administrative history of Court and parliament, which he covered in a series of studies between the 1950s and the 1980s.[7] He also made several forays into the intellectual and theoretical underpinnings of historical writing, providing a vigorous defence of the idea that political history should be studied for its own sake and on its own terms. He advocated objectivity and the primacy of sources in the study of the past and the rejection of the idea that history could in some way explain the present. As we shall see, he was writing at a time when social science and Marxist approaches were reformulating the writing of political history, but Elton shunned such methods, believing them to be corrupted because of the extent to which they imposed ahistorical organizing principles on the past. Elton was rather the most vocal advocate of a more 'traditional', Rankean, political history as the 'proper' lens through which the past should be studied. It was no accident that Elton chose the deliberately provocative title of 'Professor of English Political and Constitutional History' at Cambridge in 1967, when a good deal of the history then produced had turned its back on the kinds of political history he wished to see written.

Elton was a staunch supporter of empirical method and the primacy of (particularly governmental) sources. He believed in an inductive relationship with these materials, where questions and the structure of the answers would emerge naturally from the sources: he claimed his ideas on an administrative 'Revolution' in the 1530s 'came to my mind . . . because the evidence called them forth'.[8] He highlighted human agency and autonomy in history, based on reason and independent of grand social forces and trends, arguing that the activity of men (women did not loom large in his world-view) was the proper focus for the reconstruction of the past. Elton's insistence on the examination of discrete periods of political history for the 'truths' they could reveal led him also to reject the teleological organizing framework of 'Whiggish' history, which charted historical narratives with the aim of explaining a result that was already known. This saw him effectively becoming the first so-called 'revisionist' in his denial of the linkages between the Tudor and Stuart periods in the grand narrative of a 'high road' to civil war.

Despite these claims, however, Elton can be seen to have written political histories which contained their own modernizing paradigms, seeing the early modern period as a crucial era of transition in the formation of the modern English state. His emphasis on the administrative 'revolution' of the 1530s, under Henry VIII's minister Thomas Cromwell (1489–1540), locates a clear break between medieval (personal) and modern (bureaucratized) government, and he wrote that historians were entitled to 'speak of a revolution from the medieval to the modern state' in this period.[9] Additionally, for all his vocal rejection of attempts to systematize the past through grand social and economic theories, his presentation of the purity and pre-eminence of political action and organization assumes a similar function: his account of 'the organizational aspects' of high politics offers a progressive organizing narrative through which the 'truths' of the past are made known to the historian.[10]

Revisionism

Although Elton's work demonstrates significant genealogical lineages from Ranke, he provided an important inspiration to a revolution in the study of England's high politics in the 1970s and 1980s, which became known as revisionism. From the early twentieth century, constitutional and parliamentary history had, for the most part, constituted the central raw materials from which the structures of early modern political history had been built. Following Gardiner and A.F. Pollard (1869–1948), scholars such as Wallace Notestein (1878–1969), Sir John Neale (1890–1975) and, more recently, Robert Zaller wrote political histories which dealt primarily with the House of Commons rather than the other two elements of the parliamentary triumvirate. This concentration on parliament in early modern English political histories was largely the product of the teleological necessity of explaining the crisis of the mid-seventeenth century. In many ways, then, the Tudor and early Stuart periods were rendered as prologues and 'politics' was formulated as the constitutional and ideological differences which emerged between monarchs and their subjects within the walls of Westminster. The narratives that these historians produced continued to be shaped as stories of 'evolution' and 'progress', of explaining the precocious constitutional development of England through set-piece confrontations between a reactionary monarchy and a modernizing Commons.

This kind of teleology was attacked by the emerging wave of revisionist scholars from the early 1970s. Revisionists rejected the underlying modernization narratives and ideological and social determinism which characterized the writing of much Tudor and Stuart history to this point. They abandoned the dialectical framework within which much of this history operated, as political history was apparently corralled into a narrative which was *required* to explain consequences such as the Civil War or the Glorious Revolution of 1688, through a clash of progress versus conservatism, or a more Marxist idea of conflict between ideologically motivated classes. In their place, the revisionists stressed the contingent and pragmatic rather than the structural, the epiphenomena of politics rather than viewing it simply as the expression of long-term, structural developments. Politics, however, largely remained that which emerged from the apparatus of governmental machinery, and it continued to be located very much within Westminster and Whitehall. Although many 'revisionists' attested to the importance of provincial contexts, for the most part this was used only to enrich and help explain the political narratives at the centre.

A good deal of this revision, particularly associated with Conrad Russell (1937–2004), was centred about reclaiming the Gardinerian ideal of judging periods on their own terms, of providing a new political narrative, particularly for early Stuart England, and focusing on 'the last redoubt of "whiggery"', the high politics of parliament.[11] In Russell's classic, *Parliaments in English Politics, 1621–1629* (1979), he rejected the tendency to analyse the parliaments of the 1620s in a rising crescendo of antagonism which was effectively a precursor of civil war. Rather he stressed the degree to which these parliaments were characterized by agreement, and the extent to which divisions between elements within the Court and government were often as responsible for political tensions as any institutional antagonism between king and parliament. The prevailing discourse of this political world was the search for consensus and cooperation in place of the conflict and division which had dominated almost all previous discussions. (This stress on social harmony may be seen in part, too, as a response to the Marxist emphasis on conflict.) Here parliament was not a rising but a declining institution, its inability adequately to finance a war rendering it an increasing irrelevance for the hard-pressed Stuarts. The puritan elements within the Commons were not the proto-revolutionaries of Neale and Gardiner, but were now cast as the conservatives, seeking to shore up the Calvinist barrage against the increasing tide of new crypto-Catholic Arminianism emanating from the Court. This was the Whiggish interpretation of Gardiner turned on its head; a paradigm shift in the study of early modern political history whose shock waves continue to shape the writing of political history to the present day. Interestingly, Russell, like Gardiner, adopted the narrative form to establish the proper chronology of events, and rejected the teleologies which had blighted earlier accounts of these parliaments.

Such revisions caused a good deal of consternation within the historical community for challenging the basic framework of the parliamentary politics of Elizabethan and early Stuart England which had been in place since Gardiner's time. The stridency of the opposition to the revisionist challenge, however, was in no small measure due to their redefinition of what the 'political' was. Revisionists rejected institutional and constitutional opposition to the monarch by the Commons, and thus broke the established causal chain between the late Tudor/early Stuart era and the Civil War. As we shall see below, they also rejected the emphasis on long-term structural change in politics associated with influential scholars such as Christopher Hill (1912–2003) and Lawrence Stone (1919–99) in favour of a close scrutiny of political events within relatively circumscribed physical and temporal spaces. In place of grand explanatory theses, the critics of the revisionists maintained, they substituted short-term narratives of patronage divested of any ideological character. It was claimed that historians like Russell had reconstituted 'politics' as the meaningless dance of MPs between the twin poles of the interests of the Court and their constituencies. This was much more the world of place and patronage which Lewis Namier (1888–1960) had so influentially described for the eighteenth century, than that riven with dispute and ideological ferment familiar from almost all previous treatments of seventeenth-century politics. Scholars wondered after the 'principles', the ideological elements, which apparently had been lost in this recasting of politics. 'Revisionism' was articulated through some very traditional forms, however, with a narrative concentration on parliament and the Court, on high politics and debates in London. As the revisionist wave broke over early modern studies, an alarmed Lawrence Stone labelled its practitioners 'young antiquarian empiricists', who 'deny that there is any deep-seated meaning to history except the accidental whims of fortune and personality'.[12] For Stone, their methodologies looked backwards rather than forwards and had divested this period of history of its special importance and significance. Stone's view of its politics was very different, and it is to historians of his ilk, who viewed politics principally within longer-term social and economic developments, that we now turn.

Political history and the social sciences: Tawney, Hill and Stone

The revisionist attack on some established shibboleths of parliamentary history was also largely a response to trends in the sociological and functionalist discussions of early modern politics. Although for many the writing of political history remained the writing of parliamentary narratives, from the early twentieth century the influence of ideas derived from the social sciences and a reinterpretation of the socio-economic landscape of the early modern period helped reconfigure understandings of the political among a highly influential group of historians. From the 1920s, the socialist R.H. Tawney (1880–1962) was a prominent advocate of a structuralist approach to early modern society which dwelt upon the connection between the economy and political and religious developments. Responding to Max Weber's (1864–1920) interpretations of the relationship between capitalism and puritanism, Tawney was concerned mostly with changing patterns of landholding and commercial attitudes, asserting that 'political' events were essentially functions of underlying socio-economic trends. For him, the Civil War was the product of a rising gentry order seeking political power commensurate with their new economic power.[13] Concerned with grand themes and long-term structural change rather than the minutiae of parliamentary debate, Tawney demonstrated a sympathy for the masses, but did not seek to analyse early modern politics in a genuinely Marxist schema.

Although arriving at rather different conclusions, the writings of Lawrence Stone on early modern politics reflected the influence of Tawney, his intellectual mentor, as Stone, too, emphasized how social forces explained the political complexion of early modern England. In his approach he was greatly influenced by methods drawn from the social sciences, employing quantitative measurement, sampling and statistical testing in his study of the English aristocracy, for example.[14] Stone was representative of a historical profession in the 1960s and early 1970s which concluded that 'economic transformation . . . brought about social development, which in turn set the parameters and determined the possibilities of political outcomes' in history.[15] He asserted that 'every historian, whatever their political persuasion, lays great stress on social forces as operative factors in history', and noted approvingly the view that there was 'a direct relationship between social structure and political institutions and that the former tends to dictate the latter'.[16] Politics was almost a by-product of such metanarratives, which possessed an underlying agenda of explaining the transition from 'medieval' to 'modern' political structures, and thus reflected and perpetuated the modernizing paradigm that had organized Gardiner's story. Stone's work eschewed narrative exegesis for a more structured, analytical approach, such as the tripartite organization of 'preconditions', 'precipitants' and 'triggers' in his *Causes of the English Revolution* (1972), which owed more than a passing debt to the method of *Annaliste* Fernand Braudel (1902–85).[17] Although Stone's interpretation lay very much within a leftist tradition (for example, his insistence that economics formed a kind of base which defined the nature of other cultural phenomena such as politics), it too was far from the 'full-blown' social determinism of Marxist theory. The latter, however, can be discerned in the writings of Christopher Hill.

Hill's oeuvre is enormous, and his works so diverse and wide-ranging that it is impossible to provide a simple assessment of his interpretation of early modern politics. Hill emerged as a towering figure in early modern studies between the 1950s and the 1970s. He was a member of the Communist Party Historians' Group and founding member of the (originally Marxist) journal *Past & Present*. In *The English Revolution, 1640* (1940), he posited the view that the Civil War was 'a class war' in which the old feudal order was overthrown by a rising capitalist class of gentry and upper yeomanry. Individualist forces of enterprise and capitalism were the key to understanding this essentially bourgeois revolution, during which the reactionary structures of medieval England were finally dismantled.[18] In his later works, and after his departure from the Communist Party in 1957 (following the Soviet invasion of Hungary in 1956), this kind of imitative 'Soviet'-style interpretation was refined and modified as he turned his attention to the marginal and neglected political ideas of Civil War radicals like the Diggers, who were seen as very much the precursors of modern-day socialists and Communists. He wrote later that his aim had always been to 'emphasize *interaction* between politics and economics, seeing neither as a sufficient cause in itself', and acknowledged that the 'connection between economics and politics is not simple'.[19] To cite Hill as the exemplar of a British Marxist historian imposing economic determinism on early modern England misses much of the subtlety of his writing. Throughout his work, however, Hill sought to reveal the effects of long-term social and economic change, within a broadly Marxist construction, on early modern political, religious and intellectual history. He also always represented this period as one of struggle and conflict, conflict based upon inequalities and class difference.

At the heart of all Hill's writings, then, was the idea which could be found in much 'political history' of this period, that the early modern era was worth studying as a transitional stage in which the restraints of medieval society, such as a powerful monarchy and feudalism, were discarded, while the curtain was being raised on the modern era and progressive ideas and principles such as liberty and democracy. The English experienced a 'Revolution' in the mid-seventeenth century which was of similar importance to those in America in 1776 and France in 1789, yet this one failed to realize its revolutionary potential, producing only a short-lived republic. Yet Hill asserted that it had released forces which could not be contained, and within it lay the germ of modern Britain and, possibly, a Britain which was yet to be. Hill consciously avoided getting 'too immersed in the detail' of high political narratives. Instead he adopted a longer view, believing that this allowed historians to 'appreciate the colossal transformations which ushered England into the modern world'.

The importance Hill attached to the political preoccupations of those lower down the social order did much to bring together social history's concerns with sub-gentry society and Whiggish preoccupations with liberty and progress. He explored the political ideas of those who were traditionally excluded from the definition of 'political nation' in early modern society, and recognized that he was writing a quite different political history to the traditional constitutional and 'institutional' studies which continued to be produced. Indeed, in his highly influential exploration of the radical ideas of the minority political and religious groups of the 1640s and 1650s, he noted that a reader wishing to 'restore his perspective' on the politics of the period should rather read David Underdown's 'high political' study of the Long Parliament between 1647 and 1649, *Pride's Purge*, which dealt 'with almost exactly the same period as I do, but from an entirely different angle. His is the view from the top, from Whitehall, mine the worm's eye view. His index and mine contain totally different lists of names'.[20] He rejected out of hand the Eltonian concentration on 'government rather than the people of a country'. Yet here, too, we find in Hill echoes of the Gardinerian preoccupation with those who embodied an idea of national progress. For Gardiner, it was those parliamentarians who prefigured Liberal Victorian ideas; for Hill, it was the 'freeborn Englishmen' and proto-Communists like the Diggers – a radical group of men and women who attempted to live communally on common land in 1649–50 – who articulated the progressive democratic and libertarian ideals which lay at the heart of England's unrealized revolution, ideals which he believed were taken up more effectively by the working classes after the Industrial Revolution.

Hill was aware of the shifting contemporary climate which had contributed to his thesis becoming more acceptable to the historical community. The questioning of many established norms and social values in England during the 1960s and 1970s had encouraged a leftist sympathy with marginal and radical groups. Hill believed that the contemporary challenges to the dominant Protestant ethic in western bourgeois society were encouraging the study of radical movements which had 'refused to bow down and worship it' in the seventeenth century.[21] He related his historical focus explicitly to a political programme in modern society, of the need to realize the potentialities to change society glimpsed in the early modern revolutions.

However, his concentration on the socio-economic origins of civil war and the left-wing radical minority of the 1640s and 1650s, helped provoke a backlash from those who believed that the truly important elements of politics and the genuine narrative of political change had been left out. In many ways the influence of social science approaches in early modern history helped undermine the traditional dominance of political history in research and university curricula. The kind of social determinism and long-term structural narratives underpinning the works of Tawney, Stone and Hill on the Civil War rendered political history as essentially superficial, a product of other forces rather than the subject of study itself, and this helped provide a major impetus for the revisionist reinterpretation of the political discussed above.

Political culture and social histories of politics

Influenced by Marxist approaches such as that pioneered by Hill, the 1960s and 1970s witnessed a surge of interest in early modern social history and the writing of 'history from below'. The concentration in such approaches on elements which lay outside the gentry orders rendered it largely beyond of the purview of strictly 'political history', which continued to emphasize the high politics of institutions, social elites and key turning points, like the accession of the Stuarts or the Glorious Revolution. The revisionists' emphasis on high political narratives and their rejection of social interpretations of political change helped entrench this continued bifurcation within the profession. As has been seen, the revisionist challenge was directed squarely at the modernizing political narratives of the Whigs and Marxists, but it continued to write political history as the story of the great and the good, of parliaments and ministers, although it did so in a manner which was more sensitive to context, contingency and individual agency than structural determinism and class antagonism. Hill's writings did much to emphasize the interconnectedness of politics with economic and social conditions, but in his own work and in that of historians influenced by him – such as Keith Thomas – the political was never adequately integrated with the social. Thus the study of early modern political and social history continued to proceed largely along their own discrete paths.

The traditional boundaries between these two approaches to early modern society have increasingly been broken down in recent decades, however, impelled by the need for a broader social understanding of politics which, in part, comes from a reaction against the revisionist project's myopic focus on the high politics of the centre. A pioneering voice in this was the hugely respected historian of early modern religion and Puritanism, Patrick Collinson (b. 1929). In a path-breaking article, he advocated the need for a 'social depth' to the writing of early modern political history, for a reintegration of the social and the political or, as he put it, 'a new political history, which is social history with the politics put back in, or an account of political process which is also social'.[22] This process has proceeded in tandem with a cross-fertilization of ideas and approaches with disciplines such as literary criticism and the opening up of political history to the potentialities of the linguistic and cultural 'turns' and the influence of poststructuralist theory. The writings of the so-called post-revisionists have drawn on such approaches, for example, acknowledging the gains made by rejecting overly totalizing accounts of early modern politics, while seeking to reintegrate politics properly within its social and cultural contexts. As a consequence, politics in its early modern incarnations have come to be much more widely defined than the epiphenomena of parliamentary debates or a product of economic and social forces which prefigure 'modernity' in political life and ideas. Many of these developments have come to be encompassed under the ambiguous and widely conceived penumbra of a history of 'political culture' rather than a history of politics.[23] Political historians of Tudor and Stuart England have largely moved away from administrative and constitutional studies to examine the contexts within which political actions were performed and the intellectual and social materials from which they were created. The 'high political' histories of the parliament, Privy Council and government ministers in the Tudor period, for example, have recently been largely superseded by studies which emphasize the operation of social networks at Court, the iconographies of power and the use of language in the conduct of political debate.[24]

A greater emphasis on interdisciplinarity in modern scholarship has encouraged the scrutiny of plays, masques, architecture and painting as texts in seeking to illuminate the contemporary culture of political power relations. A highly prominent 'revisionist' of the 1970s and 1980s, Kevin Sharpe, has been among the most vociferous and influential in calling for a broadened, integrative reconceptualization of seventeenth-century politics, arguing for a 'move from politics conceived (anachronistically) as the business of institutions, bureaucracies and officers to the broader politics of discourse and symbols, anxieties and aspirations, myths and memories', although he still generally understands this reformulation of politics to include elites only.[25] Examination of political vocabularies, rhetorics and iconographies has become increasingly common in discussions of high politics in early modern England. Oliver Cromwell's recent treatment is suggestive of these developments, with Laura Knoppers's (significantly a professor of English literature) *Constructing Cromwell: Ceremony, Portrait and Print, 1645–1661* (2000). Knoppers avoids any simple political biography or assessment of Cromwell's political actions, but rather examines the way in which this enigmatic figure's image was composed and disseminated within a number of overlapping contexts in the 1640s and 1650s. Sensitive to ephemeral literature, woodcuts, portraits and satires, she uses the various representations of Cromwell to explore the manner in which political debate and opinion was conducted and constructed within early modern society.[26] Kevin Sharpe and Sean Kelsey similarly utilize evidence of the iconographic languages employed during the 1650s, in the case of the former to suggest how the Commonwealth managed to articulate a powerful and vigorous symbolism of Republicanism in presenting itself to a wary nation, while the latter emphasizes the lack of an imaginative republican iconographic vocabulary for the failure of the regimes of the 1650s adequately to establish themselves in the popular mentality of seventeenth-century England.[27] The degree to which the historiographical landscape has shifted is suggested by Geoffrey Elton's foreword to *Tudor Political Culture* (1995), edited by Dale Hoak. Although five of the volume's contributors were his graduate students, Elton notes that none 'bothers to argue about my views, and Thomas Cromwell hardly appears!'[28] Indeed, the treatment of parliaments and courts in this volume, with its concentration on rhetoric, iconography and gesture, is drastically different to Eltonian emphases; the focus and configuration of politics in the sixteenth century had altered radically within an academic generation.

The proper locales of politics have also been reinterpreted and redefined in more expansive and inclusive ways in recent times. Keith Wrightson wrote an influential essay in 1996 on conceptualizing in a truly political way the relations within the small arena of the parish by examining the 'social distribution and use of power' within it.[29] His student, Andy Wood, meanwhile, rejecting the universalizing schemata of Marxist and modernist historians, sought to redefine class as a real and experienced category within early modern history, by locating it within a local context of the mining communities in the Derbyshire Peak, characterizing this from the perspective of what he described as a 'plebeian political culture'.[30] Historians have also paid greater attention to political voices and evidence which were largely discounted or overlooked by earlier generations. Alastair Bellany's study of *The Politics of Court Scandal* (2002), for example, criticizes the narrowness of the revisionists' definition of politics and their lack of engagement with the significance of contemporary scandal and libel and its capacity to reveal the political tensions and cultural assumptions of early seventeenth-century society. Gender history has also influenced this redefinition of the political, with works such as James Daybell's study 'defining "politics" broadly in order to incorporate women excluded from formal, male-dominated state institutions'.[31] Similarly, Sara Mendelson and Patricia Crawford argue that the study of early modern politics needs to be rethought along these lines, 'to take account of the presence and influence of women' and 'to restore women to politics, and politics to women'.[32] Asymmetrical power relations within households, villages and counties have thus come to be understood as 'political'.

If these 'new' political histories have expanded the spatial and gender locales of politics, their intellectual debt to the sociological and Marxist interpretations of the mid-twentieth century can be seen in their interest in the political attitudes of those outside traditional elites. The public, collective action of 'ordinary' men and women responding to grain shortages, land enclosures, religious change and factional difference have increasingly been dissected for what they reveal about the political attitudes and assumptions of their participants and the politics of the cultures within which they operated. The invigoration of 'popular politics' as a worthwhile topic can be seen in Tim Harris's work on the London crowd in the reign of Charles II, and his edited volume, *The Politics of the Excluded* (2001), with its stated aim of shedding 'light on the politics of those who are often thought of as being excluded from the "political nation" '.[33] Similarly, Andy Wood has argued for an understanding of early modern popular politics, which includes friction over the control of resources and the distribution of power in society.[34] The emergence of a more capacious and generous definition of political activity has allowed it to advance confidently in recent years and occupy what may be described as the 'mainstream' of early modern political studies.

These developments have left the politics of early modern England in a rather disjointed state, with the foci about which politics previously gravitated – parliament, monarchs and councillors – replaced by a burgeoning and fragmented constellation of concepts and actions which have been rebranded as 'political'. In recent times, perhaps, there has been a failure to engage with the 'traditional' political elements of parliaments, elections and legislation within this 'socially enriched' understanding of early modern politics. The emphasis on the symbols, languages and gestures of politics needs to be reconnected with the policies of monarchs and the power of elites for a more satisfying understanding of early modern politics.[35] In addition, the increasing fragmentation and specialization of political histories in the aftermath of the Whig and Marxist grand narratives has left political history with neither the vocabulary nor the perspective to chart and explain change across what was clearly a period which was less modern at its beginning and less medieval at its end, and to posit possibilities for the causes of such change. In a postmodern world, perhaps 'politics' is more than ever in the eye of the beholder, but, as Wood and Harris have cautioned, we need to be wary of constructing too broad a notion of politics wherein it loses all meaning and conceptual power. The writing of early modern political history has always been fundamentally concerned with power: its nature, distribution and usage. The reformulations of recent years have afforded the opportunity to move beyond simply telling narratives of the exercise of that power by elites towards a more sensitive understanding of the normative assumptions from which it was composed and wherein it operated.

The remainder of this chapter will consider how the redefinitions and reconfigurations of 'the political', which have been charted in the foregoing discussion, can be followed more closely by examining a single topic within the historiography on early modern politics: parliamentary elections.

Case study: parliamentary elections

The interface between electors and candidates at parliamentary elections was one of the clearest political actions of early modern England, yet a brief genealogy of its discussion and treatment in the historiography illuminates some of the shifts and underlying assumptions discussed above. The processes of election in early modern England and Wales were very different to those which prevail today. Each county only had two members allotted to it (only one in Wales), and in these elections only individuals who were 40-shilling freeholders, and thus had a stake in the property of the country, were eligible to vote. There were many more borough seats, however, which were distributed around the country rather inequitably – Cornwall and Wiltshire, for example, had a disproportionately large number of borough members. In these constituencies, a whole variety of franchises prevailed, but generally the vote was restricted to freemen and residents. There were no ballot boxes or private voting and, for the most part, the (often very large) electorates declared their choices by a general acclamation; if a contest prevailed, only then would a poll or canvass of voters take place. The nature of this electorate and the principles which underwrote its actions at the hustings have been the central concerns of historians examining elections in early modern England and Wales.

In Gardiner's narrative, parliamentary elections, perhaps surprisingly given his Westminster-centric view of things, receive hardly any treatment. MPs appear fully formed in the Commons almost out of the ether, ready to do battle with the Stuart kings. They are held to represent and articulate a kind of embodiment of the national spirit, but the mechanisms by which they were chosen as the mouthpieces of these sentiments remain obscure. The electors are passive, unseen actors through which the national spirit of England operated. When he did analyse the franchise, it was to proclaim that through the various interests 'the House [of Commons] came to represent not merely the mass of electors, but also the effective strength of the nation'.[36] He did note also, however, the responsibility which members felt towards being accountable to this great national sentiment while they operated within the House.

Sir John Neale approached the Elizabethan Commons with a prosopographer's eye, and his attitude to elections reflected this. More than three-quarters of his highly influential book, *The Elizabethan House of Commons*, was directly concerned with elections and the routes by which members arrived at Westminster. However, in this and other pieces, Neale stressed elections essentially as reflections of social hierarchies, foregrounding in the choice of members the patronage of great men, which he described as 'a vestige of feudalism adapted to new social purposes'. Although Neale portrayed elections as essentially apolitical contests over prestige and social hierarchies (he acknowledged that the 'constitutional theme' of these parliaments would be treated in his other volumes on Elizabethan assemblies), his approach was actually rooted within a modernization narrative which highlighted the Elizabethan era as a crucial period in the rising significance of parliament as a national institution. The patronage of great men and the election of outsiders by communities were necessary to provide parliament with the kind of overarching political outlook required to articulate national sentiments and embody national progress. The election of outsiders was significant, Neale asserted, for 'how else could the House of Commons have greatly surpassed the average ability of the community; how else have provided room for the nation's best available skill and leadership; how else have secured that parliament should be nationally rather than locally minded?'[37] The voice of Gardiner can still be heard in Neale's accounts of elections.

When Christopher Hill mentioned early modern elections, it was usually with a view of stressing their increasingly 'democratic' nature and the progressive attitudes towards elections emphasized among radical groups like the Levellers. He wrote of the sixteenth-century 'agitations' for a wider franchise in the boroughs, prefiguring the seventeenth-century demands for a wider national electorate which articulated some kind of 'spirit of individualism'.[38] Stone similarly emphasized the demands for a wider electorate, subtly integrating it into his broader thesis of a declining aristocratic order and a rising gentry class in early modern England. He spoke of the early modern period as a time when the hold of great magnates on parliamentary seats was broken by the gentry, who had to ally themselves with the political aspirations of those lower down the social scale in order to secure political gains.[39] Elections here essentially reflected the broader development of social trends. Within both the Liberal/Whig and Marxist paradigms the electoral history of the early modern period prefigured later 'democratic' developments. John H. Plumb (1911–2001), student of the Whig G.M. Trevelyan (1876– 1962), opponent of the narrowly 'political' Elton and a socialist, wrote in 1969 on the manner in which rising inflation had reduced the social exclusiveness of voters in early modern England and led to a growing and politically actuated parliamentary franchise.[40] His thesis was grafted onto an essentially Gardinerian understanding of increasing constitutional tensions, remarking that the changing social base of the electorate 'gave Parliament much of its strength to oppose the Crown'. A man for whom history spelt social progress and political reform, Plumb's emphasis on increasing social participation in the political process reflected his own socio-intellectual interests. His topic influenced his research student, Derek Hirst, whose extremely influential 1975 book, *The Representative of the People?*, argued that the early modern period witnessed an expanding electorate which could pressurize potential candidates for parliament into acknowledging and acting upon their wishes. For example, a reaction to the unpopular royal policies of Charles I's Personal Rule saw some electorates resolving not to elect 'courtiers', who were closely associated with such initiatives. The increasing incidence of contested elections during the seventeenth century saw a corollary intensification of appeals to the electorate on issues of principle. Politics, then, penetrated much deeper into society than many accounts, focused solely on parliament and the manoeuvres of elites, had allowed. Hirst's massively detailed study appeared to support a 'traditional' interpretation of cumulative conflict and opposition within the early modern body politic, with political principles and an increasing social participation in politics at its heart. However, Hirst's work became one of the central planks underpinning the revisionist project, as Conrad Russell suggested that it was an MP's accountability to his constituents rather than his opposition to the king which could explain instances such as the Commons' reluctance to vote the Crown taxes in the 1620s.[41]

Elections themselves became subject to a thorough revisionist reworking by the American academic, Mark Kishlansky in his *Parliamentary Selection* (1986). Kishlansky challenged the inherently Whiggish paradigm which surrounded the treatment of elections and focused instead on those elections where no contest took place. He suggested that elections, contests between opposing candidates, were the aberration rather than the norm, and that generally these phenomena should be termed *selections*, wherein local elites presented the electorate with a fait accompli, a single candidate whom they usually confirmed in a reaffirmation of the hierarchical political structures at the centre of revisionists' views of early modern politics. Kishlansky considered the 1624 Cheshire election, for example, to show the manner in which magistrates nominated two candidates 'behind the scenes' who were then presented to the electorate by the sheriff, Sir Richard Grosvenor, and the voters duly endorsed their choice. There was little evidence here of ideological engagement on the part of the masses or a crescendo of political tension from the Tudor period to the Civil War. Kishlansky's work reinforced the revisionist emphasis on consensus and the rhetorical languages of hierarchy within the early modern polity. However, although rejecting Hirst's account, which he characterized as part of the 'Whig canon', Kishlansky was forced to recognize the Civil War as a kind of climacteric in the changing nature of parliamentary elections, and the rise of 'adversary politics', which he acknowledged as characterizing s/elections in the post-Restoration world. The fracture between 'pre-modern' and 'proto-modern' electoral politics remains, but it has been pushed back into a different chronological period from that of traditional historiography.

'Post-revisionist' scholars, dissatisfied with Kishlansky's apparent rejection of the ideological in politics, have sought to modify his picture of early modern elections. Most prominent of these is Richard Cust, a former student of Conrad Russell, who has engaged in a constructive dialogue with his mentor but has placed a greater emphasis on divisions of political principle in pre-Civil War England. Kishlansky had grounded his account firmly in a study of the rhetorical strategies and discourses of early modern elections and, in an interesting nod to the growing influence of cultural histories and literary theory, opened his work with a study of an election as portrayed in Shakespeare's *Coriolanus*. Cust was similarly attuned to the growing emphasis within early modern studies on languages and rhetorics, and sought to challenge Kishlansky's findings on his own ground. He offered an interpretation wherein the languages of elections, particularly contested elections, were often wholly situated in principled politics. A primary feature of this was the emphasis on anti-Catholicism which was incorporated within a nexus of attitudes and ideas contemporaries characterized as standing for the 'country'. 'Country' values included a whole complex of positions towards issues such as religion, taxation and unsuitable ministers advising the king. Contrasted with this were the values of the 'Court', used as a shorthand for crypto-popery and unpopular financial policies like ship money. Although the voters might be presented with a candidate by the gentry, Cust suggests, they were liable to reject him if he had politico-religious associations with which they were not happy. Candidates who fitted the image of a 'patriot', who stood for the values of the 'country', were thus often chosen: simply because there was no contest, then, did not mean that there was no political choice involved.[42] Cust's interpretation of the 1624 Cheshire election is very different from that of Kishlansky, for example. Although he recognizes that an agreement on potential candidates had been made, he suggests that Sir Richard Grosvenor's speech to the assembled electorate *reinforced* their capacity for choice by stressing that if these were unworthy candidates (Catholics, for example) the political community should reject them. Polarized languages, then, suggested a politically and ideologically fractured context for early Stuart elections, which recovered something of the Whiggish emphasis on principles within politics, but did not necessarily force it into the mouths of a monolithic 'opposition' contesting with the king. This was a refined and nuanced reintegration of the 'ideological' into parliamentary elections.

The study of elections, then, mirrors and elucidates many of the trends and developments in the historiography of early modern politics discussed above. The emphasis on the institutional generally has given way to examinations of the functioning of politics within its milieu, to the examination of politics as a product of its social situation rather than something separate from it. Politics was once considered to be the very essence of all historical investigation, closely associated with the rise of the professional discipline and the social function it needed to fulfil in the emergent nation states of nineteenth-century Europe. Its traditional dominance within the academy has declined significantly in recent decades, but its pervasiveness and significance has grown, perhaps, as it is increasingly recognized how 'politics' can be found in parishes as well as parliaments.

Guide to further reading

J.S.A. Adamson, 'Eminent Victorians: S.R. Gardiner and the Liberal as Hero', *Historical Journal* 33(3) (1990), pp. 641–57.

David Cannadine, 'Historians in "the Liberal Hour": Lawrence Stone and J.H. Plumb Re-Visited', *Historical Research* 75 (2002), pp. 316–54.

Patrick Collinson, '*De Republica Anglorum*: or, History with the Politics Put Back', in his *Elizabethan Essays* (London, 1994).

Geoff Eley and William Hunt (eds), *Reviving the English Revolution: Reflections and Elaborations on the Work of Christopher Hill* (London and New York, 1988).

G.R. Elton, *Political History: Principles and Practice* (London, 1970).

Ronald Hutton, *Debates in Stuart History* (Basingstoke, 2004).

Jon Lawrence, 'Political History', in Stefan Berger, Heiko Feldner and Kevin Passmore (eds), *Writing History: Theory and Practice* (London, 2003), pp. 183–202.

Susan Pedersen, 'What is Political History Now?', in D. Cannadine (ed.), *What is History Now?* (Basingstoke, 2002), pp. 36–56.

R.C. Richardson, *The Debate on the English Revolution* (3rd edn, Glasgow, 1998).

Andy Wood, *Riot, Rebellion and Popular Politics in Early Modern England* (Basingstoke, 2002).

Notes

1 T. Carlyle, *Oliver Cromwell's Letters and Speeches* (London, 1846), vol. 1, p. 1.
2 Leopold von Ranke, *A History of England, Principally in the Seventeenth Century*, 6 vols (Oxford, 1875).
3 S.R. Gardiner, *History of England, 1603–1642* (London, 1883–84), vol. 10, p. vii; 'Leopold von Ranke', *The Academy* 29 (1886), pp. 380–1.
4 J.S.A. Adamson, 'Eminent Victorians: S.R. Gardiner and the Liberal as Hero', *Historical Journal* 33 (1990), pp. 641–57.
5 S.R. Gardiner, *Constitutional Documents of the Puritan Revolution* (Oxford, 1899), p. lxiv.
6 Austin Woolrych, *Britain in Revolution, 1625–1660* (Oxford, 2002).
7 There are problems with Elton's treatment of 'the political' as he claimed to be principally a historian of political institutions rather than everyday politics. He asserted that his influential 'Tudor Revolution' thesis was 'not about politics . . . it was about administration': to many observers the difference may seem a moot one. S. Adams, 'Politics', *Transactions of the Royal Historical Society*, 6th ser., 7 (1997), pp. 247–65; G.R. Elton, 'Tudor Government', *Historical Journal* 31 (1988), p. 428.

8 G.R. Elton, *The Practice of History* (Sydney, 1967), p. 121.
9 Peter Lake, 'Retrospective: Wentworth's Political World in Revisionist and Post-Revisionist Perspective', in J.F. Merritt (ed.), *The Political World of Thomas Wentworth, Earl of Strafford, 1621–1641* (Cambridge, 1996), pp. 255–6; G.R. Elton, *The Tudor Revolution in Government: Administrative Changes in the Reign of Henry VIII* (Cambridge, 1953), p. 8.
10 G.R. Elton, *Political History: Principles and Practice* (London, 1970), pp. 3–4.
11 Thomas Cogswell, Richard Cust and Peter Lake, 'Revisionism and its Legacies', in their (eds), *Politics, Religion and Popularity in Early Stuart Britain* (Cambridge, 2002), p. 7.
12 Lawrence Stone, 'The Revival of Narrative: Reflections on a New Old History', *Past & Present* 85 (1979), p. 20.
13 See, for example, R.H. Tawney, *The Agrarian Problem in the Sixteenth-Century* (London, 1912); 'The Rise of the Gentry, 1558–1640', *Economic History Review*, 1st ser., 11 (1941).
14 Lawrence Stone, *The Crisis of the Aristocracy, 1558–1641* (abridged edn, Oxford, 1967), p. 3; Lawrence Stone, 'History and the Social Sciences', in his *The Past and the Present Revisited* (London and New York, 1987), pp. 3–44.
15 David Cannadine, 'Historians in "The Liberal Hour": Lawrence Stone and J.H. Plumb Re-Visited', *Historical Research* 75 (2002), p. 321.
16 Lawrence Stone, *The Causes of the English Revolution, 1529–1642* (London, 1972), pp. 31, 39.
17 Matthias Middell, 'The *Annales*', in Stefan Berger, Heiko Feldner and Kevin Passmore (eds), *Writing History: Theory and Practice* (London and New York, 2003), pp. 110–12.
18 Christopher Hill, *The English Revolution, 1640* (London, 1940).
19 Christopher Hill, *Reformation to Industrial Revolution* (London, 1967), p. 4; original italic.
20 Christopher Hill, *The World Turned Upside Down* (Harmondsworth, 1972), pp. 13–14; David Underdown, *Pride's Purge: Politics in the Puritan Revolution* (Oxford, 1971).
21 Christopher Hill, *World Turned Upside Down*, p. 15.
22 Patrick Collinson, '*De Republica Anglorum*: Or, History with the Politics Put Back', in his *Elizabethan Essays* (London, 1994), p. 11.
23 At the time of writing, the Royal Historical Society's *Bibliography* lists 50 titles containing the term 'political culture' which relate to the period 1500–1700. *All* were written after 1986, with the vast majority appearing since 1994.
24 Natalie Mears, 'Courts, Courtiers and Culture in Tudor England', *Historical Journal* 46 (2003), pp. 703–22; Stephen Alford, 'Politics and Political History in the Tudor Century', *Historical Journal* 42 (1999), pp. 535–48.

25 Kevin Sharpe, *Remapping Early Modern England: The Culture of Seventeenth-Century Politics* (Cambridge, 2000), p. 3. An important reflection of Sharpe's method and approach is his recent appointment as Professor of English and Comparative Literature rather than of History.
26 Laura Knoppers, *Constructing Cromwell: Ceremony, Portrait and Print, 1645–1661* (Cambridge, 2000).
27 Kevin Sharpe, ' "An Image Doting Rabble": The Failure of Republican Culture in Seventeenth-Century England', in his *Remapping Early Modern England*, pp. 223–65; Sean Kelsey, *'Inventing a Republic': The Political Culture of the English Commonwealth* (Manchester, 1997).
28 Dale Hoak (ed.), *Tudor Political Culture* (Cambridge, 1995), p. xxi.
29 Keith Wrightson, 'The Politics of the Parish in Early Modern England', in Paul Griffiths, Adam Fox and Steve Hindle (eds), *The Experience of Authority in Early Modern England* (Basingstoke, 1996), pp. 10–46.
30 Andy Wood, *The Politics of Social Conflict: The Peak Country, 1520–1770* (Cambridge, 1999).
31 James Daybell (ed.), *Women and Politics in Early Modern England, 1450–1700* (Aldershot, 2004).
32 Sara Mendelson and Patricia Crawford, *Women in Early Modern England* (Oxford, 1998), p. 345.
33 Tim Harris, *London Crowds in the Reign of Charles II: Propaganda and Politics from the Restoration until the Exclusion Crisis* (Cambridge, 1987); Harris (ed.), *The Politics of the Excluded, c.1500–1850* (Basingstoke, 2001), p. 1.
34 Andy Wood, *Riot, Rebellion and Popular Politics in Early Modern England* (Basingstoke, 2002).
35 Cf. Jon Lawrence, 'Political History', in Berger, Feldner and Passmore (eds), *Writing History*, pp. 195–9.
36 Gardiner, *History*, vol. 5, p. 181.
37 J.E. Neale, *The Elizabethan House of Commons* (1949; London, 1976), p. 14.
38 Christopher Hill, *Society and Puritanism* (London, 1964), pp. 468–9.
39 Stone, *Causes*, p. 130.
40 J.H. Plumb, 'The Growth of the Electorate in England from 1600 to 1715', *Past & Present* 45 (1969), pp. 90–116.
41 Derek Hirst, *The Representative of the People?: Voters and Voting in England under the Early Stuarts* (Cambridge, 1975).
42 Richard Cust, 'Politics and the Electorate in the 1620s', in Richard Cust and A. Hughes (eds), *Conflict in Early Stuart England* (Harlow, 1989), pp. 134–67; Richard Cust, 'Election and Selection in Stuart England', *Parliamentary History* 7 (1988), pp. 344–50; Richard Cust and Peter Lake, 'Sir Richard Grosvenor and the Rhetoric of Magistracy', *Bulletin of the Institute of Historical Research* 54 (1981), pp. 40–53.

10

The body

Kevin Stagg

The human body emerged as a specific subject of historical analysis in the later 1970s.[1] By the late 1990s, such was the abundance of theoretical works, journals, conferences and undergraduate and postgraduate courses addressing the history of the body, that scholars were described as being gripped by a 'body craze'.[2] The genesis of the history of the body is contemporaneous with and related to the interdisciplinarity of the 'new' social history of the 1960s and 1970s, and the advances of histories of women and sexuality. Since then it has developed in tandem with the 'new' cultural history and gender history, both of which owe much to the discipline's general engagement with the linguistic turn. Body history thus exemplifies general reorientations in historical study.

Of course, the body was not entirely absent from historical writing before the 1970s. Throughout the nineteenth and much of the twentieth centuries, historians regarded the human body as a source of weakness to be overcome, instead privileging the mind as the source of rationality, consciousness and identity. This dualism of mind/body was a feature of the Classical, Christian and Enlightenment traditions that dominated western intellectual thought. Thus, for Max Weber (1864–1920) the work ethic that emerged from new Protestant theologies in the sixteenth century, in which people's relationship to their labours was transformed by a rationalization of action and the development of bureaucracy, can be seen in terms of the victory of the rational and ordered mind over the licentious, disordered, instinctive body.[3] In the writings of Karl Marx (1818–83) and Friedrich Engels (1820–95), too, the human body was weak and passive. The state of factory workers' bodies – exhausted, diseased, mutilated and propelled to premature death – represented the physical manifestations of capitalist exploitation.[4] Twentieth-century historians influenced by Marxism have described the bodies of the lower orders being punished, tortured, executed, killed in battles, regimented into new fighting forces, left starving or robbed of their common land. In none of these accounts, though, are bodies central. As Foucault remarked of Marxism, the history it inspired 'has had a terrible tendency to occlude the question of the body, in favour of consciousness and ideology'.[5] There were, however, glimpses of body history's potential. *Annales* school founder Marc Bloch's (1886–1944) 1924 examination of royal healing in England and France might be termed a prototype of body history;[6] co-founder Lucien Febvre's (1878–1956) calls for quantitative histories of family life, sexuality and death also encouraged historians to historicize aspects of the body.[7]

In this chapter, particular consideration will be given to three key theorists and historians of the body – German sociologist Norbert Elias (1897–1990), Russian literary theorist Mikhail Bakhtin (1895–1975), and the French poststructuralist philosopher Michel Foucault (1926–84) – and to the groundbreaking work of feminists in this field. First, though, what *is* the body?

What is the 'body'?

There are numerous notions of what a 'body' is and thus what the history of the body consists of. As medievalist Carolyn Walker Bynum pointed out, the body 'can refer to the organs on which a physician operates or to the assumptions about race and gender implicit in a medical textbook, to the particular trajectory of one person's desires or to inheritance patterns and family structure'.[8] In many historical studies, the term 'the body' simply serves as a proxy for 'sexuality, reproduction or gender'.[9] Others have termed it cultural history 'in the most general meaning of the concept'.[10] Distinctions between studies of the body and of related subjects are sometimes blurred because bodies participate in all aspects of human activity.[11] While Kathleen Canning points to implicit and explicit histories of the body, Michel Feher notes the important distinction between studies of the body's representations (focusing on a natural and biological body) and a history of the human body that focuses on the body's 'modes of construction'.[12] Much body history hangs on this formulation, wherein the human body exists as an entity only in so far as we invest it with social and cultural meanings and functions. Some feminist scholars bemoan the degree to which adopting gender (often seen to be culturally constructed in and by language) as a category of historical analysis has been at the expense of the body and of sex, which have in turn been associated with an unchanging biological determinism. Such associations might have inhibited a more detailed evaluation of the historical body.[13]

Radical political scientist and cultural critic Ivan Illich (1926–2002) made another important distinction between the experiences of the lived body – that is, embodiment – and the body as the subject of representation. 'In every epoch, bodies exist only in context. They form the felt equivalent of an age, in so far as that age can be experienced by a specific group'.[14] Embodiment, however, might be difficult for early modern historians to explore. Historical sources such as institutional codes, laws and procedures are likely to privilege the represented body rather than the experiential body, which requires detailed personal observations. Historical studies are therefore in danger of being overly abstract and too general. Although historians might explore embodiment through analysing diaries, autobiographies, letters and other personal papers, such sources pose the opposite problem of being too specific, narrow and less amenable to generalization.

Scholarship on the body has focused primarily on three areas: first, representations of the body and how it symbolizes social relationships; second, issues of health and sickness; and third, the ways in which discourses of religion, law and medicine construct sex. In assessing the theoretical approaches adopted, I shall consider the key theoretical models, the subject areas in which body history has been utilized, the relationship between bodies and historical change and the play-off between representations and embodiment.

Norbert Elias (1897–1990)

The most influential sociologist for the history of the body is Norbert Elias.[15] Elias published works between the 1930s and the 1980s, but the key work for our purposes, *The Civilizing Process,* first published in German in 1939, had a major impact in the late 1970s, at which time it became available in English translation.[16]

Elias examined changes in forms of acceptable social conduct and the treatment of the body, particularly in relation to bodily functions, from the medieval to the modern period. He distinguished between two historical bodies. Echoing classic modernization theory, the medieval body was childlike, uncivilized, irrational and uninhibited in expressing emotions and bodily functions. In order for a more mature stage of individualization to develop, repression and education were needed. During the early modern period, the medieval body gave way to the modern, 'bourgeois' body, which was restrained, mannered and decorous. The medieval body's uncontrolled impulses were replaced by the modern body's emotional self-control. For Elias, degrees of embarrassment separated the two bodies. Farting, belching and eating with one's hands became defined as shameful and inappropriate among certain social groups. Elias here drew on Marxist notions of group distinction, focusing on the group that constituted the social elite, which changed from feudal nobility to the bourgeoisie. However, his prevailing concern was with the gradual development of democracy in the broadest sense. Whereas increased control over the body and the emotions initially developed among noble royal courtiers (and was related to power struggles among them), in the early modern period, these courtly forms of conduct filtered down first to the emerging bourgeoisie and afterwards to the rest of society. This trajectory, in which the rationalization of western society increases along with modesty, is again informed by Weberian modernization theory.[17] Elias's work also owes something to the psychoanalyst Sigmund Freud (1856–1939). Over time, the rules of appropriate conduct became internalized so that the conscience (superego, in Freudian terms) took over the task of social regulation. 'The pressure to restrain impulses and the . . . shame surrounding them – these are turned so completely into habits that we cannot resist them even when alone'.[18] External sanctions evolved into psychic change.

Elias envisaged an evolutionary process wherein bodily instincts became increasingly restrained and a more sophisticated mental attitude (internalizing feelings, holding one's tongue, and so on) developed. He presented medieval people as prone to unpredictable and extreme reactions in a society where violence was endemic and where there was a constant need for physical self-defence. In early modern royal courts, however, foresight and the adjustment of personal behaviour, rather than violence, came to be seen as the key to advancement. A more complex social environment thus emerged, requiring a greater degree of interdependence. As the state became a more prominent presence in people's lives by establishing a monopoly over both violence and taxation, the upper body strength of the combative nobility gave way to the calculating stratagems of the courtier. External constraints became internalized, thereby making 'civilized' conduct seem natural. The breaking of such internalized codes elicited negative responses in the form of shame, disgust and embarrassment. This is typical of body history – changes in the body are predicated on broader changes, such as the emergence of modernity in terms of a centralized state or a capitalist order. With Elias, the development of absolutism initiates bodily reorientation.

Some historians have challenged elements of Elias's argument. Hans Peter Duerr, for example, has argued that forms of privacy and shame were not particularly early modern developments, but exist in all historical periods.[19] Alan Hunt contends that Elias overlooked the degree to which social constraints were matters of contest and struggle.[20] Lyndal Roper questioned whether political changes in the state can be easily predicated upon changes in social conduct; in early modern Germany, 'discipline' was locally specific and contested. In addition, her gendered analysis of discipline modifies Elias's broader sweep.[21]

Nonetheless, Elias's argument positing a historical shift from disorganized to organized bodies via social regulation has been enormously influential. Numerous early modern studies utilize Elias's model of the internalization of emotions over the *longue durée*. Pieter Spierenburg's *The Broken Spell* (1991), which deals with death, madness and violence, relates bodily issues to the increasing regulation of human conduct and state formation. Spierenburg identifies three key processes: first, an increase in self-awareness and, consequently, compassion for others; second, privatization, manifest in bodily functions increasingly being concealed from public view and in the nuclear family becoming privileged over communal life; third, secularization. Altogether, the early modern period witnessed the 'taming of aggressive impulses'.[22] Public punishment declined as execution shifted from the open scaffold to the prison interior. This, like the secular treatment of criminals and the poor (in workhouses), is linked to the state's growing monopoly of violence. Following Elias's schema, Spierenburg posits a transition from tradition to modernity.

One obvious problem with surveys of large-scale historical transitions, like those of Elias and Spierenburg, is that their explanations of change are too general. State intervention is presented as capable of initiating all aspects of change across the vast expanse of centuries. Bodies become inert emblems of change shorn of any embodied dynamic. In such ways bodies reveal the quality of otherness afforded them by the assumptions of a western culture still engaged with an intellectual tradition that stresses bodily inferiority. Thus bodies align with women and ethnic 'others' in being consistently represented as mute and marginal witnesses to their own history. Another problem is that a pan-European sweep allows little consideration of specific national contexts. While Spierenburg presents examples to support his views of the modernization of attitudes to death, his general picture occludes many ways in which historicized bodies are transformed by the interplay of *specific* religious, political, economic and cultural ideas and actions. Craig Koslofsky, for instance, has shown that in eighteenth-century Saxony, the civil administration's attempts to secularize the burials of suicides failed in the face of popular and ecclesiastical opposition.[23] Historical change is far from smooth and linear.

Mikhail Bakhtin (1895–1975)

Russian literary theorist and philosopher of language Mikhail Bakhtin's study of the culture of folk humour in the context of the French writer François Rabelais (*c.*1490–*c.*1553), has become enormously influential in body history. Bakhtin identified two distinct bodies, the 'grotesque', which he discussed at length, and the 'classical'. These bodies were associated, respectively, with low and high cultures. The classical body of elite culture was easily described and recognized, but the grotesque body was difficult to categorize and appraise. It was defined primarily in opposition to the classical body. Where the classical body was individual, the grotesque was collective. While the classical body emphasized the head, traditionally associated with honour, the grotesque body accentuated the belly and genitals, and embraced organic bodily functions – defecation, lactation, menstruation and conception. The complete and immaculate classical body's interactions with the world were clearly defined. In contrast, the grotesque body's boundaries between inside and outside, between the self and the other, the body and the world, were blurred. In short, the grotesque body of popular culture was disorganized, overflowing, exaggerated and excessive; not static, but dynamic, always being renewed. This grotesque body was most easily found not in the everyday life of peasants, but in the spirit of carnival, an anarchic celebratory release of feelings involving rituals of inversion.[24]

Bakhtin's formulation of the grotesque body has informed a number of historical studies. For example, Sarah Juster's study of female mysticism owes a debt to Bakhtin (and Elias). The medicalization of childbirth and doctrines of civility and piety meant that the mystical pregnancy of Joanna Southcott in the early nineteenth century was seen as belonging to a previous age. Juster notes that the 'grotesque lived on in the spiritual imaginings of holy women long after it had been tamed by the reforming disciplines of the Enlightenment'.[25] Mark Jenner, in 2002, also evoked the Bakhtinian grotesque to understand how images of monstrous bodies were used in the 1660s to depict England and Wales's 'Rump' Parliament as means of expressing the horror of regicide and treacherous divisions within the realm. (The Rump was the nickname for England and Wales's Long Parliament, which technically lasted from November 1640 to March 1660, after it was purged of moderates by Colonel Pride in 1648 upon Oliver Cromwell's orders.)[26] Ulinka Rublack, too, describes early modern bodies as prone to 'sudden changes', with vulnerable boundaries between inside and outside, across which emotions flowed and because of which people worried 'about the stagnation or misdirection of bodily fluids'. Rublack extends Bakhtin's descriptions of turbulent and chaotic bodies to describe how personal perceptions of the body were very different in early modern Germany from our own.[27]

Bakhtin's model of the body is problematic on three counts: it is insufficiently specific about gender and race; it privileges carnival over everyday life; and, most pertinently, it offers an unsatisfactory account of change over time. Given that Bakhtin was writing in the 1930s, his lack of attention to gender and race is unsurprising. He interprets an indicatively grotesque collection of terracotta figurines of 'senile pregnant hags' and the two types of grotesque body ('the one giving birth and dying, the other conceived, generated and born'), as *universal* rather than gendered bodily forms.[28] His notion of the 'people' occludes the significance of gendered and racially different bodies and overlooks the strategies of exclusion and resistance, the forms of violence and hybridization, that inform them. There are also dangers in favouring the special festive dynamics of the carnival over the everyday. Additionally, addressing the carnivalesque as it appears in an idealized literary form (such as Rabelais's texts) tells historians little about how the concept operated in other cultural contexts. Indeed, Bakhtin himself acknowledged that the bodily life of grotesque realism does not 'reflect the drabness of everyday existence'.[29]

As regards change over time, Bakhtin merely hinted at a historical shift in the relationship of the grotesque and classical bodies. In line with the modernizing account that influenced so many early twentieth-century thinkers, Bakhtin imagined the fifteenth century to be a period of 'considerable freedom' of expression, where scatological and sexual references were commonplace. However, 'the norms of language' became stricter in the sixteenth century, with 'the canon of polite speech' being formed by the seventeenth.[30] The language of the grotesque and the carnival celebrated the body's orifices and their functions, a mode that increasingly sat uneasily with a developing official culture. Like Elias, Bakhtin assumed that restraint and politeness were the guiding principles of this shift. Bakhtin saw the sixteenth century as the apotheosis of the grotesque, when widespread publication of literature in the vernacular obscured the distinction between official (high) and non-official (low or popular) culture. The seventeenth-century rise of absolutism and rationalism left no place in official culture for the grotesque's ambivalent qualities.[31] The new official culture sought 'stability and completeness of being . . . one single meaning, one single tone of seriousness', and so was underpinned by the closed classical bodily form.[32] Unlike Elias, however, for whom the change from an older to a newer, more restrained bodily expression was a result of courtly values becoming accepted or imitated by the bourgeoisie, Bakhtin acknowledged that there were elements of resistance to the shift to a new body. The carnival and grotesque continued 'to live and struggle for its existence', finding expression in the 'lower' genres such as satire, comedy, fable, the novel and burlesque, even as it was degraded to become court masquerade, parade or a mere 'holiday mood'.[33] Such resistance can be seen in struggles over the reformation of popular sports and entertainments, and over the workplace, although Bakhtin did not describe them.[34]

Some historians have accepted Bakhtin's modernizing narrative without taking account of such resistance. Piero Camporesi relates the vivid experiences of hunger and defecation to descriptions of grotesque, pre-modern bodies that are notably at odds with the civilized and controlled body that emerged towards the end of the early modern period.[35] In another study, Tom Cheesman points out that 'Carnival, as prototypically manifested in pre-modern, pre-individualistic culture, was never absolutely present and never disappeared', but his work on gluttonous and freakish appetite in early modern Germany in fact posits a more uncomplicated chronology, in which the collective grotesque body of carnival gives way around 1700 (a 'watershed of modernization in Germany') to a modern body, characterized by 'disciplined individualism'.[36]

The importance of Bakhtin's original formulation lies in its scope for resistance to the imposition of official culture, whereby representations of the grotesque body can be viewed as parodic assertions of the popular festive culture. Where Elias posits a smooth transition, an unproblematic assimilation of elite courtly values regarding the body, the Bakhtinian approach potentially allows for a more complex and nuanced course of historical change.

Michel Foucault (1926–1984)

Michel Foucault was one of the key poststructuralist philosophers of the twentieth century. Within the poststructuralist tradition, bodies are viewed not as constant biological entities, but – like books, films and language itself – as 'texts'. Bodies can be 'read' by interpreting bodily signs and symbols. This semiotic conceptualization has led to a focus on social construction – how the meanings given to the supposedly 'natural' or biological body are not fixed but constructed socially and culturally. Hence the body is understood differently in different historical periods. Foucault's approach is a social constructionist one. For Foucault, bodies were constructed to legitimate dominant forms of power. The power relationships between rulers and their subjects are enacted on the bodies of the dominated. As modern forms of power relationships developed, so there was a change from an older to a new, modern body. The major shift towards this new form of power and body occurred in the early modern period – though Foucault's attention to chronology lacked rigour. The old fluid body of humours and astrological correspondences gave way to a new body, defined by observation, intervention and scientific rigour.

In *Discipline and Punish: the Birth of the Prison* (1977), Foucault examined the use of discipline and punishment as a social force to control the bodies of the ruled by producing self-regulated behaviour.[37] The pre-modern system of punishment, exemplified by the torturous and gory public execution of a French regicide in 1757, involved ritualistic, symbolic and public demonstrations of the sovereign's power. After the French Revolution, a more subtle modern system developed that used strict regulation and constant surveillance within closed institutions, exemplified by the English utilitarian political and social activist Jeremy Bentham's (1748–1832) plan in 1791 for the panopticon, a model prison in which each inmate would discipline him- or herself in the belief that they were under constant surveillance. (The same principle lies behind CCTV, road speed cameras and school reports.) Disciplinary power made bodies more docile and obedient. Whereas pre-modern punishment was enacted on the body, modern punishment was enacted on the mind. Foucault saw similar shifts occurring in other spheres. Alongside this penal shift from flesh to mind, modern government began to focus on the welfare of the population. Fertility, diet, housing and body habits become important. Bodies are regulated within a whole population – a far cry from the old, sovereign practice of controlling anonymous individual criminals.

Foucault identified similar shifts in other manifestations of modern power: hospitals, mental asylums, schools and military academies. Like the modern prison system, these institutions are conventionally heralded as positive, more humane systems than those that preceded them. All these modern institutions sought to observe and constrain their subjects. New ideas about health and new techniques of analysing patients led to a new 'scientific' conceptualization of the body, in which the human body was viewed as a machine and as a species (*Homo sapiens*). This scientific model focused on the body's docility, how it could be disciplined, organized and efficiently made use of. The Linnaean classification of the natural world – after the Swedish scientist Carolus Linnaeus (aka Carl von Linné, 1707–78), who laid the foundations for the modern taxonomical schema in which everything in the natural world is put into a hierarchical order – also incorporated humans as a species. Here the focus was on biology. The order concerned itself with the 'disciplines of the body and the regulations of the population'.[38]

In the first volume of his *History of Sexuality*, Foucault set out the familiar hypothesis that the sexual body became subjected to a new range of restrictions and prohibitions during the eighteenth and nineteenth centuries.[39] Foucault acknowledged that bowdlerization had occurred: there was a move to restrict the kinds of speech considered socially acceptable. However, there was, at the same time, an increase in institutional discussion about sex and how it needed to be policed and regulated, whether in terms of governmental response to demographic changes (age of marriage, contraception) or the layout and regimen of schools, hospitals and prisons. Foucault reversed the hypothesis that the Victorian era was characterized by a repressive sexuality. Rather, it was obsessed with sexuality. The new scientific model of the body became central to the way in which power was maintained.

For Foucault, sex was always bound up with notions of what constituted 'truth'. In the pre-modern era, the Catholic confession served as the main vehicle for eliciting such truths, but by the nineteenth century the confessional mode was secularized and more widely utilized in the form of 'interrogations, consultations, autobiographical narratives, letters'.[40] The truth of personal motivation was still bound up with a hidden sexuality, while the interests of power were served not by repression and censorship, but by the 'incitement' of discussion about sex.

Both the value and limitations of Foucault's approach to the body can be seen in Michael Stolberg's 2000 article on eighteenth-century campaigns against masturbation. The English surgeon and writer John Marten, the Swiss physician Samuel Tissot and the anonymous author of the 1716 work *Onania* were some of those who dispensed advice about the medical dangers of masturbation. Stolberg acknowledges the value of a theoretical approach that focuses on minute aspects of sexuality and their relation to power interests. In Foucauldian mode, he states that the campaign

> forced a very common form of sexuality into secrecy and silence only to allow scientists and pedagogues to 'discover' it, to extract it from clandestiny.

> Thus transformed, it justified the establishment of a pervasive net of surveillance, maintained by parents, teachers, and the like, and exposed the most private and intimate areas of human life to the strategies of power. The ultimate success of the anti-onanist [anti-masturbation] campaign was achieved when censor and censored, sinner and confessor were one and the same, when the prohibitions were internalized and became the source of constant scrutiny and confession.[41]

Where masturbation had formerly been an unnatural practice to confess to a priest, under the new bodily regimen people policed themselves. The confessional mode was appropriated from exploring sinful practices to engaging with medical hazards. Just as prisoners modified their conduct under the pervasive gaze of the panopticon, so anti-masturbation literature prompted 'self-enquiry and profuse talking (or writing) about sex'. Such confessions enabled a return to good health, but also served to justify later disorders. Sexual 'malfunctions' like masturbation could cause 'almost any kind of serious physical disorder in later life'.[42] Thus were the dangers of the act both confirmed and reformed, while power was extended over the most private bodily activity.

This is the strength of utilizing Foucault's approach, but Stolberg also notes the weaknesses. Foucault offers only vague notions as to what exactly constitutes power, with no apparent active agent in operation. Foucault's rather abstract concept of power (while sharing assumptions of conventional modernization theory, such as that power is bound up with a 'system' and historical change occurs to allow the system to achieve specific goals) does not clarify the diverging interests of the groups involved. Stolberg finds French sociologist and critical theorist Pierre Bourdieu's (1930–2002) notion of the *habitus* useful in locating more specifically the agents of power. The term *habitus* refers to the ways in which bodies incorporate a range of habits (manners, postures, ways of speaking and making things) that reflect prevailing social values and beliefs, and thus offers a more contextualized notion of power. The anti-masturbation campaigners did not just act as mediators of anonymous power, but rather shared with their audience a *habitus* of similar attitudes to their bodies. In the eighteenth century, this shared element was a comprehension of bodies and bodily emissions in terms of the new, modern body, identified by Foucault, which was coming to replace the traditional understanding of the body based on the idea of a balance of bodily humours or fluids. Echoing Elias's civilizing process, the new body 'turned human excretions, in their physical materiality, into increasingly powerful sources of anxiety and disgust'.[43] The new bodily ideal emerged alongside other changes; the eighteenth-century works on masturbation 'expressed and promoted the political and economic interests of the ascending bourgeoisie and an increasingly commercialized society'.[44] The medical concern of the campaigners was not invented as a moral panic, but arose out of the shifts in their *habitus* that valued rational self-control.

While identifying power with a specific social grouping, Stolberg leaves a number of questions unanswered. Is the *habitus* defined by class – would the lower classes not identify with the same concerns? Was the *habitus* uncontested within the bourgeoisie? After all, the eighteenth century also witnessed a growth of erotic and pornographic literature which, it could be argued, encouraged masturbation.[45] Stolberg fails to explain satisfactorily how a new body emerged from an oversimplified and sweeping field of social change.

Foucault's influence is seen most notably, perhaps, in the work of Thomas Laqueur, who, in 1992, challenged an apparently unassailable natural distinction – the sexually differentiated body. Laqueur describes a shift during the early modern period from a one-sex to a two-sex model of the body. The older one-sex model was based on the classical humoural system outlined by the first-century physician Galen, wherein sexual difference was the consequence of the physiological mixture of cold, wet, hot and dry qualities in a body. According to this schema, men and women's sexual organs were essentially the same, but took different forms because of the individual's particular balance of humours. Women, whose bodies were colder and moister than men's, lacked the necessary heat to expel their sexual organs. Hence theirs remained inside the body, ovaries corresponding to testes, and the vagina an inside-out penis, and so on. Women were inferior to men, but the differences between them were relative, not biologically fixed. This meant that maleness could lapse into effeminacy at any time. In a reversal worthy of Foucault, Laqueur argues that it is sex that is constructed and gender that is real. During the late seventeenth and eighteenth centuries 'natural' difference and notions of the 'opposite sex' appeared. Only then was 'sex', as we know it, invented.[46]

While there were several interconnected reasons for these changes, the key dynamic was concern about the changing social status of women: 'As the natural body itself became the gold standard of social discourse, the bodies of women – the perennial other – thus became the battleground for redefining the ancient, intimate, fundamental social relation: that of woman to man . . . Two sexes . . . were invented as a new foundation for gender'.[47] It became important for women to be defined as different from men, and, subsequently, physical attributes of male and female bodies were noted for their distinctive features. The vagina, skeleton and nervous system defined the female body as other, along with women's passivity, passionlessness and redundant orgasm, which in the new reproductive order was no longer seen as being essential for conception.

Laqueur has been criticized for simplifying the sexual revolution of the period, for overlooking the rise of separate spheres, for focusing too exclusively on elite medical and scientific works (and thus overlooking the importance of vernacular medical books and erotic writings).[48] Laqueur does relate his own history to the pattern identified by Elias and Bakhtin in that the civilizing of the grotesque, which was part and parcel of the changes in the state, 'also became attacks on the Renaissance model of sex and gender'. The new male and female bodies that appeared in the eighteenth century offered 'new metaphors of reproduction' to underpin the changed political culture, with a public sphere distinct from a private world.[49] The eighteenth century becomes the turning point between the earlier 'golden age of freedom in sex/gender identity', characterized by what Foucault described as 'direct gestures, shameless discourse, and open transgressions', and the Victorian era of the 'imperial prude'.[50]

The lack of concern with chronological specifics that characterizes some cultural history is evident in early modern body history. Longer-term trends of social formation inform changes in knowledge and models of the body. Dominant discourses of a new body do not eliminate the older bodily forms, but marginalize them and confer on them the status of 'others'. The value of the poststructuralist deconstruction of common assumptions is in reversing the accepted provenance of notions of the sexed body and gender. However, it is largely played out on familiar and generalized historical narratives. Laqueur does not *explain* the momentous shift, but rather notes it. The details of such crucial changes are blurred and vaguely bound up with the kind of historical metanarratives (such as industrialization, professionalization, democratization and the rise of separate spheres) consistently repudiated by poststructuralist theorists like Foucault, Jean-François Lyotard (1924–98) and Jacques Derrida (1930–2004).

Feminist theory and body history: a brief and partial account

As well as the influence of individual theorists such as Elias, Bakhtin and Foucault, discussed above, feminist scholarship across academic disciplines, including women's and gender history, has contributed enormously to the nature and trajectory of body history. Whereas some women's history in the 1970s tended to perceive women as a homogeneous interest group (taking little account, for example, of differences in women's experiences according to culture, class, race and ethnicity), the gender history that emerged in the 1980s acknowledged the importance of examining women in relation to men, and of considering different gender systems in particular historical periods. Indeed, gender history has been instrumental in problematizing foundational categories such as nature and culture, sex and gender. Feminist criticism of the mind/body dualism has shown that the privileging of mind (associated with masculinity) over body (associated with femininity) 'masked a distinctively masculine fear of femininity and a desire to keep the female body and all the unruliness which it represented at bay'.[51] Such ideas, in analysing the way that masculinity and femininity were mapped onto other binary oppositions, such as mind/body, demonstrate the cross-fertilization of feminist studies and poststructuralism, especially Foucauldian perspectives. Poststructuralism, however, was not solely responsible for developing insights in this area. Long before Foucault, feminists analysed how women's bodies have been shaped, normalized and subjected to scrutiny and appraisal by patriarchal cultures, and thus effectively noted that the female body was socially constructed (although not always by using those terms) by those (alpha males) holding social power. The writer Mary Wollstonecraft (1759–97), in *A Vindication of the Rights of Woman* (1792), documented procedures for making the female body docile, for example.

> To preserve personal beauty . . . the limbs and faculties are cramped with worse than Chinese bands, and the sedentary life which they are condemned to live . . . weakens the muscles and relaxes the nerves . . . artificial notions of beauty, and false descriptions of sensibility, have been early entangled with her motives of action.[52]

Such analysis of the strategic shaping of the female body is also evident in feminist writing in the 1910s and during the 1960s and 1970s. Feminists increasingly articulated that the practices of everyday life, such as what one wears and the jobs one is expected to do (cooking, cleaning, child-rearing), subordinated women. It was clear that, as Wollstonecraft stated, 'the mind shapes itself to the body, and, roaming round its gilt cage, only seeks to adorn its prison'.[53]

An emphasis on how everyday life impacts on embodiment – how people experience their bodies – is a feature of many anthropological and *Annales* works as well as feminist studies. For example, the influential anthropologist Marcel Mauss's (1872–1950) *Techniques of the Body* (1935) offered important insights into the ways in which cultures shaped bodies in terms of rites of passage, forms of walking and conversation and fashion identities.[54] Many scholars have argued that the female body, in terms of both sexuality and maternity, has been (and still is) used to underpin female inferiority and male superiority. In response, much feminist work has affirmed a positive female embodiment. This is predicated upon a fundamental sexual difference. Feminist philosopher and political scientist Iris Marion Young (b. 1949), for instance, demonstrates the importance of gender difference in relation to lived bodies, arguing that the pregnant body offers a specifically sexed form of embodiment. Young develops Mauss's body techniques in asserting that men and women possess different bodily styles, evident in the ways they sit, stand or walk, so that women 'generally are not as open with their bodies as are men in their gait and style'.[55] Drawing on French existentialist feminist writer Simone de Beauvoir (1909–86), Young argues that the distinct orientations of feminine disposition derive from sexist conditioning, with the result that women 'in sexist society are physically handicapped'.[56] The downside of this approach to embodiment is that male and female bodies may become essentialized.

German body historian Barbara Duden draws on these and other works on embodiment in describing her seen and unseen history of the female body. The visible history is that which is viewed 'by physicians, artists, and women themselves', while the hidden history is one of 'touch and vision, which grope in the darkness beneath the skin'. Duden's is an experiential history: in examining early modern women's accounts of visiting physicians, she uncovers 'experiences that have lost all meaning for us'.[57] The importance of religion, for example, with feelings of being more in touch with God, angels and the dead, meant that the unseen had a greater resonance culturally in the early modern period than it does in modern western culture, where, since the Enlightenment, sight has become the primary sense. But in early modern culture, there existed an older sense of the body based on what was not, as well as what was, seen. Duden's insights have been elaborated on by other early modern historians. Laura Gowing's *Common Bodies* (2003), for instance, is written from the perspective that touch, as much as sight, was a crucial component in how women experienced their bodies.[58]

Another recent trend in feminist accounts of the early modern body is that informed by various psychoanalytic theories. Influential elaborations and modifications of theories first posited by Sigmund Freud (1856–1939) in the late nineteenth and early twentieth centuries have included those of Melanie Klein (1882–1960) and Julia Kristeva (b. 1941), both of whom emphasized the maternal function and its importance in the development of subjectivity. Garthine Walker has discussed elsewhere how Diane Purkiss draws on Kristeva in viewing the early modern witch as a 'fantasy-image of the huge, controlling, scattered, polluted, leaky fantasy of the maternal body of the Imaginary', and relating this body to 'specific cultural circumstances'.[59] Purkiss considers how early modern people negotiated supposedly universal aspects of the psyche or unconscious mind in the context of specific cultural and historical phenomena, such as humoural understandings of physiology in which the coldness and moistness attributed to the female body made it more likely to be considered as flowing and polluting, for example. Purkiss thus juxtaposes a transhistorical psychic structure with historical elements – this could be seen as one way of negotiating the problem of a transhistorical psyche and answering the charge of determinism frequently made of psychohistory. By downplaying the reductive elements in psychoanalysis, the problem of falsifiability (that is, that any interpretation is possible as none can be disproved) is evaded.[60]

Feminist thought has led to a clearer understanding of the degree to which gender differences are not biologically inevitable, but rather are culturally, hence historically, constructed. Work on femininities as well as masculinities has assisted in reconfiguring the old dualisms and, as a result, a more complex and varied historical body has been acknowledged. Psychoanalysis has offered the opportunity of exploring new sources (fantasies, dreams, emotions) to develop an appreciation of the unconscious, the body-image and how the body has been imagined.

Conclusion

It has only been possible here to highlight some of the main trends in and approaches to the history of the body. Social and cultural history's ongoing engagement with anthropology, psychology and other social sciences distanced academic history from the positivist, empirical-narrative (and invariably nationalistic) Rankean model, with its subject focus on high politics. Body history has roots in social history's exploration of popular agency and mentalities and part of the semiotic cultural turn that grew out of social history. However, body history can stand accused of restoring 'history from above', with royal bodies and aristocratic manners becoming once more subjects of research. Elias's association of the modern body with the development of shame and civilized restraint has parallels with Rankean history's emphasis on progress as demarcated by constitutions, parliaments and centralized nation states in that the driving force for historical change is state power. Foucault's focus on dominant discourses similarly emphasized top-down solutions over popular resistance and construction. Of the three theorists, Bakhtin's approach is potentially the most useful for historians as it allows for much greater agency on the part of subordinate groups.[61]

As we have seen, several perspectives on body history posit a change over time from one perception of the body to another, a shift that is often situated in the early modern period. The older bodily form is typically presented as instinctual, openly expressing its desires, urges and functions, while the new, modern one is rational and self-controlled. Such dualistic theories are problematic for two main reasons. First, their tendency towards conceptual and chronological generalization means that insufficient attention is paid to anomalies and temporal, regional and cultural context. Although body history has been successful in opening up new areas of research, in this respect it merely reconfigures conventional historical discourses. Political history in the form of the new body politics thus returns triumphant. Second, the dichotomy between representation and experience is usually merely perpetuated rather than interrogated. Although historians such as Ulinka Rublack have pointed to the different experiences early modern people had of their bodies, there is very little material that seeks to gain an insight into the lived experience that would constitute the embodied Eliasian uncivilized body, Bakhtinian grotesque body or Foucauldian sovereign body. These stand as models but are devoid of the elements that make them vitally human. A sensitive use of literary and personal sources (including diaries and journals) would make such an approach at least feasible.

The widespread practice among scholars to 'pick and mix' from theoretical models often serves to reinforce common characteristics in approaches to the early modern body. For example, Gail Kern Paster's *The Body Embarrassed*, which explores expressions of bodily embarrassment over incontinence, bleeding, purging, childbirth and lactation in Elizabethan and Jacobean drama, draws on several theoretical models. Paster emphasizes the 'structural resemblance' of Bakhtin's grotesque body to the early modern humoural body, with its openness and instability, while resisting Bakhtin's model of collective festivity. Arguing that her focus on vernacular medical writings authenticates the grotesque model from another source, Paster is keen to emphasize its relation to a sense of personal self. Bakhtin's symbolic representation of the people's body is rejected in favour of the individual 'subjects being-in-the-body'.[62] At the same time, she adapts the insights of the anthropologist Mary Douglas (b. 1920) concerning the duality of a physical and a social body: 'The social body constrains the way the physical body is perceived. The physical experience of the body, always modified by the social categories through which it is known, sustains a particular view of society. There is a continual exchange of meanings between the two . . .'[63] Paster seeks to establish a contrast between the internal and external body, between subjective experience and 'the body visible in different ways to self and other'.[64] Representation and embodiment are seen as distinct elements, interacting via an ideologically inscribed culture. To explore the stage at which the body becomes 'enculturated', Paster draws on the psychoanalytic theory of Jacques Lacan (1901–81), which has been so influential for feminist literary theory. By establishing that it is culture that imposes meanings on the body, including sexual difference, Lacan's work has been crucial in deconstructing the belief in biological essentialism (the notion that sex is a natural, biological attribute), and Paster utilizes his notion of the 'mirror stage' of infant development to establish a convergence between psychoanalytical and historical assessments of embarrassment.[65] She also seeks to connect Laqueur's 'one-sex' model with the experience of embodiment.[66] Within this elaborate and plural (and highly promising) theoretical framework, Paster goes beyond the dichotomy between the older (in this case) humoural bodily order of 'somatic uncontrol' and the new body ideology of Eliasian refinement and Foucauldian discipline. With accounts of such topics as cross-species suckling, excretion, incontinence and menstruation, Paster explores not only the degree to which humoural theory operated to account for the body's activities, but also the language associated with these physiological processes. Challenging Laqueur's thesis that female pleasure in conception was as important as male, Paster uncovers an alternative narrative of reproduction, which reveals a 'deep ambivalence toward the maternal body'.[67] She notes how ideologies of class and gender informed the obstetric literature of the period and concludes that an 'unstable oscillation between shame and celebration' informed the practices of pregnancy, birth and wetnursing.[68] Most historians would be happy with evidence derived from the representation of pregnancy and childbirth in midwifery manuals. To test her thesis though, Paster draws on Rabelais's 1534 account of the birth of the giant, Gargantua, and the lying-in of his mother, Gargamelle. As a piece of literary assessment, Paster's analysis is well observed. Being a work of comic fiction, however, it does not meet the criteria for embodied experience that most historians would demand – subjective accounts (albeit mediated by the genre) provided by autobiographies, journals, letters or even more personal fictional records. Ultimately, therefore, Paster's overwhelming reliance on dramatic and fictional sources does not successfully resolve the gap between the two bodily dimensions of embodiment and representation.

The development of a clearer understanding of popular feelings and embodied experience remains a challenge for early modern historians. If historians wish to grasp the complexity of historical experiences of the body, they must cease to reproduce arguments about broad sequential shifts and the over-simplistic dualities the latter generate. In uniting experience and representation, body history may produce a far more intriguing series of historical narratives. Body history has much potential. Attending a conference in 2002 on the history of the body, I was struck by the diversity of papers presented, which included, among other things, explorations of the representation and experience of both clothed and naked bodies, and consideration of diet, illness and disability.[69] The expanding remit of the history of the body is setting the pace in historical scholarship in the early twenty-first century. Its ultimate impact on historical theory remains to be seen.

Guide to further reading

Barbara Brook, *Feminist Perspectives on the Body* (Harlow, 1999).

Barbara Duden, *The Woman Beneath the Skin: A Doctor's Patients in Eighteenth-Century Germany*, trans. Thomas Dunlap (1987; Cambridge, MA, 1991).

Norbert Elias, *The Civilizing Process: Sociogenetic and Psychogenetic Investigations*, trans. Edmund Jephcott, ed. Eric Dunning, Johan Goudsblom and Stephen Mennell (1939; Oxford, 2000).

Michel Foucault, *Discipline and Punish: the Birth of the Prison*, trans. Alan Sheridan (1975; London, 1977).

Michel Foucault, *The History of Sexuality*, 3 vols, trans. Robert Hurley (1976; Harmondsworth, 1990–98).

Thomas Laqueur, *Making Sex: Body and Sex From the Greeks to Freud* (Cambridge, MA and London, 1992).

Ulinka Rublack, 'Pregnancy, Childbirth and the Female Body in Early Modern Germany', *Past & Present* 150 (1996), pp. 84–110.

Ulinka Rublack, 'Fluxes: The Early Modern Body and the Emotions', trans. Pamela Selwyn, *History Workshop Journal* 53 (2002), pp. 1–16.

Londa Schiebinger (ed.), *Feminism and the Body* (Oxford, 2000).

Chris Shilling, *The Body and Social Theory* (1993; 2nd edn, London, 2003).

Garthine Walker, 'Psychoanalysis and History', in Stefan Berger, Heiko Feldner and Kevin Passmore (eds), *Writing History: Theory and Practice* (London, 2003), pp. 141–60.

Notes

1 The present discussion does not consider the separate discipline of art history or the specialized field of medical history, in both of which representations of the body are commonplace. Additionally, it is worth noting that histories of costume and marital practices were 'only banished from academic history to become the preserve of the antiquarian or amateur enthusiast in the late-nineteenth and early-twentieth centuries when the discipline became entrenched in the universities': Mark S.R. Jenner and Bertrand O. Taithe, 'The Historiographical Body', in Roger Cooter and John Pickstone (eds), *Companion to Medicine in the Twentieth Century* (London and New York, 2003), p. 188.

2 Kathy Davis, 'Embody-ing Theory: Beyond Modernist and Postmodernist Readings of the Body', in Kathy Davis (ed.), *Embodied Practices: Feminist Perspectives on the Body* (London, 1997), p. 1.

3 Max Weber, *The Protestant Work Ethic and the Spirit of Capitalism* (London, 1904–5). For a later engagement with Weber's ideas about the body, see Natalie Zemon Davis, 'The Sacred and the Body Social in Sixteenth-century Lyons', *Past & Present* 90 (1981), pp. 40–70.

4 See, for example, Friedrich Engels, *The Condition of the Working Class in England in 1844*, trans. Florence Kelley Wischnewtzky (1845; London, 1892). Max Horkheimer (1895–1973) and Theodor W. Adorno (1903–69) of the Marxist Frankfurt School saw the body as part of an 'underground' history related to the 'instincts and passions which are displaced and distorted by civilization': Horkheimer and Adorno, *Dialectic of Enlightenment*, trans. John Cumming (1944; London, 1973), p. 231.

5 Michel Foucault, *Power/Knowledge: Selected Interviews and Other Writings, 1972–1977*, trans. Colin Gordon, Leo Marshall, John Mepham and Kate Soper, ed. Colin Gordon (Harlow, 1980), pp. 58–9.

6 Marc Bloch, *The Royal Touch: Sacred Monarchy and Scrofula in England and France*, trans. J.E. Anderson (1924; London, 1973).

7 Patrick H. Hutton, 'The History of Mentalities: The New Map of Cultural History', in Stuart Clark (ed.), *The Annales School: Critical Assessments* (London, 1999), vol. 2, p. 387; Lucien Febvre, 'A New Kind of History', in Peter Burke (ed.), *A New Kind of History: From the Writings of Febvre*, trans. K. Folca (London, 1973), pp. 27–43.

8 Caroline Walker Bynum, 'Why All the Fuss about the Body? A Medievalist's Perspective', *Critical Inquiry* 22 (1995), p. 5.

9 Kathleen Canning, 'The Body as Method? Reflections on the Place of the Body in Gender History', *Gender & History* 11(3) (1999), p. 499.

10 Pasi Falk, *The Consuming Body* (London, 1994), p. 45.

11 Barbara Duden, 'A Repertory of Body History', in Michel Feher, with Ramona Nadaff and Nadia Tazi (eds), *Fragments for a History of the Human Body: Part Three* (New York, 1990), p. 472.

12 Michel Feher, 'Introduction' to Michel Feher, with Ramona Nadaff and Nadia Tazi (eds), *Fragments for a History of the Human Body: Part One* (New York, 1990), p. 11.

13 Canning, 'Body as Method?', p. 501.

14 Ivan Illich, *In the Mirror of the Past: Lectures and Addresses, 1978–1990* (New York and London, 1992), p. 215.

15 A more recent sociological treatment of the body is Bryan Turner, *The Body and Society: Explorations in Social Theory* (Oxford, 1984). Turner's preference for top-down functionalist models and abstract theorization renders his argument of limited use for historians.

16 Norbert Elias, *The Civilizing Process*, 2 vols, trans. Edmund Jephcott (1939; Oxford, 1978 and 1982).

17 Lucien Febvre identified a similar shift. André Burguière, 'The Fate of the History of *Mentalités* in the Annales', in Clark (ed.), *The Annales School*, vol. 2, p. 414.

18 Elias, *The Civilizing Process: Sociogenetic and Psychogenetic Investigations*, trans. Edmund Jephcott, ed. Eric Dunning, Johan Goudsblom and Stephen Mennell (Oxford, 2000), p. 160. Elias also drew on Freud's *Civilization and its Discontents* (1930) in arguing that bodies evolve towards civilization.

19 Hans-Peter Duerr, *Der Mythos vom Zivilsationsprozess*, 4 vols (Frankfurt-am-Main, 1988–97).

20 Alan Hunt, *Governing Morals: A Social History of Moral Regulation* (Cambridge, 1999), p. 13.

21 Lyndal Roper, *Oedipus and the Devil: Witchcraft, Sexuality and Religion in Early Modern Europe* (London, 1997), pp. 148–54.

22 Peter Spierenburg, *The Broken Spell: A Cultural and Anthropological History of Pre-industrial Europe* (Basingstoke, 1991), p. 196.
23 Craig Koslofsky, 'Suicide and the Secularization of the Body in Early Modern Saxony', *Continuity and Change* 16(1) (2001), pp. 45–70, 63.
24 Mikhail Bakhtin, *Rabelais and His World*, trans. Helene Iswolsky (1965; Bloomington, 1984), esp. ch. 5.
25 Sarah Juster, 'Mystical Pregnancy and Holy Bleeding: Visionary Experience in Early Modern Britain and America', *William and Mary Quarterly*, 3rd ser., 57(2) (2000), p. 288.
26 Mark S.R. Jenner, 'The Roasting of the Rump: Scatology and the Body Politic in Restoration England', *Past & Present* 177 (2002), pp. 107–12.
27 Ulinka Rublack, 'Pregnancy, Childbirth and the Female Body in Early Modern Germany', *Past & Present* 150 (1996), pp. 84–110; Ulinka Rublack, 'Fluxes: the Early Modern Body and the Emotions', trans. Pamela Selwyn, *History Workshop Journal* 53 (2002), pp. 1–16.
28 Bakhtin, *Rabelais*, pp. 25, 26.
29 Bakhtin, *Rabelais*, p. 19.
30 Bakhtin, *Rabelais*, p. 320.
31 Bakhtin, *Rabelais*, pp. 72, 101.
32 Bakhtin, *Rabelais*, p. 101.
33 Bakhtin, *Rabelais*, pp. 101–2, 33.
34 See Adam Fox, 'Ballads, Libels and Popular Ridicule in Jacobean England', *Past & Present* 145 (1994), pp. 47–83; Emma Griffin, 'Popular Culture in Industrializing England', *The Historical Journal* 45(3) (2002), pp. 619–35; Martin Ingram, 'Ridings, Rough Music and Mocking Rhymes in Early Modern England', in Barry Reay (ed.), *Popular Culture in Early Modern England* (New York, 1985), pp. 166–97; John Rule, 'Against Innovation? Custom and Resistance in the Workplace, 1700–1850', in Tim Harris (ed.), *Popular Culture in England, c.1500–1850* (Basingstoke, 1995), pp. 168–88.
35 Piero Camporesi, *The Incorruptible Flesh: Bodily Mutation and Mortification in Religion and Folklore*, trans. Tania Croft-Murray (1983; New York, 1988).
36 Tom Cheesman, 'Modernity/Monstrosity: Eating Freaks (Germany, c.1700)', *Body and Society* 2(2) (1996), pp. 8, 7.
37 Michel Foucault, *Discipline and Punish: The Birth of the Prison*, trans. Alan Sheridan (1975; London, 1977).
38 Michel Foucault, *The History of Sexuality. Volume 1: An Introduction*, trans. Robert Hurley (1976; Harmondsworth, 1990), p. 139.
39 Foucault, *History of Sexuality*, pp. 3–13. For a version of this 'familiar hypothesis', see Walter E. Houghton, *The Victorian Frame of Mind, 1830–1870* (New Haven and London, 1963), ch. 13.
40 Foucault, *History of Sexuality*, p. 63.

41 Michael Stolberg, 'An Unmanly Vice: Self-pollution, Anxiety, and the Body in the Eighteenth Century', *Social History of Medicine* 13(1), p. 16.
42 Stolberg, 'Unmanly Vice', p. 17.
43 Stolberg, 'Unmanly Vice', p. 19.
44 Stolberg, 'Unmanly Vice', pp. 20–1.
45 Peter Wagner, *Eros Revived: Erotica of the Enlightenment in England and America* (London, 1990); Lynn Hunt (ed.), *The Invention of Pornography: Obscenity and the Origins of Modernity, 1500–1800* (New York, 1993).
46 Thomas Laqueur, *Making Sex: Body and Gender from the Greeks to Freud* (Cambridge, MA and London, 1992), p. 149.
47 Laqueur, *Making Sex*, p. 150.
48 Randolph Trumbach, *Sex and the Gender Revolution, Vol. 1: Heterosexuality and the Third Gender in Enlightenment London* (Chicago, 1999); Tim Hitchcock, *English Sexualities, 1700–1800* (London, 1997); Karen Harvey, 'The Substance of Sexual Difference: Change and Persistence in Representations of the Body in Eighteenth-Century England', *Gender & History* 14(2) (2002), pp. 202–23.
49 Laqueur, *Making Sex*, p. 122.
50 Harvey, 'Substance of Sexual Difference', p. 908; Foucault, *History of Sexuality*, p. 3.
51 Davis, *Embodied Practices*, p. 5.
52 Quoted in Susan Bordo, *Unbearable Weight: Feminism, Western Culture and the Body* (London, 1995), p. 18.
53 Bordo, *Unbearable Weight*, p. 18. For an overview of feminist writings in this vein, see Susan Bordo, 'Feminism, Foucault and the Politics of the Body', in Carole Ramazanoglu (ed.), *Up Against Foucault* (London and New York, 1993), pp. 185–8.
54 Marcel Mauss, 'Techniques of the Body', *Economy and Society* 2 (1973), pp. 70–88.
55 Iris Marion Young, *Throwing Like a Girl and Other Essays in Feminist Philosophy and Social Theory* (Bloomington, 1990), p. 145.
56 Young, *Throwing Like a Girl*, p. 153.
57 Barbara Duden, *Disembodying Women: Perspectives on Pregnancy and the Unborn*, trans. Lee Hoinacki (Cambridge, MA, 1993), p. 8.
58 Laura Gowing, *Common Bodies: Women, Touch and Power in Seventeenth-Century England* (New Haven and London, 2003).
59 Diane Purkiss, *The Witch in History: Early Modern and Twentieth-Century Representations* (London, 1996), p. 119.
60 Garthine Walker, 'Psychoanalysis and History', in Stefan Berger, Heiko Feldner and Kevin Passmore (eds), *Writing History: Theory and Practice* (London, 2003), pp. 151–5. In the same chapter, Walker provides a useful critique of Lyndal Roper's engagement with object-relations theory.

61 Raphael Samuel, 'Reading the Signs: II. Fact-grubbers and Mind-Readers', *History Workshop Journal* 33 (1992), pp. 228–31.
62 Gail Kern Paster, *The Body Embarrassed: Drama and the Disciplines of Shame in Early Modern England* (Ithaca, 1993), p. 16.
63 Mary Douglas, *Natural Symbols: Explorations in Cosmology* (London, 1978), p. 93.
64 Paster, *Body Embarrassed*, p. 3.
65 On Lacan's usefulness for history, see Sally Alexander, 'Women, Class and Sexual Differences in the 1830s and 1840s: Some Reflections on the Writings of a Feminist History', *History Workshop Journal* 17 (1984), pp. 125–49; Teresa Brennan, *History after Lacan* (London, 1993); Walker, 'Psychoanalysis and History', esp. pp. 151–3.
66 Paster, *Body Embarrassed*, p. 17.
67 Paster, *Body Embarrassed*, p. 167.
68 Paster, *Body Embarrassed*, p. 208.
69 Conference on 'Controlling Bodies. The Regulation of the Body, 1650–2000', University of Glamorgan, 24–26 June 2002.

Index

A
Act of Union (1536) (England and Wales) 35
actors, understanding historical 172–3, 174, 175, 176
Adams, John 58
Albigensianism 53
Allen, Robert C. 171
Alltagsgeschichte 59
Anecdotes typographiques 63
Anglophone historiography xiii, xvn12
Annales school xii, 19, 161
  body history 206, 217
  ethnographic history 53
  'history from below' 78
  longe durée, importance of 26, 145, 147
  Malthusian model 163–4
  mentalités, study of 36–7, 59, 78, 144–5, 146
  power relationships 78
  quantitative approaches 145
  sources 145
  see also Le Roy Ladurie
anthropological history *see* historical anthropology
anthropology
  culture, as resource 52
  functional anthropology 50–2
  'pidgin paradigm' 63–4
  and postmodernism 63–4
  scale, question of 60–2
  standards of proof 55–7
  structural anthropology 26, 52–3
  texts, and meanings 62–3
  value of to historians 49
  see also historical anthropology
Aram Veeser, H. 41
Artemidorus of Daldis 119

B
Bacon, Francis 4, 43
Baker, Keith Michael 79–80
Bakhtin, Mikhail 57, 128, 206, 209–12
Barnes, Barry 84
Barzun, Jacques 115
Becker, Marjorie 123, 124
Behme, Jacob 121
Bellany, Alastair 196
Bennett, Judith 101–2
Bentham, Jeremy 77–8, 212
Biagioli, Mario 85
biography 142–3
  see also psychobiography
Birth of the Clinic (Foucault) 77
Black Death 6, 7 163
Bloch, Marc 10, 26, 163, 206
Bloor, David 84
Blum, Carol 79
Body Embarrassed, The (Paster) 220
body history
  classical body 209–10

body history (*continued*)
  control of bodies 212–13
  democracy, development of 207–8
  embodiment *versus* representation 205–6, 220
  gender differences 217–19, 220
  grotesque body (Bakhtin) 209–11, 220
  and 'history from above' 219
  masturbation, campaigns against 213–15
  maternal body, ambivalence towards 220–1
  medieval *versus* modern body 207–9
  mind/body dualism 205–6, 216–17, 219, 220, 221
  modernization theory, influence of 208–9
  physical *versus* social body 220
  and poststructuralism 212–16, 219
  power relationships, and bodies 212–15
  psychoanalytic theory, influence of 218, 220
  scientific model, of body 213
  seen and unseen 218
  sexual body 213–15
  sexually differentiated body (Laqueur) 215–16, 220
  shame, development of 207, 208, 219, 220
  social constructionist approach 212
  and social regulation 207–9
  'texts', bodies as 212
  theoretical models, drawing from several 220
Boettcher, Susan R. vi, 71–88
Bossy, John 145–6
Bourdieu, Pierre 86, 214
Bowen, Lloyd vi, 183–201
Bowker, G.Q. 29–31, 33
Boyle, Leonard 55
Boyle, Robert 85
Brailsford, H.N. 14
Braudel, Fernand 19, 78, 163, 174, 191
Brauner, Sigrid 83
Brenner, Robert 11
Breviate of the Life of William Laud, Archbishop of Canterbury (Prynne) 120
Brewer, John 167
Briggs, Robin 42–4, 117
British Marxist historians
  bottom-up history 13
  bourgeois history, artificial divisions of 9, 10
  bourgeois revolution, English 12–13
  capitalist development 9–10, 12, 14
  enduring controversies, emergence of 11–12, 14–15
  'humanist' Marxists 11, 13
  hypothetical approach 10–11, 13, 15–16
  modernization theory 28–9
  superstructural elements 10–11
  'vulgar Marxist' model 13
  working class, making of 13–14
Broken Spell, The (Spierenburg) 36, 208–9
Brown, Judith 152
Burckhardt, Jacob xi
Burke, Peter xii, 60–1, 146

C
Cade's Rebellion (1450) 16
Calvin, John 140, 165
Calvinism 166–7
Cambridge Group 15–16
Cameron, Euan 35, 42, 155
Camporesi, Piero 211
Canning, Kathleen 206
Capital (Marx) 3, 10, 14
capitalism
  development of 4, 5–10, 12, 14, 161
  and patriarchy 102–3
  and Protestant Reformation 26, 36, 165–7
Carlton, Charles 119–21, 127, 128
Carlyle, James Mill 5
Carlyle, Thomas 4, 184
Carnival in Romans (Le Roy Ladurie) 78
Carr, E.H. 33
Catholicism between Luther and Voltaire (Delumeau) 145
Causes of the English Revolution (Stone) 191
Certeau, Michel de 128
Cervantes, Fernando 149
Charles I, king of England 125, 126–7, 131–2, 185, 186
Chartier, Roger 63, 79, 80, 81, 148
Cheese and the Worms, The, (Ginzburg) 61, 147
Cheesman, Tom 211
Christian, William 58
Civilizing Process, The (Elias) 28, 35, 207
Cixous, Hélène 128
Clark, Alice xii, 95, 102

Clément, Catherine 128
Cobban, Alfred 78
Cobbett, William 5
Cohn, Bernard 59
Collins, Harry 84
Collinson, Patrick 194
colonial studies
  acculturation concept 148–9
  capital 6
  'consumer goods' 103–4
  and historical anthropology 59
  racial categories 106–7
  see also postcolonial theory
Committee of Both Kingdoms 186
Common Bodies (Gowing) 218
Communist Party Historians' Group 192
Confessio augustana (Luther) 140
confessionalization 150–1
constitutional monarchy 161
Constructing Cromwell (Knopper) 195
consumption
  colonial context of 103–4, 169
  'consumer revolution' 168–9
  gendered patterns of 167–8
  production, shift away from 167, 168
  and social emulation 168
Contat, Nicolas 63
Copernicus, Nicolas 84
Coriolanus (Shakespeare) 200
Council of the North (1537) 34–5
Council of Trent (1545-1563) 141, 152
Crafts, N.F.R. 171
Crawford, Patricia 121–2, 127, 128, 196
critical race theory 99
Cromwell, Oliver 125, 184, 185, 186, 195, 210
Cromwell, Thomas 34–5, 188
Crowston, Clare Haru vi, 159–77
cultural turn, and popular religion 144–9
Cust, Richard 200

D
Darkened Room, The (Owen) 116–17
Darnton, Robert xii, 62–3
Davies, Eleanor 127, 128
Davies, Godfrey 186, 187
Davis, Natalie Demon 58, 59, 81–2, 100, 123, 124, 148, 165
Davis, Natalie Zemon xii
Daybell, James 196
de Beauvoir, Simone 217
de Martino, Ernesto 56
de Pizan, Christine 101
de Saussure, Ferdinand 72
de Tocqueville, Alexis de 79
de Vries, Jan 167–8
Dear, Peter 84
decapitation, symbolism of 127
Delumeau, Jean 78, 145
Derrida, Jacques 72, 216
Diggers 192, 193
Discipline and Punish (Foucault) 41–2, 77, 212
discourses
  discourse analysis, and social constructivism 75
  and power relationships 73–4
  and the self 76, 86
  and sources 74–5
  see also poststructuralism
Ditchfield, Simon 144, 155
Dobb, Maurice 11
Douglas, Mary 220
dreams, and psychoanalytic theory
  anxiety dreams 119–20
  dream texts, suspicion of 121
  expression of what cannot be said 119
  historical questions, relating dreams to 120–1
  oneness with God, Anne Bathurst's dreams of 121–2
  oracular dreams 127
  sexual revelation, in dreams 120
  visions, and dreams 121
  William Laud's dreams, interpretation of 119–21
  wish-fulfilling dreams 119
Duden, Barbara 218
Duerr, Hans Peter 208
Durkheim, Emile xi, 26, 27, 28
Dutch Calvinism 166–7

E
Early Modern Europe: An Oxford History 42
early modern history, study of
  historians, underlying assumptions of xi–xii, xiii–xiv

early modern history, study of (*continued*)
historical periodization, constructed nature of xvi
low-key status of xi
modern world, making of xi, xvi
tradition of theoretical application to xi–xii
economic history
collectivities, and reciprocal exchange 164–5
consumption, and material culture 159, 167–9
early modern period, modernist reading of 159, 160–1
economic theory, historians' distrust of 160
and gender history 102–3
gift economy 164–5
Industrial Revolution, and creation of the 'modern' 159
Malthusian metanarrative 163–4
Marxian metanarrative 161–3
moral economy 164
and new cultural history 176
other disciplines, insights from 173–4
Protestant Reformation, and birth of capitalist spirit 165–7
see also newer economic history
election processes *see* parliamentary elections case study
Elias, Norbert xi, 28, 35–6, 38, 206, 207–9, 219
Elizabeth I, queen of England 104, 105
Elizabethan House of Commons, The (Neale) 198–9
Elliott, John 61
Elton, Geoffrey R. xiv, 33–5, 187–8, 196, 199
enclosure movement 7, 161
Encyclopedia of European Social History (Stearns) 25
Engels, Friedrich 4, 14, 205
English Civil War (1642-1649)
as 'class war' 192
fiction, drawing on resources of 123–4
masculinity, notions of 105
psychoanalytic explanations 125–6
scientific, chronological approach (Gardiner) 184, 185
English Revolution, The (Hill) 192
Enlightenment project 75, 86
Erasmus, Disiderius 140
Erikson, Eric xii, 114, 115, 142
ethnographic history
ethnographer, role of 54
inquisitorial evidence, objectivity/authority of 53–5
Montaillou, Le Roy's study of 53–5
Europe in the Sixteenth Century (Koenigsberger, Mosse & Bowker) 29–31
European Reformation (Cameron) 35
European Society in Upheaval (Stearns) 25
Evans, Richard 123
Evans-Pritchard, E.E. 50, 54

F

family, histories of 31–3
Febvre, Lucien 206
Feher, Michel 206
feminist theory
and body history 216–19
see also gender history
feudalism 4, 161
fiction, exploring resources of 123–7
Fiction in the Archives (Davis) 81
Filde, Valerie 121
Firth, Charles 186
Fortescue, John 4, 8
Foucault, Michel xi, 29, 41–2, 77–8, 154, 206, 212–16, 217, 219
Fournier, Jacques 53
Frankfurt school 29
Frazer, James 52
French Revolution 87, 159, 161–2
case study 78–80
Freud, Sigmund 28, 119, 121, 208, 218
Froude, James Anthony 34, 35
functional anthropology
magic and religion 50–2
and modernization theory 37, 38–9
primitivism, language of 51
witchcraft, charity-refusal model of 50–1
Furet, François 79

G

Galilei, Galileo 84, 85
Galileo, Courtier (Baigioli) 85
Gardiner, Samuel Rawson 184–7, 198
gay liberation movement 96–7
Geertz, Clifford 58, 61, 62, 147

Geertz, Hildred 50–3
gender history
 and body history 97, 205
 colonial contexts 103–4, 106–7
 critical race theory 99, 100
 and economic history 102–3
 feminist movement 95
 gay liberation movement 96–7
 gender, shift of focus to 96
 hermaphrodites, fascination with 104
 historical documents, constructed nature of 98
 'intersection', notion of 107–8
 masculinity, constructions of 104–6
 and patriarchy 102–3
 and postcolonial theory 99–100, 107
 and poststructuralism 97–9, 154, 217
 and psychoanalytic theory 115–16
 public/private divide 102
 and queer theory 99, 100, 106, 107
 and redefinition of the political 196
 and religion 151–4
 sex/gender distinction 96, 97, 104
 and sexuality, history of 96–7, 106
 theoretical perspectives of 100
 as totalizing 107–8
 women, and central developments 100–2
 work, gendered meaning of 103
Gender of History, The: Men, Women and Historical Practice (Smith) 129
Genovese, Eugene D. 17
Gentilcore, David vii, 49–64, 146–7
Gentileschi, Artemisia 101
German Reformation 145, 150–1
 see also Protestant Reformation
Gift, The (Mauss) 164
gift economy 164–5
Gift in Sixteenth-Century France, The 165
Ginzburg, Carlo xii, 55–7, 61, 143, 147–8
Gladstone, William 184
Glorious Revolution (1688-1689) 161
Gowing, Laura 218
Goya, Francisco de 84
Gramsci, Antonio 17–18
Great Arch, The (Corrigan & Sayer) 14
'great cat massacre' 62–3
Greenblatt, Stephen 76, 86, 122–3
Gregory, Brad 83
Grendi, Edoardo 57
Growth in a Traditional Society (Hoffman) 170–1

H
Harley, C.K. 171
Harris, Tim 196–7
Harrison, William 4
Hegel, G.W.F. 33, 34
Henrician Reformation 34–5, 188
Henry VII, king of England 34
Henry VIII, king of England 34–5, 188
Hill, Christopher 11, 12–13, 15, 28, 190, 192–4, 199
Hilton, Rodney H. 10, 11, 14, 16
Himmelfarb, Gertrude xii
Hirst, Derek 199–200
historical anthropology
 as 'anthropological history' 58
 and archival sources 64
 as sub-discipline 58, 59
 use of term 58–9
 see also anthropology
history from below
 and *Annales* school 78
 versus high political narratives 194–6
 local and regional archives, opening up of 15–16
 and Marxism 4, 5, 8
 people, effect of transformations on 80
 see also popular religion
History of England (Gardiner) 184–6
History of Sexuality (Foucault) 213
Hoak, Dale 196
Hobbes, Thomas 4, 85
Hobsbawm, E.J. 11, 16, 161
Hoffman, Phillip 164, 170–2, 173, 175–6
Hollar, Wenceslaus 123
homosexuality 106
Huizinga, Johan 29, 37
Hume, David 4
Hunt, Alan 208
Hunt, Lynn 79

I
ideological theory, and historical writing xii–xiii
Illich, Ivan 206

Industrial Revolution
  challenge to traditional views of 171–2, 174
  and creation of the 'modern' 36, 159
  and proto-industrialization theory 162–3
Inquisition records 53–5, 57, 143, 146–7
intellectual history, and religion 140–4
interdisciplinarity, of historical writing xv–xvi, 61, 71, 194–5
Interpreting the French Revolution (Furet) 79

J
James I, king of England 184
James II, king of England 161
Jenner, Mark 210
Jews, persecution of 83, 86, 140
Johnson, Trevor vii, 139–55
Jordan, Constance 104
Jordanova, Ludmilla xiii
Journal of Interdisciplinary History 58
Juster, Sarah 210
justification by faith 142

K
Kelly, Joan 101
Kelsey, Sean 195
Kepler, Johannes 43
Keynes, John Maynard 160
Kishlansky, Mark 200
Klein, Melanie 122, 153, 218
Knopper, Laura 195
Koenigsberger, H.K. 29–31, 33
Koslofsklý, Craig 209
Kriedte, Peter 162
Kristeva, Julia 218

L
labour force, proletarianization of 7–9
Labrousse, Ernest 161
Lacan, Jacques 129, 220
Laqueur, Thomas 215–16, 220
Laslett, Peter 15, 17
Laud, Archbishop William 119–21
Le Bras, Gabriel 144, 145
Le Roy Ladurie, Emmanuel 53–5, 63, 78, 148, 163, 175–6
Lead, Jane 121
Lefebvre, Georges 78, 161, 163
Leveller Movement 14
Levi, Giovanni 172, 173
Lévi-Strauss, Claude 26, 52
Leviathan and the Air Pump (Shaffer) 85
linguistic theory
  attraction of 71–2
  discourses 72–3
  intertextuality 73
  metanarratives 73
  metaphor for modernity, Benthams' panopticon as 77–8
  modernist narrative, continuing dominance of 87–8
linguistic turn
  'change over time', explanations of 87
  criticisms of 86–7
  French Revolution case study 78–80
  and gender history 97–8, 154
  modernist narrative, and history of science 84–5
  narrative interpretation *versus* reconstruction 86
  and power relationships 85–6
  precarious definitions of 72
  rationality, and progress 82–6
  reality, issue of 86–7
  self, discourse of 76, 86
  and structuralism 71, 72
  and textual analysis 80–2
  see also postmodernism; poststructuralism
Linnaeus, Carolus 213
logocentrism, critique of 75–7
Long Parliament 210
Louis XIV, king of France 165
Louis XVI, king of France 80, 86
Loyola, St Ignatius 142
Lucas, Colin 79
Luther, Martin 114, 140, 141
Lyotard, Jean Francois 75, 216

M
Macfarlane, Alan 58, 147
Machiavelli, Niccolò 106
Madness and Civilization (Foucault) 77
Making of the English Working Class, The (Thompson) 13
Making of the Modern Family (Shorter) 31–3
Malinowski, Bronislaw 38

Malthus, Thomas Robert 5, 6, 163–4
Malthusian metanarrative 163–4
Mandeville, Bernard 4
Marshall, Alfred 160
Marten, John 213
Marx, Karl xi, 205
Marxism
body, as weak and passive 205–6
'bourgeois' revolutions 4, 8
capitalism, transition to 4, 5–9, 161
class struggle, history of 14–15, 17, 78–9
culture of resistance 18
genuine paradigm shift, effecting of 15–16
globalism 8
history from below 4, 5, 8
impact of 161–2
'infrapolitics', and notion of 'hidden transcripts' 18
labour force, proletarianization of 7–9
means of production, ownership of 3–6, 8
metanarrative of 161–3
and modernization theory 28
nation state, and class 17
peasant politics 16–18
'primitive accumulation' 6, 7, 9
proto-industrialization theory 162–3
secondary sources, Marx's use of 4–5, 8–9, 11
and social determinism 192–4
social relations of production 3–4, 5
theoretical approaches to history xii–xiii
universal intellect *versus* 'the intellectual' 17–18
see also British Marxist historians
Mary II, queen of England 161
masculinity, constructions of
'effeminacy' 106
male rulers, qualities of 105
marriage, and authority 104–5
political power, access to 104–5
same-sex attachments 106
see also gender history
Mathiez, Albert 78
Mauss, Marcel 164, 165, 217
Mayer, Thomas 141
McKendrick, Neil 167, 168
McMillan, Margaret 115
Medick, Hans 162
Meissner, W.W. 142
Mendels, Franklin 162
Mendelson, Sara 196
Menocchio 55–6, 143
mentalités, study of 36–7, 59, 78, 144–5, 146
Merrick, Jeffrey 105
metanarratives
economic history 161–4
linguistic theory 73
postmodernism 75–7, 154
of progress 76, 82–6
and theory xii
see also teleology
microhistory
and newer economic history 172
and popular religion 143, 147–8, 149
scale, question of 60–2
Mill, John Stuart 5
Minard, Philippe 173–4
Misselden, Edward 4
modernization theory
barbarous/civilized dichotomy 26, 35–6
and body history 207–9
change process 36, 44
civilizing process 35–8
consensus as norm 28, 30
early modern Europe, view of 29–31
elites, focus on 28, 30, 42, 45
family, histories of 31–3, 39–40
and functional anthropology 37, 38–9
and functionalist approach 27–8, 30
habitus concept 36
individualism, development of 40
mentalités, history of 36–7
moral judgement 28–9, 30
origins of 26–7
and poststructuralism 41–2
religion, and decline of magic 38–9
secularization 43–4
teleology 34, 36, 44–5
traditional/modern distinction 25–6, 27, 32, 38–9, 40, 43, 45
Tudor revolution in government 33–5
Montaillou (Le Roy Ladurie) 53–5, 63, 78
More, Thomas 4, 8
Mosse, George L. 29–31, 33
Muchembled, Robert 52, 149

Muldrew, Craig 173
Myth of Ritual Murder, The (Po-Chia Hsia) 83

N
Namier, Lewis 190
nation states, emergence of 33–4, 130–1
Neale, Sir John 188, 198–9
new cultural history 72, 176
and history of the body 205
and popular religion 146–7, 148, 149
and religious history 153–4
new historicism 41, 72, 99
new history xii
new intellectual history 141
new social history 14–16, 205
newer economic history
1780-1815 as key transitional moment, challenge to 174
choice, emphasis on 175
discourse, lack of attention to 175–6
economic theory, and history 170–1
economy, state's relation to 174–5
historical actors, understanding 172–3, 174, 175, 176
Industrial Revolution, challenge to traditional views of 171–2, 174
microhistory, drawing on 172
power, notion of 175
theoretical tools, use of 170
total factor productivity model 170–1
Newton, Isaac 73
Night Battles, The (Ginzburg) 147, 148
Nisbet, Robert A. 40
North American Puritans, modernity of 32–3
Notestein, Wallace 188

O
Oberman, Heiko 141
Oestreich, Gerhard 150
O'Malley, John 141, 144
Onania 213
Oneirocritica (Artemidorus of Daldis) 119
Order of Things, The (Foucault) 78
Owen, Alex 116–17

P
Paine, Tom 5
panopticon, of Bentham 77–8, 212
parliamentary elections case study
democratic developments, study of 199–200
election processes, in early modern England 197–8
ideology, in elections 200–1
modernization narrative 198
Parliamentary Enclosure Movement 7
Parliaments in English Politics (Russell) 189
Parsons, Talcott 27, 28
Past & Present 192
Paster, Gail Kern 220–1
Peace of Augsburg (1555) 150
peasant politics 16–18
Peasants of Languedoc, The (Le Roy Ladurie) 163
Peasants' Revolt (1381) 16
Pepys, Samuel 124
periodization
constructed nature of xvi
and modernization theory 27, 32
questioning of 101–2
Personal Rule of Charles I, The (Sharpe) 126
Petty, William 4
pilgrimage literature 83
Pilgrimage of Grace (1536) 34
Plath, Sylvia 124
Plumb, John H. 199
Po-Chia Hsia, R. 83
Pocock, John 75
Pole, Cardinal Reginald 141
political culture
history from below, *versus* high political narratives 194–6
interdisciplinarity, greater emphasis on 194–5
political iconographies 195–6
popular politics 196–7
political history
'modern' society, shaping of 183–4
and moral messages 184
parliamentary elections case study 197–201
revisionism, and study of high politics 188–90, 194
social history, of politics 194–7
and social sciences 190–4
Politics of Court Scandal, The (Bellany) 196
Politics of the Excluded, The (Harris) 196–7

Pollard, A.F. 34, 188
Popper, Karl xiii
popular politics 196–7
popular religion, and cultural turn
acculturation, and colonial activities 148–9
gender 151–4
Marxist approach 144
mentalités, history of 144–5, 146
and microhistory 143, 147–8, 149
qualitative approach 145–7
and social history of religion 144, 149, 155
population growth
and captialism (Marx) 5–7
and demographic/economic stagnation (Malthus) 163–4
Population History of England 1541-1971, The (Wrigley & Schofield) 15
Porter, Roy 167
positivism 98
postcolonial theory 59, 99–100, 107, 169
Posten-Vinay, Gilles 170, 173
postmodernism
and class struggle 15
and deconstruction 76
gender, and religion 151–4
and hermeneutic of suspicion 76, 77
logocentrism, critique of 75–7
metanarratives, sceptical approach to 154
and modernist narrative 84, 87–8
see also poststructuralism
poststructuralism
and body history 212–16, 219
and class struggle 15
and empirical historical method 114
and gender history 97–9, 154, 217
and historical metanarrative xiii
and 'irrational/irrelevant' activities and sentiments 83–4
punishment, history of 41–2, 77–8
religious institutions, study of 143
and traditional/modern dichotomy 29
see also discourses; linguistic theory; linguistic turn; postmodernism; textual analysis
power, location of (Foucault) 41–2, 77–8, 212–13
Pride's Purge (Underdown) 193
progress, metanarrative of 76, 82–6
Protestant Ethic and the Spirit of Capitalism, The (Weber) 165–6
Protestant Reformation
and capitalism 26, 36, 144, 165–7
and 'crisis of gender relations' 153
and mind/body dualism 205
and modernity 43, 139, 154
reciprocity, notions of 165
and witchcraft 83
proto-industrialization theory 162–3
Prynne, William 120
psychic allohistories 125
psychoanalytic theory
aberrant moments, focus on 116, 125–6
cultural practices, analysis of 129
dreams 119–29
and empirical historical method 114–15
fantasy, concept of 116, 130–1
fiction, exploring resources of 123–7
and gender history 115–16
historian, focus on 128–9
historical psychoanalysis 129, 131–2
marginalization of 114–15
private/public split 127, 130
psychic expression, as subject to historical change 118–19
psychobiography 114, 119, 120, 124–6
social unconscious, argument for 128
and witch trials 116–19
psychobiography 114, 119, 120, 124–6, 141–2
punishment, history of (Foucault) 41–2, 77–8, 212–13
puritanism 32–3, 185
Purkiss, Diane vii, 114–32, 218
Pym, John 185

Q
qualitative approach, to study of religion
evidence, evaluation of 145
functionalism 147
new cultural history 146–7, 148, 149
social anthropology, influence of 147, 149
'thick description' 147
quantitative approaches 78, 145
queer theory 99, 100, 106, 107

R
Rabelais, François 209, 221
Rabelais and his World (Bakhtin) 128
Rabinow, Paul 77
racial categories 106–7
Raftis, J.A. 16
Rankean method 33, 219
  chronology, commitment to 185, 186
  empirical method, and primacy of sources 187–8
  high political narrative, focus on 185, 187–8
  historical objectivity 184–6, 187
  human agency and autonomy 188
  national political history 186
  parliamentary democracy, perspective of evolution of 186
  political history, defence of 187
  scientific approach 185
  social and economic theory, rejection of 187, 188
  teleological approach, rejection of 188
rationality
  of historical actors 172–3, 175
  and progress 82–6
  and secularization 43–4
reader-response theory 72
Reddy, William 175
Redfield, Robert 53
Reformation *see* Protestant Reformation
Reformation to Industrial Revolution (Hill) 12
Reinhard, Wolfgang 150
religion, and history
  confessional texts 140
  confessionalization, and religious change 150–1
  critical distance, lack of 140–1
  cultural turn, and popular religion 144–9
  doctrine, concern with 140–4
  early modern period, and historiography of religion 139
  and gender 151–4
  insularity, danger of 141
  microhistory 143, 147–8, 149
  modernization theory 27, 28–9
  psychobiography 141–2
  religious institutions, study of 143–4
  religiously idiosyncratic figures, biographies of 142–3
  social disciplining 150, 152, 153
  social history of religion 144, 149, 155
Religion and the Decline of Magic (Thomas) 38–9, 50
Renaissance Self-Fashioning (Greenblatt) 86
Renaissance studies 41, 85
Representative of the People, The (Hirst) 199
revisionism, and high politics 188–90, 194
Ricardo, David 5, 160
Ricoeur, Paul 62
ritual murder 83
Roche, Daniel xii, 167
Rollison, David vii, 3–19
Roman Catholic Church
  and Copernican Revolution 84–5
  and modernization theory 30–1, 34
Roper, Lyndal 117–18, 153, 208
Rorty, Richard 130
Rosaldo, Renato 54, 63
Rose, Jacqueline 131
Rosenthal, Jean-Laurent 170, 173
Rublack, Ulinka 210
Rump Parliament 210
Russell, Conrad 189, 200

S
Sahlins, Marshall 59
Schama, Simon 166, 167
Schapera, Isaac 50
Schilling, Heinz 150
Schleitheim Articles (1527) 140
Schlumbohm, Jürgen 162
Schofield, R.S. 15
science, history of 84–5
Scott, James C. 17, 18
Scott, Joan xiii, 115
Scribner, Bob 64, 147, 148
secondary sources, Marx's use of 4–5, 8–9, 11
selfhood, changing notions of 76, 86, 122–3
Sexton, Anne 124
sexuality, history of 96–7, 106
Shaffer, Steven 85
Shakespeare, William 4
Shapin, Steven 85, 141
Sharpe, J.A. 42
Sharpe, Kevin 123, 126, 195

Shorter, Edward 31–3
Sin and Fear (Delumeau) 78
Skinner, Quentin xii, 75
Smith, Adam 5, 160
Smith, Bonnie 129
Smith, Thomas 4
Soboul, Albert 78, 163
social constructionist approach 75, 212
social history
  of politics 194–7
  of religion 144, 149, 155
  see also cultural turn, and popular religion; new social history; political culture
Social History of Truth, The (Shapin) 85
social science methods
  influence of 33, 35, 38
  and political history 190–4
Society and Puritanism in Pre-Revolutionary England (Hill) 12
Society of Jesus 142, 143
sociology, invention of 26
Soergel, Phil 83
Spierenburg 36–8
Spierenburg, Peter 208–9
Stagg, Kevin vii, 205–21
Stearns, Peter 25
Steedman, Carolyn 115, 120
Stolberg, Michael 213–15
Stone, Lawrence 31, 38, 39–40, 64, 190, 191, 194, 199
Strauss, Gerald 145
structural anthropology 26, 52–3
structural linguistics 72
structuralism 71, 72, 82, 191
Stuart history 85, 185–6, 188–90, 194
  see also English Civil War (1642-1649)
Subaltern Studies 99

T
Tawney, R.H. 12, 28, 191, 194
Taylor, George 79
Techniques of the Body (Mauss) 217
teleology, and modernization theory 27, 31, 34, 36, 44–5, 188–90, 200
Teresa of Ávila, St 152
textual analysis
  legal transcripts, interpretation of 81–2
  literacy rates, and reception 81
  and meanings 62–3, 82
  'reading against the grain' 76–7
  textual sources 80–1
  see also linguistic turn; poststructuralism
Thatcher, Margaret 131
theology, and historiography of religion 140
theory, and historical writing xii–xiv
theory-practice dualism 64
Thomas, Keith xii, 35, 38–9, 50–3, 58, 147
Thompson, E.P. 10–11, 13–14, 15, 17, 18, 58
Thornton, Alice 127
Tindall, Gillian 123, 124
Tissot, Samuel 213
Todd, Margo 61
Tomalin, Claire 124
traditional/modern distinction 25–6, 27, 32, 38–9, 40, 43, 45
transnational theory 169
Trevelyan, G.M. 199
Trevor-Roper, Hugh 120
Trexler, Richard 58
Trumbach, Randolph 106
Tudor history
  high political history 187–8, 195
  and modernization theory 33–5
  revisionism 188–90, 194
Tudor Political Culture (Elton) 196
Turner, Victor 58, 60
Tylor, E.B. 52

U
Underdown, David 192

V
Veblen, Thorstein 168
Victoria, queen of England 184
Villari, Rosario 60
Vindication of the Rights of Women, A (Wollstonecraft) 217
Virgin Mary , figure of 153
von Linné, Carl 213
von Ranke, Leopold xiv, 33, 98, 184
Vovelle, Michel 78, 145

W
Walker, Garthine viii, 25–45, 218
Walker Bynum, Caroline 206

Weber, Max ix, 26, 27, 28, 29, 35, 36, 39, 143, 144, 146, 165–7, 191, 205
What is History? (Carr) 33
Whiggish history 186, 189, 194, 199, 200, 221
White, Hayden 86
Wiesner-Hanks, Merry E. viii, 95–108
William III, king of England 161
Williams, Gerhild Scholz 75
witchcraft
  charity-refusal model of 50–1, 52
  gendered religious symbols 153
  and hysteria 128
  and Protestant Reformation 83
  and psychoanalytic theory 116–19
Wolf, Bernard 59
Wollstonecraft, Mary 217
women's history 15, 59, 95–6
  see also gender history
Wood, Andy 14, 17, 196, 197
Wood Middlebrook, Diane 124
Woolrych, Austin 187
Worden, Blair 123
Working Life of Women in the Seventeenth Century (Clark) xii, 95
World Turned Upside Down, The (Hill) 13
World We Have Lost, The (Laslett) 15
Wrightson, Keith 4, 5, 8, 196
Wrigley, E.A. 15

Y
Young, Iris Marion 217–18
Young Man Luther (Erikson) xii, 114, 142

Z
Zaller, Robert 188
Zambelli, Paola 56
Zeeden, Ernst Walter 150
Zizek, Slavoj 116, 129–32